Making Choices for Multicultural Education

THIRD EDITION

Making Choices for Multicultural Education

Five Approaches to Race, Class, and Gender

Christine E. Sleeter
California State University, Monterey Bay

Carl A. Grant
University of Wisconsin-Madison

 MERRILL,
an imprint of Prentice Hall
Upper Saddle River, New Jersey   Columbus, Ohio

Library of Congress Cataloging-in-Publication Data

Sleeter, Christine E., (date)
    Making choices for multicultural education : five approaches to
    race, class, and gender / Christine E. Sleeter, Carl A. Grant. —
    3rd ed.
        p. cm.
    Includes bibliographical references and index.
    ISBN 0-13-908807-5
    1. Multicultural education—United States. 2. Children of
    minorities—Education—United States. 3. Social classes—United
    States. I. Grant, Carl A. II. Title.
LC1099.3.S58   1999
370.117'0973—dc21   98-16980
                                                          CIP

Editor: Debra A. Stollenwerk
Production Editor: Mary Harlan
Design Coordinator: Diane C. Lorenzo
Production Supervision and Text Design: WordCrafters Editorial Services, Inc.
Cover Art: © Photodisc, Inc.
Cover Designer: Ken MacKay
Production Manager: Pamela D. Bennett
Director of Marketing: Kevin Flanagan
Marketing Manager: Suzanne Stanton
Marketing Coordinator: Krista Groshong

This book was set in Palatino by Maryland Composition and was printed and bound by
R. R. Donnelley & Sons Company. The cover was printed by Phoenix Color Corp.

Earlier editions © 1994 by Macmillan Publishing Company; 1988 by Merrill Publishing Company.

Printed in the United States of America
10 9 8 7 6 5 4 3 2 1

ISBN: 0-13-908807-5

Prentice-Hall International (UK) Limited, *London*
Prentice-Hall of Australia Pty. Limited, *Sydney*
Prentice-Hall of Canada, Inc., *Toronto*
Prentice-Hall Hispanoamericana, S. A., *Mexico*
Prentice-Hall of India Private Limited, *New Delhi*
Prentice-Hall of Japan, Inc., *Tokyo*
Simon & Schuster Asia Pte. Ltd., *Singapore*
Editora Prentice-Hall do Brasil, Ltda., *Rio de Janeiro*

*To Roberta, Ellen, and Ron
and Carl and Alicia*

Preface

Our primary reason for writing *Making Choices for Multicultural Education: Five Approaches to Race, Class, and Gender* was to offer to the educational community a way of thinking about race, language, culture, class, gender, and disability in teaching. The second edition was also written to serve as a major voice, a repository of references and resources, in the multicultural debate that has taken off since the publication of the first edition in 1988. This third edition incorporates the most recent literature relevant to ongoing struggles and offers continued reflection on and insight into this evolving field of study and practice. More specifically, the book includes recent demographics, an expanded discussion of sexual orientation, a reflection on the increased development and implementation of conflict resolution and peer mediation programs in schools, insights regarding the evolving role of policy in shaping teaching and curriculum, a focus on the recasting of deficit ideology, a discussion of the growing trend toward gradually replacing single-group study with multiple-group and interdisciplinary perspectives, and an emphasis on the ways multicultural education is materializing in contexts across schools and society.

For the first edition we reviewed over 200 articles and 60 books about multicultural education.[1] We have continued our review since then. This investigation is thorough, although not exhaustive, since publications about multicultural education are being released daily. The publications are in many disciplines and are aimed at students and educators at different levels of learning.

WHAT DO WE MEAN BY MULTICULTURAL EDUCATION?

People mean different things by the term *multicultural education*. For one thing, they do not always agree on what forms of diversity it addresses. Some people think only about racial or cultural diversity, while others conceptualize gender, social class, and additional forms of diversity. At the same time, many people who discuss gender equity, for example, share concerns similar to those of multicul-

---

[1]Grant, C. A., & Sleeter, C. E. (1985). The literature on multicultural education: Review and analysis. *Educational Review, 37,* 97–118; Grant, C. A., Sleeter, C. E., & Anderson, J. E. (1986). The literature on multicultural education: Review and analysis, Part II. *Educational Studies, 12,* 47–71; Sleeter, C. E., & Grant, C. A. (1987). An analysis of multicultural education in the U.S.A. *Harvard Educational Review, 57,* 421–444.

tural education advocates but virtually ignore race and culture. Still others conceptualize multicultural education in relationship to issues of public policy, such as immigration (e.g., California's Taxpayers' Protection Act) and bilingualism (e.g., English Only legislation).

In this book we focus on several forms of difference that also define unequal positions of power in the United States. These include race, language, social class, gender, disabiilty, and sexual orientation. We take the position that schools generally operate in ways that favor the "haves." In Chapter 1, we synthesize data about schooling and the wider social context to support this position. In subsequent chapters, we ask how schooling could work differently to treat diverse groups more equally. We synthesize research and theory underlying five approaches to what multicultural education could mean and illustrate with examples and vignettes applying each approach to various forms of diversity.

Chapter 2 explores "Teaching the Exceptional and Culturally Different." Teachers who advocate this approach are concerned mainly about helping low-achieving students catch up and succeed in school so they can "make it" in the mainstream of society. Teachers are concerned not with criticizing or trying to change the mainstream itself, but rather with building bridges between children and that mainstream.

Chapter 3 examines the "Human Relations" approach, which focuses on improving affective dimensions of the classroom: how students relate to each other, how they feel about themselves, and how they feel about diverse groups in the community and society.

Chapter 4 concentrates on the "Single-Group Studies" approach. Teachers who use this approach teach about one specific group, or one group at a time, such as African Americans, Native Americans, women, or people with disabilities. The approach rests on a great deal of research and theorizing being done in departments of ethnic studies as well as gay and lesbian studies in higher education, making it more complex than many classroom teachers realize at first.

The "Multicultural Education" approach is the focus of Chapter 5. This is the approach long-time advocates of multicultural education have most discussed. It involves complete reform of the entire education process to reflect and support diversity, addressing dimensions of schooling such as curriculum, tracking and grouping, staffing, and testing. It also focuses on improving student achievement, but unlike Chapter 2, supports the development of a culturally pluralistic mainstream that does not require assimilation for success.

Chapter 6 discusses "Education That Is Multicultural and Social Reconstructionist," which calls attention to social justice issues and empowering young people to make social changes. Like the "Multicultural Education" approach, this one also involves reform of the entire education process, but it focuses much more explicitly on social critique and democratic citizen participation.

We believe that educators need to be very clear about what multicultural education means to them. What goals they actually have in mind? What target student populations? What vision of society? What ideas about how to achieve a better society? What assumptions about learning? It is important for you, the reader, to be clear about your own beliefs to achieve what you are attempting.

In Chapter 7, after sharing what we have learned about each of the other approaches, we explain the one we advocate. As objective as we tried to be in writing the first six chapters, we know that what people say and how they see the world is shaped by their ideology, background, and vision of the world. Our students want to know which approach we favor, and our readers probably will as well. Also, we know that the colleagues and students with whom we work are thoughtful people who are not easily persuaded, and most are capable of making up their own minds.

HOW TO USE THIS BOOK

We have found two different uses for *Making Choices for Multicultural Education.* Some people read it to gain an overview of the history and thinking behind multicultural education. Such readers often read the book quickly, pausing to reflect mainly on differences among the approaches. This text may be used in a course that includes one or two other books on issues related to multicultural education, providing students with a comprehensive overview of the field.

A second way to use the book is to spend time examining how to use each approach to multicultural education in the classroom. The companion text, *Turning on Learning,* Second Edition (Grant & Sleeter, Merrill/Prentice-Hall, 1997), can be helpful. It is organized according to the same chapter plan as this text, but it provides examples of lesson plans using each approach. When using the books together, a student or teacher can read, for example, the theory behind the "Single-Group Studies" approach in Chapter 4 of *Making Choices,* then examine several lesson plans that illustrate the same approach in Chapter 4 of *Turning on Learning.* In addition to lesson plans, each chapter of *Turning on Learning* contains one or two action research activities, such as a textbook analysis instrument and a stereotyping quiz.

A teacher educator can structure an entire course around *Making Choices for Multicultural Education.* The book can be used alone; it can also be supplemented with other readings or texts. For example, you could spend several weeks in the semester examining various teaching strategies that help improve achievement of low-income students and/or students of color, using Chapter 2 as a base, and supplementing it with material about bilingual education or culture and cognitive style. Similarly, you could pair Chapter 6 ("Education That Is Multicultural and Social Reconstructionist") with readings on critical pedagogy and antiracist education.

We believe that *Making Choices for Multicultural Education: Five Approaches to Race, Class, and Gender* makes a vital contribution to the fields of multicultural education, gender studies, mainstreaming, and critical teaching at an important time in the development of these concepts. Enjoy the fruit of our labor, and if you are inclined, please let us know what you think, for we enjoyed and learned from your comments regarding the first and second editions, and we know that your thoughts will continue to help us to grow.

Acknowledgments

We are grateful to the wide audiences that gave our first and second editions of *Making Choices for Multicultural Education* a warm reception, making this third edition possible. This third edition reflects events and our own growth, but it is largely similar to the first two editions. Readers of the previous editions generally affirmed for us the validity of the ideas we developed; some also offered us critiques, compliments, and suggestions.

We would like to thank the students in our courses at the University of Wisconsin–Parkside, California State University, Monterey Bay, and the University of Wisconsin–Madison in which we have used this book, for their helpful feedback. Their questions, reactions, and even difficulties with portions of the text helped us to make this edition stronger. We thank Grace Thomsen for her useful and insightful contributions of information and ideas related to language-minority students. Sincere appreciation is extended to Lisa Loutzenheiser for her excellent ideas about gay, lesbian, and bisexual issues. Super thanks go to Kim Wieczorek for library research—accessing more recent resources—and insightful comments and contributions to the overall process. Great appreciation and gratitude are extended to Kristen Buras for her illuminating ideas, patience, scholarship, and excellence throughout this revision.

The following reviewers are acknowledged for their helpful suggestions and enthusiastic reception of this book: Alan Crawford, California State University–Los Angeles; Kathleen Sernak, Purdue University, and Frank Gulbrandsen, University of Minnesota–Duluth.

Brief Contents

Contents

CHAPTER FIVE
MULTICULTURAL EDUCATION   150

CHAPTER SIX
EDUCATION THAT IS MULTICULTURAL AND SOCIAL RECONSTRUCTIONIST   188

CHAPTER ONE

Illusions of Progress: Business as Usual

Picture the following class: Of its 30 students (15 girls and 15 boys), 21 are White, 5 are African American, 3 are Hispanic (2 Mexican Americans and 1 Cuban American), and 1 is second-generation Asian American. Two of the African American students, 1 Hispanic student, and 4 White students come from families who live below the poverty line, while another 4 White students are from upper-income homes. These status distinctions are not readily visible, however, because most of the students are wearing jeans and cotton shirts or T-shirts. Nevertheless, a glance at home addresses and at the free-lunch roster indicates the students' socioeconomic status. The students' families vary widely: Only 2 students come from families in which the father but not the mother works outside the home, 9 are from single-parent families (6 of which live below the poverty line), and both parents of the remaining 19 students hold or have recently held jobs at least part time. Most of the students grew up speaking English, but 2 of the Hispanic students speak Spanish at home, and 1 White student speaks French at home. The students' academic skills vary widely: Two spend part of the day in a class for children with learning disabilities; 1 is in a class for children with mental retardation; 1 is in a program for gifted students; and 1 is in a speech therapy program.

How does a teacher teach such a wide variety of students? What sort of curriculum is taught? Are all students taught the same curriculum? What teaching strategies are used? How are students grouped for instruction, or are they grouped at all? How are they seated? You may find conflicting images forming in your head. Of these images, one may depict how you believe a teacher should teach these students, another may depict how you have seen a teacher whose class you observed teach these students, and another may depict how most teachers really do teach them.

We based our hypothetical class on statistics describing the composition of public schools in the United States in the early 1990s (National Center for Education Statistics, 1991). Actually, student composition varies widely across the country, even within the same city or the same school. But given the diversity of America's students, schools, and classrooms, the same questions persist: How do teachers actually teach their students, and how should students be taught?

This book addresses these central questions. We recognize, however, that schools do not exist in a vacuum, but are closely connected to the society they serve. Therefore, when considering what kind of education would best serve the United States' increasingly diverse student population, we need to consider the nature of the society in which schools exist. This chapter will first discuss briefly the nature of society in the 1990s and predictions for the early part of the 21st century in relation to race, language, culture, gender, social class, and disability. Then it will synthesize recent research to demonstrate how teachers actually teach America's diverse student population. Finally, it will provide the framework used in subsequent chapters to address alternative approaches to teaching.

SOCIETY TODAY

It now seems in some cases that race, gender, and bias against people with disabilities are no longer serious societal problems. Increasingly, White women and African American men are elected mayors of large cities. Hispanic men and women are rising in the political structure; many Native Americans own businesses. An African American male, Douglas Wilder, was elected governor of Virginia. Thirty-nine White women have been elected to Congress (34 in the House and 5 in the Senate), 10 African American women (9 in the House and 1 in the Senate), and 1 Asian American woman. Hispanic, Asian American, and Native American political clout is growing.

Additionally, African Americans have leading roles in television entertainment, and it is becoming rather commonplace to see people of color and both sexes reporting the news or hosting television programs in large urban television markets. One can think of additional illustrations of progress in the 1990s. Women and people of color as astronauts are no longer big news; the U.S. Supreme Court has two active female members and its second African American justice. A review of many newspapers and magazines suggests that Americans are hearing more about "diversity" in regard to both national and international matters.

However, these indications of progress obscure the larger picture. For example, although the political representation of particular gender and racial groups in the House of Representatives and Senate has increased over time, such increases are minimal. In 1995, 89.2% of representatives elected to the House were male, while only 10.8% were female. In the Senate, female membership was only 8%. This same year, 85.98% of House representatives were White, and in the Senate, Whites constituted 97% (percentages based upon U.S. Bureau of the Census, *Statistical Abstract of the U.S.: 1995*, p. 281, Table 444). Thus, in spite of examples of social progress (which involve only small numbers of people) there is considerable evidence that U.S. society is still battling problems of racism and sexism and is very stratified on the basis of race, gender, and disability. In fact, stratification based on socioeconomic status is a prominent feature of U.S. society, and social policy in the last four decades has made little sustained attempt to change it.

In the past few years, Americans have been reminded repeatedly that the population of the U.S. is rapidly becoming more racially and ethnically diverse. In 1994, the U.S. population was 11.98% African American; 10.02% Hispanic; 3.24%

Asian or Pacific Islander; 73% Native American, Eskimo, or Aleut; and 74.03% non-Hispanic White (U.S. Bureau of the Census, 1995, p. 19, Table 19). In the 1980s, 6 million legal immigrants joined the U.S. population, and before the year 2000 we will probably see an even larger wave of immigrants. Most immigrants are from areas other than Europe. About 43% of the Hispanic population are immigrants from the 1970s and 1980s, and fully 70% of the Asian population are immigrants from those two decades (Riche, 1991).

This diversity certainly enlarges the pool of cultural resources existing in the United States, while at the same time engendering misunderstanding and resentment. In addition, the growing racial diversity of the United States underscores the urgent need for our nation to come to grips with racism. While European immigrants have been able to blend in with the dominant population after a generation or two, non-Europeans continue to be visibly distinct from EuroAmericans and thus experience American racism, a situation that causes disillusionment even among those who came to the United States full of hope and optimism.

When considering racism in society, Americans often cite improved racial attitudes as a sign of progress. Indeed, attitudes have improved, according to a Gallup poll taken in 1990. In 1963, when Gallup asked Whites if they would be inclined to move out if a Black family moved next door to them, 45% said they would. Presently, only 5% respond in the affirmative when asked that same question. In contrast, Gallup and Hugick (1990) reported no significant change since the late 1970s in public opinion about African Americans' success in achieving equal opportunities. The perception of how well African Americans are treated in their communities has not improved since that time. Sixty-three percent believe that African Americans are treated the same as Whites, while 24% say that African Americans are treated "not very well" or "badly." However, in a study analyzing racial attitudes toward residential integration, Bobo, Schuman, and Steeh (1986) found that

> There is evidence of a steady progressive trend toward acceptance of the goal of residential integration and toward support for enforcement of blacks' housing rights. These changes are lent further credence by expressed white willingness to take part in integrated living situations that involve more than a token blacks presence. On the other hand, support for enforcing blacks' rights to free residential choice is well below that for the principle itself. Indeed, respondents proved to be quite willing to endorse the principle and express reluctance to enforce it. (p. 165)

The last four decades may have brought about improved White attitudes and improved access to facilities such as schools, but African Americans, Hispanics, and Native Americans are still distinctly subordinate economically and politically. For example, in 1990, although the average educational attainment of African Americans was only slightly below that of Whites (12.2 years and 12.6 years, respectively), the median income of African American families was only 60% of the median income of White families and had improved little in over a decade. Hispanics with at least a high school diploma were more than 2½ times as likely as Whites to be living in poverty in 1988, and in 1990 Hispanic males had a lower annual earning rate than either Whites or African Americans (U.S. Department of

TABLE 1–1.
Earnings of Full-Time, Year-Round Workers, Age 25 and Older (1989)

Education Attained	Four Years High School	1–3 Years College	Four or More Years College
	Income Earned		
White	$24,755	$29,498	$43,314
Black	$19,813	$22,813	$32,046
Latino	$20,567	$25,620	$38,559

Source: U.S. Department of Commerce, Bureau of the Census, *Population Survey*, March 1990, Table 6.

Commerce, Bureau of the Census, 1991b). As Table 1–1 shows, education does not pay off equally for members of different racial groups: Being White has measurable economic and employment advantages. In terms of mean annual income, in 1993, Black households lived on $19,533, Hispanic families on $22,886, and White families on $32,960 (U.S. Bureau of the Census, 1995, p. 469, Table 723).

People of color continue to experience poverty and unemployment disproportionately. For example, Figure 1–1 shows the poverty rate from 1960–1995 for persons based on race. Such trends continue: In 1994, for example, Whites suffered unemployment rates of 5.3%, Hispanics, 9.9%, and Blacks, 11.5% (U.S. Bureau of the Census, 1995, p. 400, Table 628). Data on Native Americans are not reported as systematically as they are for other groups, but many tribes experience devastating poverty and unemployment. For example, in 1980 the poverty rate for Native Americans was 27.5% overall, although on the Rosebud and Navajo reservations it was 51.4% and 52.4% respectively (Tippeconnic, 1991).

Children are particularly hard hit by poverty. As Table 1–2 shows, for example, in 1994 the percentage of African American children living below the poverty line was nearly 3 times that of White children, and Hispanic children were over 2.5 times as likely as White children to live in poverty. Also, children of color living with two parents are more than twice as likely to be poor as White children living with two parents (National Commission on Children, 1991).

The gap in employment has not improved, either: Whites continue to have the greatest access to available jobs. In 1989, only about 55 percent of all African American recent high school graduates were employed, compared to about 75 percent of White recent high school graduates. In fact, White dropouts were almost as likely to be employed as African American high school graduates (Ogle, Alsalam, & Rogers, 1991). There are several reasons for this phenomenon. Racial discrimination in hiring is one of them. In spite of affirmative action—which, it should be noted, is currently under attack (e.g., California's Proposition 209)—a study by the Urban Institute found that when African American and White candidates with the same qualifications applied for the same jobs, African Americans were interviewed only 80% as often as Whites; 15% of the Whites were ultimately offered jobs while only 5% of the African Americans were offered employment (Dervarics, 1991). Another reason for the employment gap is that, increasingly,

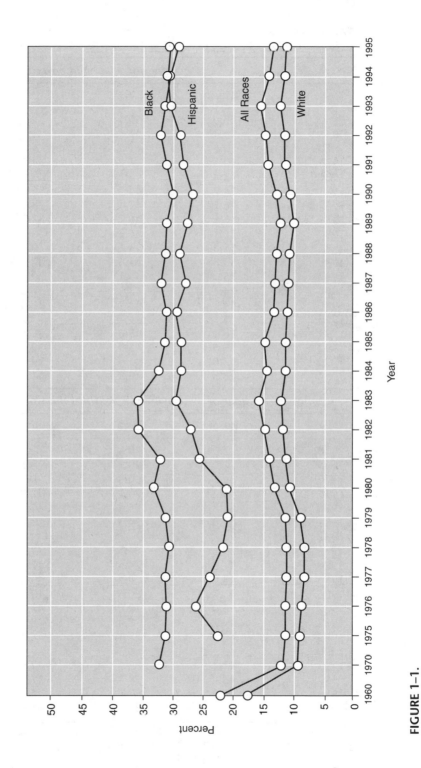

FIGURE 1–1.
U.S. Poverty Rate: Percentage of Persons Below Poverty Line

Source: Data from U.S. Department of Commerce, Bureau of the Census, *Statistical Abstract of the United States* (117th ed.), 1997, p. 475.

6

TABLE 1–2.
Children Under 18 Living in Poverty: 1960–1994

Percentage of children in poverty				
Year	White	Black	Hispanic	Total
1960	20.0	65.5	–	26.5
1965	14.4	47.4	–	20.7
1970	10.5	41.5	–	14.9
1975	12.5	41.4	34.5	16.8
1980	13.4	42.1	33.0	17.9
1981	14.7	44.2	35.4	19.5
1982	16.5	47.3	38.9	21.3
1983	17.0	46.2	37.7	21.8
1984	16.1	46.2	38.7	21.0
1985	15.6	43.1	39.6	20.1
1986	15.3	42.6	37.1	19.8
1987	15.0	45.1	39.3	20.0
1988	14.1	43.5	37.6	19.2
1989	14.1	43.2	35.5	19.0
1990	15.1	44.2	37.7	19.9
1991	16.1	45.6	39.8	21.1
1992	16.5	46.3	39.0	21.6
1993	17.0	45.9	39.9	22.0
1994	16.3	43.3	41.1	21.2

Percentage of children in poverty living with female householder				
Year	White	Black	Hispanic	Total
1960	21.0	29.4	–	23.7
1965	27.0	49.7	–	31.7
1970	36.6	60.8	–	45.8
1975	41.7	70.1	42.9	51.4
1980	41.3	75.4	47.1	52.8
1981	42.0	74.3	48.5	52.2
1982	–	–	–	–
1983	39.3	74.5	42.5	50.0
1984	41.8	74.9	47.2	52.4
1985	43.0	78.4	49.6	53.8
1986	45.7	80.5	49.5	56.6
1987	46.0	79.0	47.2	56.9
1988	49.7	78.4	48.7	58.7
1989	46.3	78.1	46.4	56.7
1990	46.9	80.3	47.8	57.9
1991	47.4	83.1	47.0	59.0
1992	43.2	79.1	37.5	55.3
1993	45.0	81.6	45.6	56.8
1994	46.4	82.2	45.6	57.7

Source: U.S. Department of Commerce, Bureau of the Census, "Poverty in the United States." *Current Population Reports*, series P-60, March, various years.

jobs are not located where people of color live. After World War II, millions of people of color moved to urban areas to take manufacturing jobs, which are now being exported to Third World countries. Job openings increasingly are located in suburban areas. People of color find it difficult to relocate, largely because of housing discrimination. Two studies of housing discrimination conducted by the Department of Housing and Urban Development (HUD) in 1987 and 1988 found that African Americans faced housing discrimination in both rental and sales markets 59% of the time, and Hispanics, 56% of the time. When people of color are matched with White home-seekers on factors such as income and family size, over half the time the White home-seekers are given more options and better chances to locate housing.

Mare and Winship (1984), after studying racial inequality and joblessness among Black youths, observed that this gap is widening because Black youths are both staying in school longer and joining the military in greater numbers—thus no longer having a "head start" in the labor market for unskilled or semiskilled jobs. Their study suggests that "worsening labor force statistics for Black youths do not denote increasing racial inequality, but rather persistent racial inequalities previously hidden by race differences in other aspects of young adulthood" (p. 54).

As a result of differential access to jobs, housing, and health institutions, other estimates of quality of life vary according to race. For example, in 1993, 88.8% of White Americans were covered by health insurance, while 79.5% of African Americans and only 68.4% of Hispanic Americans were similarly covered. The percentage of all Americans without health insurance rose from 14.0% to 15.3% between 1990 and 1993 (U.S. Bureau of the Census, 1995, p. 118, Table 169). Moreover, Whites enjoy a longer life expectancy than Americans of color. In 1990, for instance, the life expectancy of the Black male at birth was age 65 compared to 73.2 years for the White male (U.S. Bureau of the Census., 1995, p. 87, Table 116). Native Americans are especially short-changed on life span, the average life expectancy for Native Americans being 6 years less than that of other groups of color (U.S. Department of Health and Human Services, 1985). As life expectancy for the general population increases, a racial gap persists (Figure 1–2).

People of color are also more likely than Whites to be imprisoned. In 1990, jail inmates were 47.4% Black, 13.3% Hispanic, .8% Native American and Alaskan Native, .3% Asian and Pacific Islander, and 3.7% not known, while 34.5% were non-Hispanic White. However, as of December 31, 1990, of the 2,356 prisoners under sentence of death, 943 (40%) were Black, 38 (1%) were listed as "other races," and 1,375 (59%) were White. (U.S. Department of Justice, 1990).

People of color are also still locked out of much of the political system, even though increasing numbers of big-city mayors are men of color. Since 1971 there have been only 2 African American U.S. senators; the number of other senators of color has fluctuated between 2 and 4. Between 1971 and 1993, the number of African American elected to Congress increased from 12 to 39, but still constituted only 9% of the House of Representatives, a significant underrepresentation for the 12% of Americans who are Black. Four percent (4%) of the House in 1993 was Hispanic; Hispanic representation had grown over the decade but still underrepre-

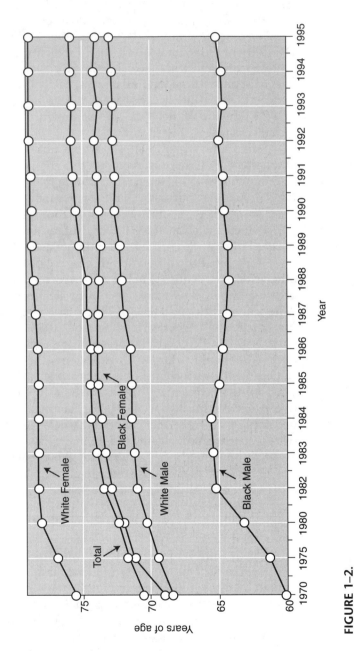

FIGURE 1–2.
Life Expectancy at Birth

Source: Data from U.S. Center for Health Statistics, U.S. Department of Health and Human Services, *Vital Statistics of the United States,* annual, and Monthly Vital Statistics Reports. Washington, DC: U.S. Government Printing Office.

TABLE 1 3.
The Wage Gap Over Time: Earnings of Full-time Female Workers Compared to Each Dollar Earned by Full-time Male Workers (1955–1990)

Year	Female earnings per dollar of male earnings	Year	Female earnings per dollar of male earnings
1955	63.9¢	1979	59.6¢
1959	61.3¢	1980	60.2¢
1960	60.8¢	1981	59.2¢
1962	59.5¢	1982	61.7¢
1965	60.0¢	1983	63.8¢
1967	57.8¢	1984	67.8¢
1970	59.4¢	1985	68.2¢
1972	57.9¢	1986	69.2¢
1973	56.6¢	1989	68.0¢
1975	58.8¢	1990	71.0¢
1977	58.9¢		

Source: U.S. Department of Commerce, Bureau of the Census, U.S. Department of Labor Statistics, *Employment and Earnings*, 1991.

sented the 9% of Americans who are Hispanic. There are 2 Asian senators and 6 Asian members of the House. There is 1 Native American senator in Congress. In 1984 Jesse Jackson ran as the first Black presidential candidate, but his White constituency was small and his support of the Democratic nominee was considered a liability by many Whites.

Women, too, are still distinctly subordinate, both economically and politically, in spite of recent gains. Women are participating in the labor market in ever-growing numbers. However, the earnings of full-time working women are only about 71% the earnings of full-time working White men. This wage gap has fluctuated over the last three decades and appears to be shrinking currently as women enter male-dominated fields (Table 1–3). As Table 1–4 shows, this gap exists between men and women who have attained the same levels of education. A number of studies have examined human capital factors (e.g., work experience, evidence of work commitment) that might explain this differential; however, taken together, Treiman and Hartman (1981) report that these "factors usually account for less than a quarter and never more than half of the observed earnings differences" (p. 42). One major institutional factor perpetuating this situation is that "women are concentrated in low-paying occupations and, within occupations, in low-paying firms" (p. 42). Women are making substantial inroads into some high-paying, traditionally male occupations, such as law. Nevertheless, in 1995, most female workers were still concentrated in low-paying "pink collar" ghettos, with only 14.2% in administrative positions as compared to 40.3% in technical, sales, and administrative support positions and 15.83% in service occupations (U.S. Department of Education, 1996, p. 414, Table 373). Additionally, the median weekly earnings of women in these occupations were less than men's (Table 1–5).

TABLE 1–4.
Average Earnings of Full-Time, Year-Round Workers, by Educational Attainment
and Sex (1994)

Education	Average Earnings	
	Men	Women
Less than 8 years	$16,863	$10,163
Eight years	$18,946	$12,655
9–11 years	$21,327	$13,136
Completed high school	$24,745	$16,223
1–3 years college	$29,253	$19,336
Four years college	$38,117	$23,506
5+ years college	$47,903	$30,255

Source: U.S. Department of Commerce, Bureau of the Census (1996). *Digest of Education Statistics 1996*. Washington, DC: U.S. Government Printing Office, p. 416.

As women increasingly become heads of households, this persistent wage gap contributes heavily to the growing pauperization of women and children. In 1993, while the average married-couple family earned $43,129, and the average unmarried male earned $21,372, the average unmarried female earned only $12,995 (U.S. Bureau of the Census, 1995, p. 471, Table 727). Currently, about half of all female-headed households live below the poverty line. This situation heavily affects children: Women are given custody of children in about 90% of divorce cases and often must attempt to support the family on a low-wage budget. According to the National Center for Children in Poverty (McGowan, 1991), nearly one of every four children in the nation under 6 years of age is poor. Additionally, children represent a declining proportion of the population, whereas the elderly represent a rising proportion (Figure 1–3). One implication of this demographic shift, according to the National Commission on Children (1991), is that "each worker will bear a greater burden of support for the nation's retirees" (p. 5).

The influx of women into the labor market is taking another toll on women as well: Because housework and child care continue to be regarded as women's responsibilities, most husbands do not yet assume an equal share of these roles, although they share more now than they did 20 years ago. Consequently, married women who hold jobs are finding themselves with less and less leisure time. For example, researchers in a 1986 study of a company in Boston found that

> Women work twice as many hours on child care and homemaking as men, even when the woman's income is greater than the man's. They also found that women are more likely to stay home if the children are sick and that married female parents spend a total of eighty-five hours a week on work, in and outside of the home, while married male parents spend sixty-five hours. (Sidel, 1990, pp. 202–203)

Because they anticipate being the primary domestic workers, many women do not enter careers that require long hours, one reason why women's earning power continues to lag. For example, "a recent detailed study by the Boston Bar Associa-

TABLE 1–5.
The Wage Gap Between Men and Women

Basic Data— U.S. Dept. of Labor Occupations	Women's Median Weekly Earnings	Women's Median Weekly Earnings as a Share of Men's Wages	Men's Median Weekly Earnings
Computer Programmers	$573.00	83%	$ 691.00
Financial Managers	$558.00	67%	$ 833.00
Lawyers and Judges	$834.00	70%	$1184.00
Managers, Marketing, Advertising, and Public Relations	$616.00	68%	$ 902.00
Personnel and Labor Relations Managers	$604.00	69%	$ 881.00
Registered Nurses	$608.00	99%	$ 616.00
Secretaries, Stenographers, and Typists	$341.00	88%	$ 387.00
Teachers, College and University	$620.00	77%	$ 808.00
Teachers, Elementary	$513.00	89%	$ 575.00
Waiters and Waitresses	$194.00	73%	$ 266.00

Source: *U.S. News and World Report*, U.S. Department of Labor.

tion of 2,000 lawyers in the Boston area found that women were significantly more likely than men to be single, divorced, and without children" (Sidel, 1990, p. 174). These developments and divorce settlements in which women are viewed as the primary caretakers of children are leading some female attorneys and scholars to argue, according to Gest (1991), that the landscape of the legal world needs to be redrawn to replace the "male" value system of rights, rules, and hierarchies with "female" values based upon relations, responsibilities, and caring.

Violence against women is another manifestation of women's devalued status in society. Statistics on battered women vary from 15 million physically abused women to one-third of the female population (Sidel, 1990). For example, in Wisconsin during 1991 there were 24,163 reported incidents of domestic abuse; 80% of the victims were female. Physicians were being instructed to ask more about domestic abuse when female patients showed physical injuries (Buelow, 1992). Many women regard violence against women as a power issue, the act of beating representing an attempt to reaffirm women's subordinate status.

The political position of women has improved somewhat, but is still no better than women's economic position. Although greatly increasing numbers of women have been elected to local and state offices, women still constitute only a small minority of officeholders at the state level, and an even smaller minority at the national level. Only about 14% of state legislators in 1985 were women. In 1993,

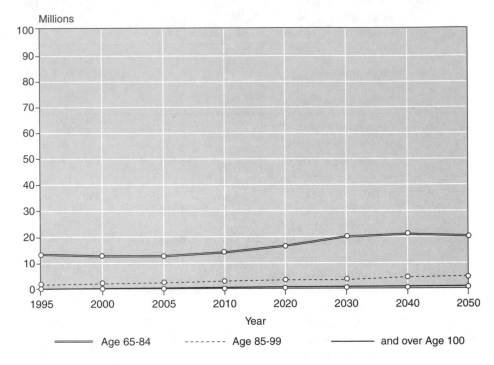

FIGURE 1–3.
Growth in the Elderly Population

Source: U.S. Department of Commerce, Bureau of the Census, *Current Population Reports*, series p-25, no. 1130. *Population Projections of the United States by Age, Sex, Race, and Hispenic Origin: 1995 to 2050*. (Washington, DC: U.S. Government Printing Office, 1996), page 12, Figure 8.

11% of the members of the House and .013% of all U.S. senators were women. In 1993, furthermore, only 14% of the women in Congress were of color (*Black Congressional Monitor*, January 5, 1993, p. 6). Only one or two states at a time have a female governor. While in 1984, Geraldine Ferraro became the first woman nominated by a major political party for vice president, she needed to make herself acceptable to the public by emphasizing that she had fulfilled the traditional roles of wife and mother in addition to pursuing a career.

As women gained ground both in the political sphere and in the job market during the late 1970s and 1980s, a backlash grew—one that many women regard as a move to keep women in their place domestically and to protect male access to better-paying jobs. For example, the American Anorexia/Bulimia Association has estimated 1,000 deaths a year from anorexia nervosa (National Mental Illness Screening Project, 1996). Also, Wolf (1991) analyzed the growth of the beauty industry, arguing that media are projecting an increasingly thin and "perfect" beauty image to women, who are responding by becoming increasingly obsessed with losing weight and changing how they look. She reports, for example, that 90% of young American women believe they weigh too much, 5% to 10% are anorexic, most would rather lose 10 to 15 pounds than achieve any other goal in life. Wolf (1991) traces this obsession with beauty to profit-making beauty industries, beauty requirements for some careers (such as television reporting), and media images that are sold to women. The entire feminist movement itself has been cast as the "ravings" of a fringe group of women who would rather be men. As a result, contemporary young women are often ambivalent about gender issues and tend to regard equality as having been achieved, with choices now open to everyone regardless of sex (Sidel, 1990).

Similarly, as the political and social climates have improved for women, there has also been some improvement for gay men, lesbians, and bisexual men and women. Issues surrounding sexual orientation have slowly been brought into the public eye, particularly since the 1969 Stonewall Riots in New York City. Stonewall is considered a turning point in the modern fight for gay, lesbian, and bisexual rights because it was one of the first incidents where gay men, transexuals, and lesbians fought back when harrassed by the police. In the ensuing years, being gay, lesbian, or bisexual was less often framed as an illness, but as a struggle for civil rights. In many ways, it has grown easier for the estimated 10 percent of the population who is gay, lesbian, or bisexual to be "out," yet prejudice and discrimination still exist. The U.S. has no federal law protecting the rights of gay men, lesbians, and bisexual men and women, and many states still have laws on their books outlawing "homosexual conduct." This lingering prejudice has a profound effect on children.

While many gay, lesbian, and bisexual youth find little conflict in terms of their own sexual orientations, others are not so fortunate. Overall, gay, lesbian, and bisexual youth compare favorably with heterosexually identified adolescents in regard to resilience, reactions to distress, or insecurities (Herdt & Boxer, 1993). The often quoted 1989 study of suicide risk among gay and lesbian youth cited that gay and lesbian youth are 2 to 3 times more likely to try suicide and may comprise up to 30% of all youth suicides (United States Dept. of Health and Human Services, 1989). A more recent study confirms the high level of suicide risk among gay and lesbian youth (Herdt & Boxer, 1993). Gay, lesbian, and bisexual teens are not only at risk when it comes to suicide, but they are more likely to use and abuse drugs, become victims of violence and harassment, and get thrown out of their homes and end up on the street (Buce & Obolensky, 1990; Krucks, 1991; Remafedi, 1987; Uribe & Harbeck, 1991).

The United States is a distinctly social-class-stratified society, and appears to be becoming more so. Although debates about racism and sexism have always existed, and in the last three decades have been quite plentiful, Americans have devoted much less attention to social class stratification. Yet there are tremendous inequities in the distribution of wealth. In 1989, the wealthiest 4% of the population earned as much as the bottom 51%. In 1970, the wealthiest 4% earned as much as the bottom 38%, and in 1959, as much as the bottom 35% (Barlett & Steele, 1992). In other words, more and more Americans have been downwardly mobile over the past three decades, and the gap between the wealthiest Americans and the majority has widened. As Figure 1–4 shows, between 1978 and 1986, a time of rapid

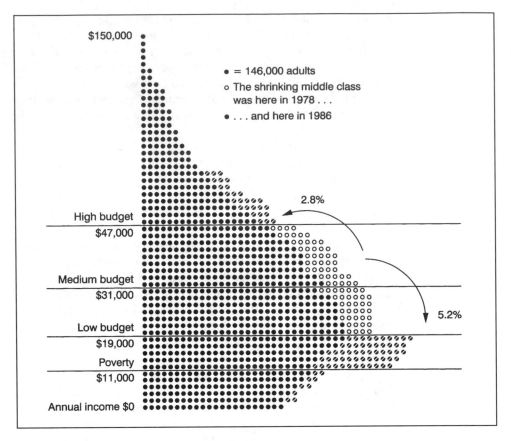

FIGURE 1–4.
The Shrinking Middle Class: 1978–1986

Source: S. J. Rose (1986). *The American profile poster.* New York: Pantheon Books, a Division of Random House, Inc. Reprinted by permission.

change in wealth distribution, the middle class shrank and the lower class grew over twice as much as the upper class.

The poverty rate in the United States in 1990 was 13.5% (U.S. Department of Commerce, Bureau of the Census, 1991a). Although the United States is a relatively wealthy nation, it has not been able to rid itself of poverty. Many find it tempting to blame the poor for poverty, arguing that the unemployed do not want to work. However, our economy sustains an unemployment rate that rarely falls below 7%. This statistic means that there are not enough jobs to go around, and 7% of Americans actively seeking work are unable to find it; this figure does not include those who have given up and stopped looking. Furthermore, many of the poor are employed but are paid very low wages.

For example, Figure 1–5 shows the income of a woman with two children in Kenosha, Wisconsin, in 1991 if she is on AFDC (Aid for Families with Dependent

---

Woman with Two Children in Kenosha in 1991

What she lives on per month:
- No earned income:
  $517 AFDC + $112 food stamps:
- Full-time minimum wage worker:
  $3.80/hr. =$576/month + $57 food stamps
- Full-time worker: $4.25/hr. = $731/month + $48 food stamps

FIGURE 1–5.
Options for mothers on welfare

Source: What welfare moms live on. *Kenosha News* Special Report, *No place to call home*. February 22, 1992, pp. 2–3.

Children), or if she is employed in a minimum-wage job. In either case, her financial resources are minimal. Try constructing a budget for her that includes rent, utilities, food, transportation, toiletries, medical expenses, and clothing.

In *The New American Poverty*, Harrington (1984) argued that there was a growing gap between rich and poor in the United States and that the middle class today was shrinking as a result of changes in the economic structure:

> People who, twenty or even ten years ago, were secure in their jobs and communities now live somewhere between poverty and semiaffluence, walking the edge of an economic precipice. Their problems will be ameliorated, but far from ended, by economic recovery, if this really does come. For they, or people like them, are likely to face downward social mobility for twenty or thirty years, unless this country turns around. These are not, then, the instant "new poor" that the media discovered in that winter of American discontent, 1982–83. (p. 64)

Almost a decade later, with the U.S. economy still operating at a sub-par level, Hacker (1992) points out in *Two Nations* that the economic situation for many is still very dismal. He observes that many who have jobs are employed for less than a full day's work or for only a part of the year. He also discloses that in addition to the number of men and women who are officially recorded as unemployed, at least an equal number have given up the search for a job. Because of the inability of these people to find work, the Bureau of Labor Statistics has created a category called "discouraged worker" (p. 105).

In spite of the popular belief that anyone who desires it can attain wealth through individual effort, Jencks et al. (1972) found occupation to be predicted largely by educational attainment, which in turn is predicated mainly by family socioeconomic background. In other words, children tend to grow up to occupy the same social class position as their parents. Similarly, Hacker (1992) reports that "there is a close association between economic status and SAT scores ..." (p. 144). Even among those with the same level of education, the children of wealthy parents are much more likely to attain high-paying jobs than are children of lower- or middle-class parents (Rumberger, 1983).

In addition, those controlling the greatest proportion of wealth tend to have the most political power. As Parenti (1978) points out, those who are most likely to sit on state and local boards, boards for colleges and universities, and boards of corporations are from the upper socioeconomic classes and make the rules by which society operates. For example, in the 1980s, while the paychecks of top corporation executives increased by 149%, the pay to workers at the largest corporations decreased by 5%. While the income taxes of the richest one percent of Americans dropped 25%, income taxes for the average family rose about $400 (Reeves, 1990). In their analysis of "what went wrong" with the distribution of wealth, Barlett and Steele (1992) argue that the wealthiest rulemakers on Wall Street and in Washington have constructed laws and rules for corporations that are dismantling the middle class and channeling wealth upward to a small minority.

Finally, people with disabilities constitute a subordinate group, although not as many statistics are kept on them as on other groups. Historically, public concern for their welfare has risen and fallen. With the passage in 1990 of the Americans With Disabilities Act, it is hoped that public concern will remain active, but if history is an accurate guide, this concern may wane. Federal and state laws for disabled people do make a difference in that they offer greater protection for the rights of people with disabilities and they demand that support services be expanded. However, laws and services on behalf of people with disabilities are usually made by nondisabled people and often are not as comprehensive as people with disabilities would recommend. Further, disabled people as a group are overrepresented in the ranks of the poor, and they are somewhat invisible as an impoverished group because statistics on their employment and income are not widely kept and published.

Nevertheless, there are some patterns. Most disabled adults are either unemployed or employed part time, and their earnings are often below the poverty level. For example, Hasazi, Gordon, and Roe (1985) followed up on 459 youths exiting special education programs in Vermont. The youths' employment rate was only 54%. In a similar follow-up study in Colorado, Mithaug, Horiuchi, and Fanning (1985) found an employment rate of 69%, but almost half of those employed were earning less than $3.00 per hour. In 1984, only 27.4% of disabled people were employed full time, a decrease of two percentage points since 1972. Of those employed, the poverty rate is 26% (Habeck, Galvid, Frey, Chadderden, & Tate, 1985). Unemployment and poverty are particularly severe among disabled people of color, who face double discrimination in the job market.

Disabled people lack access to facilities and the opportunities that most citizens enjoy. For example, zoning laws restrict locations of homes for deinstitutionalized people with mental retardation. Blind, deaf, and physically impaired people have legal rights to public facilities, but in practice find it difficult or impossible to get around in many buildings, communicate with public service workers, or use certain public channels of communication.

The speed with which the Americans With Disabilities Act (1990) removes these barriers will greatly impact the successful mainstreaming of people with disabilities. Disability advocates, however, are wary and issue cautions. An article in *The Disability Rag* points out that the act "drew national attention to the fact that the problems disabled people face are primarily discrimination—not health—problems" (The Americans with Disabilities Act, 1991, p. 11). However, many people working on the act's implementation still treat those with disabilities as incapable persons rather than as intelligent collaborators. Further, opposition to the act is mounting because of the costs it will incur.

In addition, there are issues the act does not solve. For example, although the act specifies that housing is to be accessible, many builders are not familiar with or interested in accessibility (Johnson, 1991), and the legislation does not address the scarcity of low-cost housing. Chicago's Access Living, for example, refers people with disabilities to housing, but has run out of low-cost housing to which they can refer people, partly because the federal funds for low-income housing have been slashed drastically ("No housing," 1990). People with disabilities are often targets of violence and hate crimes. "Data about rape, child sexual abuse, incest, sexual harassment, battery, neglect, defamation, and other forms of violence directed at disabled people indicate that they are much more likely to be targeted for violence than their nondisabled cohorts" ("Hate," 1992, p. 5). *The Disability Rag*, a disability activist publication, regularly creates attention for access and discrimination issues of which people without disabilities are usually simply unaware.

People with disabilities also bear stereotypes of incompetence. As Gliedman and Roth (1980) have noted, public images of disabled people emphasize limitations, and disabled people have no offsetting counter-image, such as African Americans have with the "Black is beautiful" concept. Many disabled people also must depend on others to articulate their concerns. Siegel (1986) has pointed out that physically disabled people represent "an extremely vocal and powerful lobby," whereas mentally retarded and emotionally disabled people are less able to express their own interests persuasively and assertively (p. 50). Recently, nondisabled people have created alternative terms such as "physically challenged" and "differently abled" to attempt to redress this image. However, *The Disability Rag* periodically editorializes against such euphemisms, pointing out that disabilities are real and present policy issues that need action to enable real choices; euphemistic terms tend to gloss over the need for action.

BUSINESS AS USUAL

Before we discuss approaches that teachers can take to deal constructively with race, class, gender, and disability, it is important to describe what often occurs in classrooms and schools. School, it has been observed, reflects society. Just as a few improvements in society may give an incomplete or inaccurate view of progress in reducing racism, sexism, class bias, and bias against disabilities, a few improvements in our schools are similarly misleading. In many schools, one can readily observe students of color and White students socializing; girls in classes such as woodshop and autoshop, once considered the exclusive domain of the boys; boys in home economics classes, once considered no-man's-land; teachers and students speaking Spanish in mathematics classes; and students in wheelchairs attending proms and participating in many other school events. Also, in some schools the cheering squad, band, and sports teams reflect the diversity of the student body. Moreover, in integrated schools it is not unusual for a person of color to be the president of the student council, a class officer, or a member of the Homecoming queen's court.

Furthermore, most teachers and school administrators support equal opportunity and access to all courses and activities for all students enrolled in the school: They support events that recognize the contributions of people of color and women; many welcome mainstreamed special education students into their classes; most will not tolerate sexist behavior in the classroom; and virtually all support having students from different socioeconomic status attend the same school. Also, many teachers examine their curriculum materials for bias, are willing to attend workshops dealing with multicultural education, and try to avoid using any instructional materials that are obviously biased.

These examples suggest that success for all students is the order of business in classrooms and schools. However, to the discerning observer, much has been left out. Like the society we described earlier, schools are beset with problems related to race, class, gender, and disability.

Our description of "business as usual" is based on several studies published during the 1980s and 1990s in which researchers observed what actually takes place in the schools. We will describe the main patterns that emerge. We acknowledge that schools and classrooms vary, although those that vary significantly are usually few and far between. We invite you to compare this description with schools with which you may be familiar. The description is organized into five categories: how teachers teach, what teachers teach, how students are grouped, other patterns, and student culture.

HOW TEACHERS TEACH

Many studies have found strong similarities in how teachers teach (Bigler & Lockard, 1992; Cuban, 1984; Everhart, 1983; Goodlad, 1984; Grant & Sleeter, 1996; Page, 1991; Sleeter, 1992; Trueba, Jacobs, & Kirton, 1990). Cuban (1984) summarizes these well, drawing on his own research. He separates the elementary and secondary levels, acknowledging a greater diversity among elementary teachers than among secondary teachers. Cuban reports that in elementary classrooms he came to expect a number of regularities. Almost half of the teachers (43 percent) put a daily schedule on the blackboard. If it was time for reading, the teachers would work with one group and assign the same seatwork or varied tasks to the rest of the class. If it was time for math, social studies, science, or language arts, generally the teacher would work from a text with the entire class answering questions from the text, ditto sheets, or workbooks (p. 220).

Both Cuban, in his study of 6 school districts, and Goodlad (1984), in his study of 13 elementary-middle-high school feeder systems, found that many elementary teachers deviate from this pattern by individualizing instruction, using learning centers, and using small groups. However, the majority favored teacher-centered, large-group instruction in which all students work on the same tasks and in which much of the work depends on the textbook, ditto sheets, or workbooks.

At the secondary level, there is much more uniformity. Cuban describes the main pattern as "rows of tablet-arm chairs facing a teacher who is talking, asking, listening to student answers, and supervising the entire class for most of the period—a time that is occasionally punctuated by a student report, a panel, or a film" (p. 222). Cuban found that labs in science classes offered the main variation from this pattern in academic courses; Goodlad added that vocational, physical education, and art classes involve more varied activities and much more hands-on learning. Page's (1991) study of eight lower-track classrooms in two middle-class high schools revealed that the teachers arrange the classrooms so that students can proceed in simple, step-by-step routines to learn practical skills. She posits that the teachers dominate classroom talk without being domineering, and they "teach by remote control, without calling attention to themselves as teachers" (p. 147).

These patterns have several implications for student diversity. One implication is that students whose learning style diverges from predominant teaching styles are at a disadvantage. For example, Shade (1989) argues that African American students suffer academically in schools because their learning style tends to be oriented toward cooperation, content about people, discussion and hands-on work, and whole-to-part learning, which conflicts with the independent, task-oriented, reading-oriented, part-to-whole style that most teachers employ with most students. As another example, Deyhle (1985) found that young Navajo students interpret tests as games, in contrast to White students who view tests as serious business, a result of different home socialization. Whereas White children learn early to display knowledge publicly for evaluation, Navajo children learn at a young age that serious learning is private and therefore do not exert their best effort when tested. Furthermore, Goodlad notes that the activities used in nonacademic areas, such as industrial arts, attract students who prefer active involvement in learning. This approach may help lure lower-class and minority students, more than middle-class White students, into these areas and away from academics.

A second implication is that students whose skills deviate from those of the majority present a problem for the classroom teacher, because most teachers individualize very little. The main solution schools have used has been to place such students in remedial or special education classes or to track them. This has created additional problems.

Clearly, this uniformity in teaching procedures conflicts with the mainstreaming movement. In a study of one junior high school, we found that regular education teachers modified their procedures only minimally for mainstreamed students, and they expected everybody else to learn at the same rate, through the same instruction procedures and materials (Grant & Sleeter, 1996). It seems that regular and special educators often find themselves in conflict over the intent of Public Law 94–142 (The Education for All Handicapped Children Act). Many regular educators view special education as a place to put students whose skills deviate significantly from the majority, while special education teachers are trying to move students from special education back into the mainstream and wish to see regular education teachers become more flexible in how they teach.

Similarly, many bilingual education teachers find themselves in conflict with "regular" classroom teachers over the specific needs of students with limited English proficiency (LEP). Although sent to other classrooms for reading, mathematics, or other instruction, LEP students are often "mainstreamed" in art, music, and physical education. Unfortunately, some teachers refuse to alter their standard approaches to meet the needs of these students. Instead, the students' language and cultural background is sometimes perceived as a handicap, and they are then "diagnosed" and treated as learning disabled (Trueba et al., 1990).

A third implication is that much instruction given in classrooms is uninteresting and alienating for many students. In our study of a junior high school, the word students used most often to describe instruction was *boring*. Goodlad (1984) describes classrooms as emotionally flat. Students who do not readily identify with schooling, with their teachers, or with the content being taught tend to become turned off and disengaged. This seems particularly true when the content is unrelated to the students' experiential background. Everhart (1983) describes an incident in a junior high classroom in which students were filling in a worksheet after reading about Switzerland in their textbooks. Not having been to Switzerland, and not having been provided experiences to develop visual, aural, or tactile imagery about Switzerland, the students discussed the weekend football game while completing an assignment that to them was merely verbal gymnastics.

Of course, there are some excellent and dynamic teachers. Unfortunately, much of the usual classroom instruction discourages some students, turns off others, and fails to engage the minds of many. Further, those who tend to become turned off, disengaged, or frustrated are disproportionately lower-class students and students of color. (Students mainstreamed from special education may also become frustrated and disengaged, but they usually have the support and help of a special education teacher.)

There is another instructional problem that occurs in some classrooms. Research has found that many teachers interact with, call on, praise, and intellectually challenge students who are White, male, and middle class more than other students in the same classroom and that they reprimand Black male students the most (Jackson & Cosca, 1974; Sadker & Sadker, 1988). For example, Table 1–6 illustrates the average proportion of questions and praise that girls and boys received in several classrooms at three different times during the year. In the first and third observations, boys received proportionately more questions and praise than girls. During the second observation, teachers were monitoring their behavior because results of the first observation had been shared with them, but by the third observation they had returned to their earlier pattern. Further, as the year progressed, boys initiated an increasingly larger proportion of student-initiated questions (Sleeter, 1992). Teachers are usually unaware that they are showing favoritism, but such bias can benefit members of advantaged social groups when it occurs.

Bigler and Lockard (1992) observed that the teachers they interviewed reported that the reason students tell parents they did "nothing" in school is "not due to the lack of talented teachers or their desire to teach, but as a direct result of too much to do, insufficient time to do it and increasing intrusion on teaching time" (pp. 63–64). In discussing classroom life, Apple (1993) also expresses concern regarding the intensification of labor teachers are experiencing, stating, "The chronic sense of work overload ... has escalated over time. More and more has to

TABLE 1–6.
Teacher–Student Interaction: Gender Patterns

Average Classroom Composition:	*Females, 46%; Males, 54%*		
	Observation 1 *(24 classrooms)*	*Observation 2* *(14 classrooms)*	*Observation 3* *(16 classrooms)*
Who gets called on:	%	%	%
Females	39	47	38
Males	61	53	62
Who gets praised:			
Females	32	51	43
Males	68	49	57
Which students *initiate questions:*			
Females	35	22	19
Males	65	78	81

Source: Sleeter, C. E. (1992). *Keepers of the American dream*, London: Falmer Press, p. 127.

be done; less and less time is available to do it. This has led to a multitude of results" (p. 124). Unfortunately, the overtaxing of teachers, lack of teaching and planning time, and classroom interruptions most directly impact students who are marginalized and can least afford it. It is quite ironic, too, that women, who constitute the majority of the teaching force at the elementary and secondary level, are laboring not only under increasingly constrained and regulated conditions, but that much of the labor of teaching is unpaid, not unlike work in the domestic sphere. During the school year 1993–1994, for example, the average hours worked by full time teachers per week *before and after school and on weekends* ranged from 11 to 13 hours, depending upon the nature of the school setting (U. S. Department of Education, 1996, p. 27, Table 48–1).

Observations of classrooms where gay students are present note that teachers will interrupt and deal with racist and sexist name calling, but often will not intervene when homophobic comments are made. Another observed silence is the absence of resource materials in the school library for adolescent students who may have questions about gay and lesbian issues. Much like the books missing in the library, discussions of gay and lesbian issues in the classroom tend to be absent. When teachers do discuss homosexuality, they tend to do so in the context of pathology. Usually when homosexuality is discussed, it is reported as deviant behavior. The connection between those who contract AIDS and/or who are HIV positive, homosexuality, and immoral behavior is an example.

WHAT TEACHERS TEACH

Goodlad's (1984) study of 38 schools nationwide provides a comprehensive view of what teachers today are teaching. We will not provide extensive description, but will note salient findings. The main finding was school-to-school uniformity, especially at the secondary level. Goodlad summarized two subject areas as follows: "Overall, the impression that emerged from the analysis of English and language arts was one of great curricular similarity from school to school. This impression comes through even more strongly for mathematics" (p. 208). He found that teachers in both subject areas emphasized the acquisition of skills, often apart from context or real-life use. Social studies and science at the elementary level varied considerably from classroom to classroom, often being grounded in students' experiential background. For example, primary-grade social studies usually revolved around the family and neighborhood. At the secondary level, however, social studies content became increasingly alike from one classroom to another and increasingly removed from student experience. More variation was found in what was taught in the arts and vocational areas. Goodlad also found heavy emphasis on rote learning: Although teachers often said they were developing higher-level thinking skills, their tests overwhelmingly emphasized the regurgitation of memorized material.

Curricula emphasize the wealthy White male experience, although less so today than 25 years ago. In 1990, we analyzed 47 textbooks that were in use in Grades 1 through 8, with copyright dates between 1980 and 1988. The analysis included social studies, reading and language arts, science, and mathematics textbooks. The results supported the following conclusion:

> Whites consistently dominate textbooks, although their margin of dominance varies widely. Whites receive the most attention, are shown in the widest variety of roles, and dominate the story line and lists of accomplishments. Blacks are the next most included racial group. However, the books show Blacks in a more limited range of roles than Whites and give only a sketchy account of Black history and little sense of contemporary Black life. Asian Americans and Hispanic Americans appear mainly as figures on the landscape with virtually no history or contemporary ethnic experience … Native Americans appear mainly as historical figures … Males predominate in most books; but even in books in which females have a major presence, females of color are shown very little. One gains little sense of the history or culture of women, and learns very little about sexism or current issues involving gender … Social class is not treated in the books much at all … The image that books in all subject areas convey is that the United States is not stratified on the basis of social class, that almost everyone is middle-class, that there is no poverty and no great wealth … Disability is ignored as well. (Sleeter & Grant, 1991, pp. 97–98)

Furthermore, there seems to be more cultural diversity in curricular materials than in the actual content teachers teach. It is important for us to point out that, although an increasing number of teachers do use culturally pluralistic and nonsexist materials, most of these teachers do not refer very often to people of color or women when talking or lecturing (Grant & Sleeter, 1996). Thus, what teachers teach when doing "business as usual" includes people of color somewhat, and in a supplementary way, but Whites still predominate; it includes White females, but males still dominate; it includes people with disabilities; and it virtually excludes the experience of those living below the middle class.

The curriculum responds most actively to diversity when there are non-English speaking students. Since the Supreme Court decision in *Lau v. Nichols*

(1974), schools have been required to provide help in learning English as well as instruction in the child's language while the child is learning English. Under business as usual, this seems to mean providing bilingual or English as a Second Language (ESL) instruction for as short a time as possible until minimal English proficiency is achieved. For example, Guthrie (1985) studied a Chinese-English bilingual program in California. She found that the Chinese community wanted its children to learn the Chinese language and culture, whereas the school system expected bilingual education to work toward as rapid a transition to English as possible. Debates at the federal level during the 1980s and into the 1990s support the school system's expectation; they revolve around how to teach English most effectively, not how to promote bilingualism. (Interestingly, however, business as usual does encourage college-bound English-speaking students to acquire minimal competence in a second, usually Western European, language.)

So far, our description suggests that all students of a given grade level are taught much the same thing, regardless of geographic region, student interest, or cultural background, except in the case of non-English-speaking students. This characterization is only partially correct. There does appear to be a standard curriculum that most teachers use as a guide. It is not codified in a national curriculum guide; rather, it is codified in standardized achievement tests and text materials, which are more alike than different for any given subject area. Teachers tend to use the content of text materials and standardized tests as the basis for what they teach. They then modify this material to fit the average skill level of a class and, to a much lesser degree, student interest and experiential background. For example, consider the teachers in the junior high school studied by Grant and Sleeter (1996). When asked how they decided what to teach, most teachers reported starting with an idea of what students at that grade level should know in that subject area, then adjusting forward or backward to most students' current level of mastery. In this case, students were behind grade level in most areas, so teachers either retreated to earlier material or watered down grade-level material to make it simpler. Student interest rarely affected what these teachers taught.

Goodlad's (1984) study of 38 schools supports this finding. The main variation he found in content was between tracks or ability groups. Teachers beefed up or watered down content in response to student skill level. Student interest played at most a minor role in determining the curriculum. Geographic locale played no role. Student cultural background played a minor role. Because track or ability group plays the main role in determining how teachers vary both instruction and content, we will next turn to how students are grouped. But before doing so, it is important to briefly discuss a shift that is shaping both how and what teachers teach.

In the midst of widespread patterns of school failure, there is a movement to de-emphasize the study of teacher practice at the microlevel and to emphasize the formation of educational policies. The formation of policy that addresses how and what teachers teach is largely connected with the underlying belief that administrative and regulatory measures will lead to "better" teaching and therefore to increased levels of student achievement. In fact, efforts to generate "higher" standards in the content areas are related to this shift. Yet, as policy recommendations proliferate, fewer and fewer studies are being done to assess their impact upon teachers, students, and learning. It is imperative, though, that a dialogue among members of the research, policy, and practice communities take place if efforts are to successfully transform education (Cohen, McLaughlin, & Talbert, 1993).

HOW STUDENTS ARE GROUPED

Within school districts, students are grouped in various ways: by school, by ability group or track, by special education need, and by interest (in the form of electives). We will discuss aspects of grouping under business as usual as they relate to race, social class, gender, and handicap.

First, although schools are supposed to be racially desegregated, they do not need to be desegregated on the basis of social class. It is quite common for schools to serve primarily or solely upper-class, middle-class, working-class, or lower-class students, and schools serving different social classes are not alike. They differ somewhat in the availability of resources (Kozol, 1991), such as computers (Campbell, 1984), and in the salaries they are able to offer. They differ strikingly in curriculum and instruction. For example, based on observations in five schools, Anyon (1981) reported differences that are virtually the same as the differences between tracks that we will describe.

Racial desegregation is also less a reality than many of us would like to believe, particularly for language-minority students. Although the segregation of African American students has decreased, the segregation of Hispanic students has increased (Orfield, 1986). The majority of Hispanic students attend schools that serve predominantly minority populations. This increased segregation of Hispanic students interferes with their acquisition of English-language competence (Garcia, 1986) and is related to higher dropout rates in high school. In addition, the schools that Hispanic students attend are largely inferior, reporting the highest dropout rates, lowest achievement rates, and greatest problems with teacher turnover, overcrowding, and gangs (Kyle, Lane, Sween, & Triana, 1986). As Orum and Vincent (1984) put it, "Hispanics now have the dubious distinction of being not only the most undereducated group of American children, but also the most highly segregated" (p. 26).

A second important kind of grouping is ability grouping, found extensively in elementary schools, and tracking, a pervasive feature of high schools in the major academic areas. The pros and cons of ability grouping are a continuous focus of debate among teachers, as demonstrated on the "Speak Out" page of the American Federation of Teachers' publication *On Campus* (Lucas, 1992; Mitchell, 1992). Here, two teachers argued their positions on ability grouping, one basically arguing that ability grouping can create a label that lasts a lifetime and the other arguing that talented students must not be ignored. Based on a review of research on the effects of tracking, Oakes (1985) reports that although many people assume that ability grouping and tracking are best for most students, the evidence points clearly to the conclusion that "no group of students has been found to benefit consistently from being in a homogeneous group," and those in the middle and lower groups are often affected negatively (p. 7). Her own investigation of 25 secondary schools across the country in the late 1970s found considerable tracking being used. In multiracial schools, upper-track classes were disproportionately White, whereas lower-track classes were disproportionately minority and lower class. Upper-track students tended to receive the following: at least 80% of class time spent on instruction, considerable homework, more varied teaching activities, clear instruction, emphasis on higher-level thinking skills, and exposure to content that would gain them access to college. Lower-track students, on the other hand, received about 67% of class time spent on instruction, half (or less) the homework of upper-track students, varied materials but very routinized instructional activities, less clarity in instruction, emphasis on rote memory, and content oriented around everyday-life skills (which may seem practical but also may block access to college). Most upper-track students reported enthusiasm for school and feelings of personal competence, whereas lower-track students were often turned off to school and felt academically incompetent. These are the same sorts of differences Anyon (1981) found between upper-class and working-class schools.

These studies clearly show that students are grouped partly on the basis of race and social class and then are taught differently. Upper-track and upper-class students are offered more instructional time, more challenge, interesting and effective instruction, opportunities to think, and preparation for college. Lower-track and lower-class students tend to receive routine and dull instruction, less challenge, memory work, and little or no preparation for college. Middle groups receive something in between. Although people often say that these groupings meet students' instructional needs and provide opportunity for advancement, for the most part lower groups are being turned off to school and are not being pushed to catch up, causing them to grow increasingly different from other groups as they proceed through school. For this reason, schools have been very accurately described as a sorting machine, slotting the young for a stratified labor market (Spring, 1976).

A third problem is the proportionately smaller numbers of female students in upper-level mathematics and science courses and in computer courses. It appears that although girls may take almost as many mathematics and science courses as boys, they often avoid the more difficult courses, which greatly hinders access to mathematics and science majors in college (Fennema, 1984).

A fourth aspect of grouping is special education, which in many ways fits into the tracking system, although less so for the physically, visually, and hearing impaired than for other categories. Classes for gifted students are still disproportionately White, whereas classes for children with mental retardation and emotional disturbances are disproportionately African American (Table 1–7). In some schools, Hispanic students are overrepresented in special education; in some, they are placed in bilingual education whether this is appropriate or not. Learning disability classes appear to be shifting from protective areas for White, middle-class, failing children to remedial classes for students previously classified as retarded or slow (Sleeter, 1986). The nature of content and, to some extent, instruction parallels distinctions between upper and lower tracks. However, special education teachers often do a better job than most other teachers of adapting instruction to

TABLE 1–7.
Percentage of Students in Disability Categories by Race

	Enrollment by Race (%)				
	American Indian	Asian	Hispanic	Black	White
Total Enrollment in School System	1	3	10	16	70
Special Education Classifications:					
Gifted and Talented	0	5	5	8	81
Educable Mentally Retarded	1	1	5	35	58
Trainable Mentally Retarded	1	2	10	27	60
Speech Impaired	1	2	8	16	73
Severely Emotionally Disturbed	1	0	7	27	65
Specific Learning Disability	1	1	10	17	71

Source: Harry, B. (1992). *Cultural diversity, families, and the special education system.* New York: Teachers College Press, p. 62. Reprinted by permission of the publisher, © Teachers College, Columbia University. All rights reserved.

students' learning styles, skill levels, and interests and often act as advocates and helpers for their students, helping to get them through the school system to graduation (Grant & Sleeter, 1996).

A fifth aspect of grouping is vocational classes, which group students at the secondary level somewhat by interest. Even here, however, we find grouping roughly following social class, race, and gender lines. For example, Oakes (1985) found a distinct racial difference in vocational courses: Home economics and general industrial arts were by far the main vocational courses in White schools, whereas courses preparing students for specific blue-collar and clerical occupations were common in non-White and racially mixed schools. In spite of Title IX (an education amendment of 1972 that forbids schools from restricting access to courses and school activities based upon sex), one is also likely to find a gender difference, with home economics and clerical courses dominated by girls and industrial arts courses dominated by boys (DBS Corporation, 1982). Although enrollments in vocational courses depend largely on student choice, researchers find that other factors strongly affect what students choose. These factors include availability of courses at their school, how comfortable students feel with the gender composition that is usually in a given course, how useful students think the course will be in helping them attain what they consider is a realistic (although not necessarily desirable) future occupation, and the quality of guidance and encouragement they receive (Grant & Sleeter, 1996; Oakes, 1985; Valli, 1986).

A sixth aspect of grouping at the secondary level is bilingual education or English as a Second Language (ESL). Many bilingual programs at the secondary level are seen by local administrators as remedial in nature, designed primarily for the student with limited English proficiency who needs to "catch up" or minimally develop "survival" English skills. In addition, many programs segregate language-minority students within the school, making it more difficult for them to interact with Anglo students in English or to receive exposure to the curriculum that Anglo students are being taught. In some states where graduation requirements have recently been raised, bilingual and ESL classes are not counted for graduation. With the institution of minimum competency testing (in English), many language-minority students face the possibility of not receiving high school diplomas or of receiving "attendance diplomas" that will close opportunities for postsecondary education (Fernandez & Velez, 1985).

All of this suggests that when schools operate according to business as usual, students are grouped in ways that roughly parallel race, class, and gender lines and then are taught in ways that help channel them into roles currently occupied by members of their race, class, and gender groups. Grouping is usually based on tests, teacher judgment, grades, and student choice, but as ethnographic studies of schools are revealing, all of these processes are often linked in subtle but strong ways to race, social class, and gender.

OTHER PATTERNS

Additional patterns in schools tend to mirror and help reproduce prevailing race, social class, and gender patterns. Viewing school systems from top to bottom, one finds the following staffing patterns: Superintendents are overwhelmingly White and male (95%). Twenty-seven percent of the principals in the country are women, and although they make up 34% of the elementary school principals, they only account for 12% of the secondary school principalships (Pigford & Tonnsen, 1993). Therefore, women and men of color in school administration tend to be elementary school principals, central office staff, or administrators charged with duties related to Title IX, desegregation, and so forth. Over 90% of teachers are White, and this percentage is increasing. Over 80% of elementary school teachers are female; mathematics, science, and industrial arts teachers are predominantly male, whereas foreign language, English, and home economics teachers tend to be female. People of color are often custodians and aides, and over 90% of secretaries are women. These patterns offer distinct role models and authority relationships for students.

In addition, the growing lack of people of color in teaching and administration means that fewer teachers are likely to identify with and advocate concerns particular to students of color. Furthermore, the preponderance of men in decision-making positions sometimes causes insufficient attention to be paid to the concerns of female students, whereas the preponderance of women at the elementary school level makes it difficult for many boys to identify with school and its requirements.

Extracurricular activities can also mirror existing societal patterns and reinforce segregation patterns, although situations vary from school to school. However, the following patterns are not uncommon. Middle- and upper-class students often dominate the activities, especially activities that are academically oriented. In racially mixed schools, especially if Whites are clearly in the majority, Whites tend to dominate. When White domination occurs, other students often feel unwelcome in activities. Students of color sometimes dominate some of the sports. At times, sports are divided by race and class, with golf or swimming, for example, predominantly White and basketball predominantly Black. Boys' sports often receive a larger share of the budget than girls' sports and may receive better coaches, better playing schedules, and so forth. Probably the greatest change in extracurricular activities in the past several decades has been the development of girls' sports; the challenge now seems to be to make them qualitatively equal to boys' sports.

STUDENT CULTURE

The preceding discussion centered on what schools do. But students do not respond to schools in a mechanical fashion. Researchers are increasingly aware that student cultures develop in ways that often help reproduce existing social patterns, make it difficult to change student behavior, and reaffirm to teachers that their own behavior toward students is correct. Often, great gaps exist between how teachers and students perceive each other and how they perceive themselves.

Everhart (1983), for example, studied boys in a White, working-class junior high school. The boys entered school uncertain about occupational goals, familiar mainly with working-class jobs and ways of life. The teachers perceived the students as academically average or below average, with most of them probably headed for working-class jobs. Classroom instruction was teacher dominated, rarely individualized, and routine, emphasizing the memorization of predigested material. To an observer, it was immediately apparent that students spent quite a bit of time goofing off, investing only as much effort in classwork as they needed to get by. On closer examination, however, Everhart found that the students actively engaged in creating a culture that would help make school livable. The students saw school as analogous to the work world, and the school offered much on which to base this analogy: It was clearly dominated by authority figures with whom the students could not identify; the work was routine and unrelated to the students' daily lives; most of the students' time was structured; and students were rewarded for accomplishing prescribed pieces of work. Without consciously connecting their interpretation of school to the labor market or their future life chances, the students attempted to control whatever fragments of time they could and to build relationships with each other. To the teachers, the students' behavior reaffirmed that they were not interested in academic work and were incapable of managing substantive decisions, so there was no point in challenging them. The teachers seemed unaware that the student culture was generated partly in response to what they offered the students; and the low level of academic work, accepted by both teachers and students, helped ensure the students a working-class future.

Gaskell (1985) offers a similar portrait of working-class girls in clerical courses. The girls chose the courses for several reasons: These courses offered more hands-on learning than did college-preparation courses and were therefore more fun; the students were treated more like adults than were academic students; and the courses would help the girls secure secretarial jobs before settling down to raise a family. Many of the girls did not particularly like secretarial work, but given the world they grew up in, this option seemed like a more viable alternative than college preparation. In school, they developed a culture that rejected academics (academic kids being viewed as somewhat childish rather than mature). Their culture centered around building social relationships with each other and drew on traditional patterns of femininity for guidance in how to control bosses, handle male workers, make boring work fun, and so forth. To the outside observer, it seemed that these girls were predisposed to do the traditional work performed by women, that they chose secretarial work because they liked it, and that the school had nothing to do with these things. From the inside, it was found that the girls developed their secretarial culture as a way of trying to make the best of what they saw as limited career options, to cope with male co-workers, and to attain some status for themselves in relationship to middle-class, college-bound students.

Student culture has relevance to "business as usual," because it helps shape many of the decisions students make about school and because it develops as much from within the school as from outside the school. Many teachers believe that all or most of their students' values and beliefs are generated only from outside; students who fail, turn off, drop out, or choose low-ability classes are doing so in spite of the school's attempt to give all an equal chance. These teachers often blame the students' home culture or society in general.

Although society and home certainly cannot be discounted, they do not determine student behavior. In a very real sense, students determine it as they make sense of the school experience they confront every day. All the patterns described here as business as usual present students with experiences that vary somewhat according to student race, social class, and gender, among other factors; the experiences that students have outside the school give them frameworks that also vary by race, social class, and gender, and students use these frameworks to interpret school life. There has always been a gap between teachers and students, resulting at least from age and role and often compounded by differences in cultural background. This gap has recently been expanded, as an increasing number of students come from homes that have alternative life styles and family arrangements. Some teachers bridge this gap and grasp the differences in student culture and life style fairly well; many do not, interpreting student behavior as part of the natural order of things that teachers need to control and to discourage from being reproduced. As the teaching staff in the United States becomes increasingly older and increasingly White, it is quite possible that the gap between teachers and students, and especially low socioeconomic-status students and students of color, will widen to become a chasm in many schools.

APPROACHES TO MULTICULTURAL EDUCATION

The problems we have just described have existed for a long time and have been recognized and contested by many educators. In fact, the progress that we have noted has come about largely through the efforts of educators, working in conjunction with community and social movements, to make schools, along with other social institutions, fairer and more responsive to the needs of the students.

The reforms that educators have advocated bear different names but are directed toward common practices. Some of the more common names for these reforms are *multicultural education, nonsexist education, human relations, gender fair education, multiethnic education, ethnic studies, sex equity, bilingual/bicultural education, anti-racist teaching,* and *mainstreaming.* Multicultural education has emerged as an umbrella concept that deals with race, culture, language, social class, gender, and disability. Although many educators still apply it only to race, it is the term most frequently extended to include additional forms of diversity. For this reason, we will use the term *multicultural education* to refer to educational practices directed toward race, culture, language, social class, gender, and disability, although in selecting the term we do not imply that race is the primary form of social inequality that needs to be addressed. We see racism, classism, and sexism as equally important.

Educators have not advocated a single, unified plan for multicultural education. Responding to somewhat different issues in different schools, employing different conceptual views of school and society, and holding somewhat different visions of the good society, educators over the years have constructed different approaches to multicultural education.

Gibson (1976) reviewed advocacy literature in multicultural education, identifying four approaches that led her to ultimately suggest a fifth. The four approaches she identified were (a) education of the culturally different, or benevolent multiculturalism, which seeks to incorporate culturally different students more effectively into mainstream culture and society; (b) education about cultural differences, which teaches all students about cultural differences in an effort to promote better cross-cultural understanding; (c) education for cultural pluralism, which seeks to preserve ethnic cultures and increase the power of ethnic minority groups; and (d) bicultural education, which seeks to prepare students to operate successfully in two different cultures. She proposed, as an alternative, "multicultural education as the normal human experience," which teaches students to function in multiple cultural contexts, ethnic or otherwise (such as regional).

Pratte's (1983) typology of approaches was similar. He identified the following four approaches: (a) restricted multicultural education, which seeks to remediate deficiencies in culturally different students and teach majority students to tolerate minorities; (b) modified restricted multicultural education, which seeks to promote full school services for all groups and promote equality among groups within the school; (c) unrestricted multicultural education, which seeks to remediate ethnocentrism in all students by teaching them to identify with a plurality of cultural groups; and (d) modified unrestricted multicultural education, which seeks to prepare all students for active citizenship in a racially diverse society.

Combined, these two typologies distinguish fairly well among the various approaches to multicultural education, but they have some limitations, the main one being that neither author fleshed out the theory undergirding each approach. (Each approach occupied a page or less in a journal.) A second limitation is that both typologies were applied only to race and missed or glossed over distinctions related to gender and social class. A third limitation is that the two typologies did not quite capture the range of practices we have observed in schools. Finally, a fourth limitation is that they tended to focus on issues related to cultural diversity more than social inequality.

Based on our own work as teachers, administrators, college professors, and ethnographic researchers, as well as on extensive reviews of the literature on multicultural education (Grant, 1992a, 1992b; Grant & Sleeter, 1985; Grant, Sleeter, & Anderson, 1986; Sleeter, 1991, 1992; Sleeter & Grant, 1987), we constructed our own typology of approaches to multicultural education. We will briefly introduce these approaches.

During the 1960s, in efforts to desegregate schools, many White educators "discovered" students of color and saw them as culturally deprived. This view was contested vigorously by those who argued that these students were different, not deficient, and that their cultural differences should be accepted by the school. This view has been paralleled by many special educators who argue that disabled students' differences should be accepted and built on. The approach that emerged—*Teaching the Exceptional and the Culturally Different*—focuses on adapting instruction to student differences for the purpose of helping these students succeed more effectively in the mainstream. This corresponds to Gibson's first approach and Pratte's first and second.

During about the same period, but building on the post-World War II Intercultural Education Movement, other educators argued that love, respect, and more effective communication should be developed in schools to bring people who differ closer together. This developed into the *Human Relations* approach, which corresponds to Gibson's second approach. It has often been applied to race, gender, and handicap.

The 1960s also saw the emergence of more assertive approaches to change the mainstream of America rather than trying to fit people into it. Ethnic studies, women's studies, and, to a lesser extent, labor studies were developed in an effort to focus attention on specific groups, raise consciousness regarding that group's oppression, and mobilize for social action. This was a portion of Pratte's second approach.

The *Multicultural Education* approach emerged during the early 1970s, continuing to develop as some educators have grown disenchanted with earlier approaches and as others have begun conceptualizing more complete and complex plans for reforming education. This approach links race, language, culture, gender, disability, and, to a lesser extent, social class, working toward making the entire school celebrate human diversity and equal opportunity. Both Gibson and Pratte described it as their third approach, and we have subsumed Gibson's fourth and fifth approaches under it.

Finally, the 1970s and 1980s saw the development of a fifth approach, which we are calling *Education That Is Multicultural and Social Reconstructionist*. Throughout the 1990s, this approach has been gaining in recognition and credibility, in part because it extends the Multicultural Education approach into the realm of social action and focuses at least as much on challenging social stratification as on celebrating human diversity and equal opportunity. Pratte's fourth approach leaned in this direction.

PLAN OF SUBSEQUENT CHAPTERS

Our continuous reviews of the literature on multicultural education have led us to an important observation: The existing literature on these various approaches, although more analytical than when we did the first edition in 1988, is nevertheless still somewhat fragmented, and in many cases conceptually weak. Much of it simply prescribes what teachers should do, offering short and sometimes simplistic reasons. Some of the literature ignores previous writings on multicultural education and discusses the concept as if it has no history. Additionally, other writings selectively choose the approach to multicultural education that their authors wish to discuss and ignore the other approaches. Similarly, the authors of some books and articles that are well conceptualized and well researched in a specific area of multicultural education tend to present their approaches as if they were the only approaches.

The chapters that follow offer two major features to correct these shortcomings. First, they explicate the five approaches and allow the reader to compare them. A critique of each approach is offered to help with this comparison. The reader is invited to think through the goals, assumptions, and practices of each approach to determine which makes the most sense.

Second, each approach is developed here in some depth. The first part of each chapter discusses each approach's goals, assumptions, and theoretical base. This provides a clearer picture of what the approach is attempting to do and why, as well as guidance for developing strategies to implement it. Next, recommended practices are summarized, followed by one or two vignettes that illustrate the approach in action. Then the approach is critiqued from the vantage points of other approaches. Finally, a table summarizing the main goals, target audience, and recommended practices is presented, enabling the reader to see the main ideas of the approach at a glance. We invite the reader to think through carefully which approach makes the most sense. We are not without our own opinion on this. After presenting each approach in what we hope is an unbiased manner, we will argue (in our last chapter) why we feel that one approach is preferable to the other four.

REFERENCES

Alsalam, N., & Rogers, G. T. (1991). *The condition of education 1991: Volume 2. Postsecondary education*. Washington, DC: U. S. Government Printing Office.

The Americans with Disabilities Act: Where we are now. (1991, January/February). *The Disability Rag*, 11–19.

Anyon, J. (1981). Elementary schooling and distinctions of social class. *Interchange, 12*, 118–132.

Apple, M. W. (1993). *Official knowledge: Democratic education in a conservative age*. New York: Routledge.

Barlett, D. L., & Steele, J. B. (1992). *America: What went wrong?* Kansas City, MO: Andrews & McMeel.

Beulow, M. C. (1992, July 13). State doctors told to ask more about domestic abuse. *Kenosha News*, p. 1.

Bigler, P., & Lockard, K. (1992). *Failing grades*. Arlington, VA: Vandermere Press. *Black Congressional Monitor*. (1993, January 5). p. 6.

Bobo, L., Schuman, H., & Steeh, C. (1986). Changing racial attitudes toward residential integration. In J. Goering (Ed.), *Housing desegregation and federal policy* (pp. 153–169). Chapel Hill: University of North Carolina Press.

Buce, J., & Obolensky, N. (1990). Runaway and homeless youth. In M. J. Bradley & N. Obolensky (Eds.), *Planning to Live: Evaluating and treating suicidal teens in community settings*. Tulsa, OK: University of Oklahoma Press.

Campbell, P. (1984). The computer revolution: Guess who's left out? *Interracial Books for Children Bulletin, 15*, 3–6.

Cohen, D. K., McLaughlin, M. W., & Talbert, J. E. (Eds.). (1993). *Teaching for understanding: Challenges for policy and practice*. San Francisco, CA: Jossey-Bass.

Cuban, L. (1984). *How teachers taught*. New York: Longman.

DBS Corporation. (1982). *Elementary and secondary schools survey*. Unpublished paper prepared for the U. S. Office of Civil Rights, U. S. Department of Education.

Dervarics, C. (1991). Landmark study confirms widespread job bias. *Black Issues in Higher Education, 8*(7), 1 & 4.

Deyhle, D. (1985). Testing among Navajo and Anglo students: Another consideration of cultural bias. *Journal of Educational Equity and Leadership, 5*, 119–131.

Everhart, R. (1983). *Reading, writing, and resistance*. Boston: Routledge & Kegan Paul.

Fennema, E. (1984). Girls, women, and mathematics. In E. Fennema & M. I. Ayer (Eds.), *Women and education* (pp. 137–164). Berkeley: McCutchan.

Fernandez, R. R., & Velez, W. (1985). Race, color, and language in the changing public schools. In L. Maldonado & J. Moore (Eds.), *Urban ethnicity in the United States: New immigrants and old minorities* (pp. 123–144). Beverly Hills, CA: Sage.

Gallup, G., Jr., & Hugick, L. (1990). *Racial tolerance grows, progress on racial equality less evident*. Los Angeles: Gallup Poll News Service.

Garcia, E. E. (1986). Bilingual development and the education of bilingual children during early childhood. *American Journal of Education, 95*, 96–121.

Gaskell, J. (1985). Course enrollment in the high school: The perspective of working-class females. *Sociology of Education, 58*, 48–59.

Gest, T. (1991, June 17). The new meaning of equality. *U.S. News & World Report*, p. 48.

Gibson, M. A. (1976). Approaches to multicultural education in the United States: Some concepts and assumptions. *Anthropology and Education Quarterly, 7*, 7–18.

Gliedman, J., & Roth, W. (1980). *The unexpected minority*. New York: Harcourt Brace Jovanovich.

Goodlad, J. I. (1984). *A place called school*. New York: McGraw-Hill.

Grant, C. A. (1992a). *Best practices in teacher preparation for urban schools*. Paper presented at the American Educational Research Association National Conference, San Francisco.

Grant, C. A. (Ed.). (1992b). *Research and multicultural education*. London: Falmer Press.

Grant, C. A., & Sleeter, C. E. (1985). The literature on multicultural education: Review and analysis. *Educational Review, 37*, 97–118.

Grant, C. A., & Sleeter, C. E. (1996). *After the school bell rings* (2nd ed.). Barcombe, England: Falmer Press.

Grant, C. A., Sleeter, C. E., & Anderson, J. E. (1986). The literature on multicultural education: Review and analysis, Part II. *Educational Studies, 12*, 47–71.

Guthrie, G. P. (1985). *A school divided*. Hillsdale, NJ: Erlbaum.

Habeck, R. V., Galvid, D. E., Frey, W. D., Chadderden, L. M., & Tate, D. G. (1985). Economics and equity in employment of people with disabilities: International policies and practices.

Proceedings from the Symposium. East Lansing, MI: University Center for International Rehabilitation.

Hacker, A. (1992). *Two nations: Black and white, separate, hostile, and unequal*. New York: Charles Scribner's Sons.

Harrington, M. (1984). *The new American poverty*. New York: Holt, Rinehart & Winston.

Harry, B. (1992). *Cultural diversity, families, and the special education system*. New York: Teachers College Press.

Hasazi, S., Gordon, L., & Roe, C. (1985). Factors associated with the employment status of handicapped youth exiting high school from 1979 to 1983. *Exceptional Children, 51*, 455–477.

Hate. (1992, May/June). *The Disability Rag*, 4–7.

Herdt, G., & Boxer, A. (1993). *Children of Horizons: How gay and lesbian teens are leading a new way out of the closet*. Boston: Beacon Press.

Jackson, G., & Cosca, C. (1974). The inequality of educational opportunity in the Southwest: An observational study of ethnically mixed classrooms. *American Educational Research Journal, 11*, 219–229.

Jencks, C., Smith, M., Acland, H., Bane, M. J., Cohen, D., Gintis, H., Heyns, B., & Michelson, S. (1972). *Inequality: A reassessment of the effect of family and schooling in America*. New York: Harper & Row.

Johnson, M. (1991, March/April). What builders don't know. *The Disability Rag*, 12–17.

Kozol, J. (1991). *Savage inequalities: Children in America's Schools*. New York: Crown.

Krucks, G. (1991) Gay and lesbian homeless youth. *Journal of Adolescent Health, 12*(7), 515–518.

Kyle, C. L., Jr., Lane, J., Sween, A., & Triana, A. (1986). *We have a choice: Students at risk of leaving Chicago public schools*. Chicago: DePaul University Center for Research on Hispanics.

Lau v. Nichol, 414 U.S. 563 (1974).

Lucas, L. (1992) Does ability grouping do more harm than good? Don't ignore the potential of talented students. *On Campus, 11*(6), 6.

Mare, R. D., & Winship, C. (1984). The paradox of lessening racial inequality and joblessness among black youth: Enrollment, enlistment, and employment, 1964–1981. *American Sociological Review, 49*, 39–55.

McGowan, B. (1991). *Children welfare reform*. New York: National Center for Children in Poverty, Columbia University School of Public Health.

Mitchell, B. L. (1992) Does ability grouping do more harm than good? It creates labels that last a life time. *On Campus, 11*(6), 6–9

Mithaug, D. E., Horiuchi, C. N., & Fanning, P. N. (1985). A report on the Colorado statewide follow-up survey of special education students. *Exceptional Children, 51*, 397–404.

National Center for Education Statistics, Office of Education Research and Improvement. (1991). Washington, DC: U.S. Government Printing Office.

National Commission on Children. (1991). *Beyond rhetoric*. Washington, DC: U.S. Government Printing Office.

National Mental Illness Screening Project. (1996). Who suffers from eating disorders? Washington, DC: Author.

No housing to refer people to. (1990, May/June). *The Disability Rag*, 7.

Oakes, J. (1985). *Keeping track: How schools structure inequality*. New Haven: Yale University Press.

Ogle, L. T., Alsalam, N., & Rogers, G. T. (1991). *The condition of education 1991: Volume 1. Elementary and secondary education*. Washington, DC: U.S. Government Printing Office.

Orfield, G. (1986). Hispanic education: Challenges, research, and policies. *American Journal of Education, 95*, 1–25.

Orum, L., & Vincent, A. (1984). *Selected statistics in the education of Hispanics*. Washington, DC: National Council of La Raza.

Page, R. N. (1991). *Lower-track classrooms*. New York: Teachers College Press.

Parenti, M. (1978). *Power and the powerless*. New York: St. Martin's.

Pigford, A. B., & Tonnsen, S. (1993). *Women in school leadership*. Lancaster, PA: Technomic.

Pratte, R. (1983). Multicultural education: Four normative arguments. *Educational Theory, 33*, 21–32.

Reeves, R. (1990, August 30). Who got what in the 1980's. *Kenosha News*, p. 10.

Remafedi, G. (1987). Male homosexuality: The adolescents's perspective. *Pediatrics, 83(3)*.

Riche, M. F. (1991). We're all minorities now. *American Demographics*, 26–34.

Rumberger, R. W. (1983). The influence of family background in education, earnings, and wealth. *Social Forces, 3*, 755–773.

Sadker, M., & Sadker, A. (1988). *Sex equity handbook for schools* (2nd ed.). New York: Longman.

Shade, B. J. (1989). *Culture, style, and the educative process*. Springfield, IL: Charles C Thomas.

Sidel, R. (1990). *On her own: Growing up in the shadow of the American dream*. New York: Penguin.

Siegel, S. (1986). *The right to work: Public policy and the employment of the handicapped*. Unpublished doctoral dissertation, San Francisco State University and University of California, Berkeley.

Sleeter, C. E. (1986). Learning disabilities: The social construction of a special education category. *Exceptional Children, 53*, 46–54.

Sleeter, C. E. (Ed.). (1991). *Empowerment through multicultural education*. Albany, NY: SUNY Press.

Sleeter, C. E. (1992). *Keepers of the American dream*. London: Falmer Press.

Sleeter, C. E., & Grant, C. A. (1987). An analysis of multicultural education in the U.S.A. *Harvard Educational Review, 57*, 421–444.

Sleeter, C., & Grant, C. (1991). Race, class gender, and disability in current textbooks. In M. W. Apple & L. K. Christian-Smith (Eds.), *The politics of the textbook* (pp. 78–110). New York: Routledge.

Spring, J. (1976). *The sorting machine: National education policy since 1945*. New York: McKay.

Tippeconnic, J. W., III. (1991). The education of American Indians: Policy, practice, and future direction. In D. E. Green & T. V. Tonnesen (Eds.), *American Indians: Social justice and public policy* (pp. 180–207). Milwaukee, WI: University of Wisconsin System Institute for Race and Ethnicity.

Treiman, D. J., & Hartman, H. I. (1981). *Women, work, and wages: Equal pay for jobs of equal value*. Washington, DC: National Academy Press.

Trueba, H. T., Jacobs, L., & Kirton, E. (1990). *Cultural conflict and adaptation: The case of Hmong children in American society*. London: Falmer Press.

Uribe, V., & Harbeck, K. M. (1991). Addressing the needs of lesbian, gay, and bisexual youth: The origins of PROJECT 10 and school-based intervention. In K. M. Harbeck (Ed.), *Coming Out of the Classroom Closet* (pp. 9–28). New York: Harrington Park Press.

U.S. Bureau of the Census. (1995). *Statistical Abstract of the United States: 1995* (115th ed.). Washington, DC: Author.

U.S. Department of Commerce, Bureau of the Census. (1991a). *Current Population Reports*, series P-70, No. 29. Washington, DC: U.S. Government Printing Office.

U.S. Department of Commerce, Bureau of the Census. (1991b). U.S. Department of Labor Statistics. *Employment and Earnings*. Washington, DC: U.S. Government Printing Office.

U.S. Department of Education. National Center for Education Statistics. (1996). *The Condition of Education 1996*, NCES 96–304 by Thomas M. Smith. Washington, DC: U.S. Government Printing Office.

U.S. Department of Education. National Center for Education Statistics. (1996). *Digest of Education Statistics 1996*, NCES 96–133, by Thomas D. Snyder. Production Manager, Charlene M. Hoffman. Program Analyst, Claire M. Gidder. Washington, DC: Author.

U.S. Department of Health and Human Services. (1985). *Report to the secretary's task force on Black and minority health, Vol. 1, Executive summary*. Washington, DC: U.S. Department of Health and Human Services.

U.S. Department of Health and Human Services. (1989). *Gay Male and Lesbian Youth Suicide. Report of the secretary's task force on youth suicide. Volume 3: Prevention and intervention in youth suicide* (89–1623). Rockville, MD: U.S. Department of Health and Human Services, Public Health Service, Alcohol, Drug Abuse and Mental Health Administration Publication. Washington, DC: U.S. Government Printing Office.

U.S. Department of Justice. (1990). *Correctional population in the U.S.* National Prison Statistics Series. Washington, DC: U.S. Government Printing Office.

Valli, L. (1986). *Becoming clerical workers*. Boston: Routledge & Kegan Paul.

Wolf, N. (1991). *The beauty myth: How images of beauty are used against women*. New York: William Morrow.

CHAPTER TWO

Teaching the Exceptional and the Culturally Different

Often we are threatened by or want to change those who differ from ourselves and whom we do not understand. Our classrooms often have students who do not look like us, talk like us, or think like us—who have not had some of the experiences we have had. Students may have grown up in neighborhoods unlike our own. Some may not behave as we were taught to behave. Some may not show much interest in learning things we personally value. Some, because of hearing impairments, visual impairments, reading difficulties, and so forth, may not have acquired knowledge that we take for granted. However, as teachers, we very often want to make our students become more like us.

GOALS

Many teachers see themselves as responsible for helping students fit into the mainstream of American society. They believe that students who do not readily fit because of cultural background, language, learning style, or learning ability require teaching strategies that remediate deficiencies or build bridges between the student and the school. To these teachers, multicultural education means teaching exceptional or culturally different students so that they can achieve in school and better meet the traditional demands of American life.

Proponents of this approach regard United States society as basically good and just, and they believe that the main goal of schooling is to assimilate the young into that society as shown in Table 2–1. The goal of this approach is to equip students with the cognitive skills, concepts, information, language, and values required by American society in order to hold a job and function within the society's existing institutions and culture. Most proponents regard immigrants, the poor, the unemployed, people with disabilities, and alienated members of society as lacking primarily the right skills, values, and knowledge.

According to this approach, modifications are made in schooling to facilitate these students' academic achievement and their transition to the mainstream culture that White, middle-class children are learning. This approach is based on the *human capital theory* of society. After presenting it, we will discuss two quite different orientations that teachers use to interpret student differences: one that

TABLE 2–1.
Teaching the Exceptional and the Culturally different

Societal goals:	Help fit people into the existing social structure.
School goals:	Teach dominant traditional educational aims more effectively by building bridges between the student and the demands of the school.
Target students:	Lower-class, special education, limited English proficiency, female, or students of color who are behind in achievement in main school subjects.
Practices:	
Curriculum	Make relevant to students' experiential background; fill in gaps in basic skills and knowledge; teach content in language students can understand; use first language as basis for teaching standard English.
Instruction	Build on students' learning styles; adapt to students' skill levels; Teach as effectively and efficiently as possible to enable students to catch up.
Other aspects of classroom	Use decorations showing group members integrated into main stream society.
Support services	Use transitional bilingual education, ESL, remedial classes, special education as temporary and intensive aids to fill gaps in knowledge.
Other schoolwide concerns	Involve lower-class and parents of color in supporting work of the school.

views differences as deficiencies and the other that views differences simply as differences.

THE HUMAN CAPITAL THEORY OF EDUCATION AND SOCIETY

The human capital theory holds that education is a form of investment in that the individual acquires skills and knowledge that can be converted into income when used to get a job. You probably have been told that you should go to school so that you can get a good job and that the more time and energy you invest in school, the better the job you will get. In a technological society such as ours, what counts as capital is "the knowledge and skills required to take on and use efficiently the superior techniques of production" (Schultz, 1977, p. 322). Thus, schools should teach skills and attitudes appropriate for working at a very wide range of jobs as well as for consuming products. This approach assumes that opportunities open up to individuals at a level commensurate with the level of education they have acquired and that the more individuals develop their human capital through education, the better their life circumstances, our economy, and society in general will be. The approach further suggests that the poor are poor mainly because they have not developed their human capital. Theoretically, then, poverty and inequality result largely from insufficient opportunity for people of color, the poor, people with disabilities, and women to acquire the knowledge and skills society needs.

Americans frequently look to the schools to solve social problems. People who subscribe to the human capital theory often call for school reforms when they perceive the United States experiencing a national crisis. During the late 1950s, when the Soviet Union launched Sputnik (the first space vehicle), many Americans became concerned that the United States was falling behind in the Cold War and called on schools to upgrade science, math, and foreign-language instruction. Similarly, in the 1980s, as the United States experienced loss of previously undisputed economic supremacy in the world market, many people again called on schools to supply the "human capital" necessary to develop the American competitive edge. Beginning with *A Nation at Risk*, published in 1983 (National Commission on Excellence in Education), reports made recommendations such as lengthening the school day and school year, instituting more testing, raising standards for achievement, getting back to basics, and upgrading science and math instruction. Since that time, the National Board for Professional Teaching Standards (NBPTS) has been established, standards in the various content areas are being developed, and, in some states, additional and mandatory testing is becoming a prerequisite for high school graduation—with each of these efforts symbolizing an increasing national preoccupation with accountability, the efficient and successful production of human capital, and economic, global competition.

Some groups of students have tended to lag behind in achievement in school as well as in achievement in the broader mainstream society. These groups include children of color, children from low-income homes, children with disabilities, children whose native language is not English, and, in some areas such as math, girls. Even though school achievement gaps based on race and gender have been steadily closing (as measured, for example, by the National Assessment of Educational Progress and the Scholastic Assessment Test [SAT]), gaps still remain and become even more worrisome during periods when standards for students in general are rising. Like the reform movement of the late 1950s, the reform reports of the 1980s disclosed very little about how to boost the achievement of these groups (Grant & Sleeter, 1985).

Educators who adopt this approach to multicultural education fall into two quite different camps. Those educators who subscribe to the *deficiency orientation* see prevailing standards for "American culture" and "normal" human development as universally correct, and they trace failures to achieve those standards to supposed deficiencies in children's home environments and in their physiological and mental endowments or in both. Those educators who subscribe to the *difference orientation* see prevailing standards as relative to the demands of a particular culture and hold that different cultural contexts produce equally healthy but different patterns of normal development. Individuals can learn to function productively in mainstream culture as well as in their own community culture. We will present both orientations, although we are critical of the deficiency orientation and see much more promise in the difference orientation.

However, educators who subscribe to either orientation view multicultural education as Teaching the Exceptional and the Culturally Different, and these educators share a common goal: to help children who are "different" become as "mainstream" as possible through education so they can invest themselves in work that will bring them society's rewards. The approach assumes that ultimately assimilation has the best chance for eradicating poverty, unemployment, racism, sexism, and general social tensions because it helps everybody develop sufficiently to play a productive role in society and share a common culture.

DEFICIENCY ORIENTATION

Think of a person who is successful in today's society, such as a lawyer or a businessperson. That person probably has developed a high level of literacy, a respect for time schedules, competitive skills, an ability to act independently of other people, certain interpersonal skills, skill in the use of Standard English, and so forth. Now think of a person who seems unsuccessful. How would you compare the successful person with the unsuccessful one? In making such a comparison—which we do all the time—we frequently think of the less successful adult or student in terms of what we believe she or he lacks: reading ability, motivation, exposure to knowledge, discipline, language skills, and so forth.

The deficiency orientation focuses on what we believe members of another group lack, usually based on a comparison to the abilities and cultural resources we have and with which we are familiar. Adherents to the deficiency orientation regard people who exemplify the values, skills, and abilities that mainstream society requires as the standard for normal development. Psychological theories of normal development have been based on this standard and have codified it in the form of various intelligence and personality tests. People who subscribe to the deficiency orientation focus primarily on either presumed cultural deficiencies or physiological and mental deficiencies.

Cultural "Deficiency"
In our education classes, we hear students refer to poor children as *disadvantaged*, *socially deprived, low socioeconomic, culturally deprived,* and *culturally deficient*. Over the past ten years, *children at risk* has become another popular label. Although different labels highlight different images—some stressing socioeconomic disadvantage, others educational disadvantage—they all trace problems back to the child's living environment.

An examination of the education literature of the 1960s readily yields a description of students who were thought to be culturally deficient. Goldberg's description is a good example:

> Beginning with the family, the early preschool years present the child from a disadvantaged home with few of the experiences which produce readiness for academic learning either intellectually or attitudinally. The child's view of society is limited by his immediate family and neighborhood where he sees a struggle for survival which sanctions behavior viewed as immoral in the society at large. He has little preparation either for recognizing the importance of schooling in his own life or for being able to

cope with the kinds of verbal and abstract behavior which the school will demand of him. Although he generally comes to first grade neat and clean and with his mother's admonition to be a "good boy," he lacks the ability to carry out those tasks which would make him appear "good" in the eyes of his teacher.

Early difficulty in mastering the basic intellectual skills which the schools and thus the broader society demands leads to defeat and failure, a developing negative self-image, rebellion against the increasingly defeating school experiences, a search for status outside the school together with active resentment against the society which the school represents. The child early finds status and protection in the street and the gang which requires none of the skills which are needed in school but makes heavy use of the kinds of survival skills which he learned in his early home and street experiences. (1963, p. 87).

In the 1990s, you often hear similar descriptions in teachers' lounges, but descriptions of at-risk students in the education literature are more careful. For example, Ralph (1989) described who is at risk today as follows: "The descriptors vary from all-encompassing background factors—low income, low achievement, handicapping condition, minority status, inner-city household, and limited proficiency in English—to concrete, specific measures, such as dropping out of high school" (p. 396). What thinking lies behind composites of the culturally deprived or at-risk student?

One line of thinking promoted by Arthur Jensen (1969) and Herrnstein and Murray (1994) holds that children in poor families, disproportionately of color, have inherited flaws from an inferior genetic stock, and their failure in school and society simply reflects that flawed inheritance. Most educators, ourselves included, do not accept this line of thought, so we will not review it here.

Many educators who disagree with the heredity explanation for the failure of students of color (especially African American students) explain failure in terms of general environmental conditions. In their description of trends in disadvantaged populations, for example, Pallas, Natriello, and McDill (1989) explained that they "view educational experiences as coming not only from formal schooling, but also from the family and the community. Students who are educationally disadvantaged have been exposed to inappropriate educational experiences in at least one of these three institutional domains" (p. 16). A number of specific psychological deficiencies have been attributed to "substandard" environments.

One psychological deficiency is poor perceptual skills. Klaus and Gray (1968) and Deutsch (1963) argued that homes in the ghetto provided too little visual and tactile stimulation and too much disorganized aural stimulation for normal perceptual development. A bare apartment with the TV blaring constantly—the image many people have of inner-city homes—was thought to retard a child's learning to discriminate among shapes and objects and learning to listen carefully to environmental sounds. Ausubel (1966) catalogued a list of perceptual problems supposedly brought about by low-income homes that lacked sensory stimulation and systematic and ordering of stimuli: "poor perceptual discrimination skills; inability to use adults as sources of information, corrections and reality testing, and as instruments for satisfying curiosity; an impoverished language-symbolic system; and a paucity of information, concepts, and relational propositions" (p. 251).

Some educators believed that these deficiencies would not only hinder a child's ability to acquire information but would also ultimately retard the child's development through Piaget's stages of cognitive growth (Hunt, 1961).

Although these descriptions are almost forty years old and have received critism for years, they continue to re-emerge under different labels, such as "difference" or "at risk." Also, the "deficit" and "difference" models continue to hold their popularity as categories to structure discussions and writing about the learning of students of color and students living at or below the poverty level (Portes, 1996). Language is a second area of deficiency popularly attributed to the "culturally deprived." Many educators believe that the language that lower-class children have learned is so concrete and disorganized that it prevents them from learning to think abstractly. For example, Bernstein (1964) described middle-class language as *elaborated* because of its complex vocabulary and structures that enable the communication of hypotheses, relationships, and abstractions. In contrast, he saw lower-class language as *restricted* because of its high use of concrete words and short, simple sentences. More recently, Orr (1987) attributed African American students' difficulties with mathematics to the grammatical structure of Black English: "They come to school without an *as ... as* structure in the language they speak" (p. 195). She argued that in thinking through a mathematical expression like "twice as large as," Black-English-speaking students merge the structure into their own grammatical frame of reference—ending up with, in this case, "twice as larger than"—and confuse themselves in the process.

Children whose native language is not English are also not exempt from concern. It is not uncommon for language-biased teachers and counselors to place language-minority children in classes for the mentally retarded or learning disabled (Harry, 1992; San Miguel, 1987; Sheets, 1995; Trueba, 1989). Furthermore, many educators believe that Mexican migrant children fail to develop enough competence in either English or Spanish to enable complex learning, which is why their IQ scores are lower than those of Anglo children. Compensatory education for Hispanic students has focused on, as the primary determinant of underachievement, language rather than other factors (such as the quality of the teaching or the relevance of the concepts being taught). Consequently, Hispanic students' achievement is rarely discussed without reference to bilingualism, Spanish dominance, or lack of English skills, and other factors related to achievement are often overlooked (Walker, 1987).

A third supposed deficiency is moral integrity and stability. Many educators believe that poor children lack appropriate role models and that this deprivation damages their development. For example, Silber (1988) described welfare dependency and sexual hedonism as the moral code now characterizing the "underclass" and perpetuating the cycle of poverty. A recent description of inner-city families noted that "A mother is sometimes present in these homes, but she is often a drug addict or a teenager who comes and goes ... Scarred by years of abuse and neglect, many of these children are angry and disruptive" (Gross, 1992, pp. 1, 616). African American males today face enormous barriers, and many people still blame the African American family and community (for example, by attributing problems to female-headed households). African American educators, however, who address the needs of African American males much more assertively than White educators do, frame the issues in terms of access to resources and support systems rather than moral depravity and psychological instability.

Increasingly, educators are becoming aware of the effects that maternal drug use during pregnancy has on the development of children. Fetal drug addiction can have very damaging consequences for later learning. A stereotype we encounter in schools is that drug use is more common among low-income mothers than among middle-income mothers; thus, if a child from a low-income family is performing poorly in school, the child is probably "unteachable" because of brain damage resulting from the mother's drug use. Such a conclusion is a very dangerous leap for a teacher to make. A recent medical study of the use of illicit drugs during pregnancy found virtually no relationship between drug use and race or socioeconomic status. Yet, poor and African American women were much more likely to be reported to health authorities for suspected abuse than were middle-class and White women (Chasnoff, Marvey, Landress, & Barrett, 1990). Teachers who hold a deficiency orientation toward low-income people, people of color, or both may be susceptible to making unwarranted assumptions about maternal drug use, rather than looking for other reasons that a child is not learning.

In schools, we commonly encounter use of the cultural deprivation model to explain lower achievement of students from low-income and minority homes. For example:

> Where are they coming from? ... What's going on in their brains, you know? Because sometimes I realize how irrelevant it is to stand up here and talk, and I have a very close family ... [my husband and I] have been very strong disciplinarians and we encourage the work ethic ... I realize how foolish and presumptuous [it is] to think all these kids are coming from the same thing ... Just to have a totally helter skelter house where there is nothing regular and the people who are your parent figures come and go and—you don't know, you know what I mean, just what is going on in their brains and where they are coming from. (Sleeter, 1992, p. 172)

Richardson, Casanova, Placier, and Guilfoyle (1989) studied how teachers decide who is at risk and how they attribute causes of risk. They found that

> The teachers were generally unwilling to attribute a student's lack of success to a characteristic inherent in the child or to their own instructional programs. They therefore moved outside the classroom to find the cause of the student's problems. These causes most often rested on their students' home lives and parents. (p. 37)

The teachers viewed students not at risk as coming from strong families and so-called at-risk students as coming from deficient families. Therefore, "teachers appeared to accept any negative statement about families of at-risk students from other teachers or adults in the building" (p. 37).

As teachers observe changes in the demographics of schools, many interpret these changes as suggesting that more and more students are coming to school incapable of advanced learning. For example, Pallas, Natriello, and McDill (1989) reported that, "substantial numbers and troubling proportions of U.S. children may be classified as educationally disadvantaged" (p. 17). They went on to review statistics on the proportions of racial and ethnic minority students, students with backgrounds of poverty, students from single-parent families, and students whose primary language is not English. The portrait they presented was one that causes alarm: With a growing proportion of "disadvantaged" students to serve, educators are facing increasingly bigger problems. In response to such problems, Hirsch (1996) has even recommended the adoption of an official national curriculum, a measure largely understood as compensatory in nature and essential for the success of culturally deficient students.

Defining cultural diversity as more of a problem than a resource indicates adherence to the deficiency orientation. Teachers who believe that some children do not come to school able to learn often give up on them or have low expectations for them. Even though the term *at risk* is supposed to direct us toward intervention to prevent failure (Ralph, 1989), it often feeds right into assumptions about what a child lacks that prevents learning. The literature on teacher expectations documents a link between student backgrounds, teacher expectations, and how teachers teach (Brophy, 1983; Contreras & Delgado-Contreras, 1991). In practice, the cultural deficiency orientation supports low expectations and precludes many teachers from examining and improving their own teaching.

Physiological and Mental Deficiency

Historically, much of the work in special education has sought to understand and remediate physiological and mental deficiencies. You can accurately catalog these deficiencies (or supposed deficiencies) simply by listing the special education categories: visual impairment, hearing impairment, physical and health impairments, mental deficiency (in fact, a leading special education journal and professional organization both have the term *mental deficiency* in their titles), emotional or behavioral disorders, learning disabilities, and, more recently, attention disorders. For the most part, the field of special education assumes these disorders to have primarily an organic or psychological basis, although mental retardation and emotional disturbance have also been thought to be strongly linked to the cultural "deficiencies" described earlier (Dunn, 1963). Most special educators regard disabilities in school as products of the interaction of deficits within the child and characteristics of the learning environment.

> Children who enter school without a diagnostic label ... bring with them as yet unspecified cognitive, behavioral, linguistic, and affective characteristics developed over time, which interact with the academic and social ecology. Out of this interaction comes school success or, in about 10% of children, failure and referral for special education. (Cooper & Speece, 1990, p. 124)

Many of the same deficits in psychological functioning ascribed to the so-called culturally deprived have been ascribed to those students labeled mentally retarded, emotionally disturbed, learning disabled, hard of hearing, and visually impaired. Most of these students are described as deficient in language and reading skills. Children classified as mentally retarded, for example, have been described as having "deficits in memory, ability to pay attention, verbal communication, motivation, ability to generalize, and understanding of similarities and differences" (Mandell & Gold, 1984, p. 12). Children classified as learning disabled have been described as deficient in their ability to handle grammatical inflections, comprehend and create complex sentences, define words, classify objects into categories, produce sentences, and recognize their own language errors (Bryan & Bryan, 1978).

Students with language and reading problems are often described as lacking information—as well as some of the underlying concepts—that their "normal" age-mates have. For example, according to Kneedler (1984), mentally retarded children "learn concepts slowly if at all [and] have difficulty remembering things" (p. 51). Hearing impaired children are often behind academically because of their "difficulty succeeding in a system that depends primarily on the spoken word and written language to transmit knowledge" (Hardman, Drew, & Egan, 1984, p. 227). When you realize that much of what is taught in school is explained verbally or read, this conclusion makes sense: If you can't read the book, you won't learn the material in it.

Another area of deficiency attributed to most special education children is thinking skills. Hardman et al. (1984) described the moderately retarded as having "difficulty focusing on relevant stimuli, inefficient rehearsal strategies that help commit information to long-term memory, inability to learn from incidental learning cues, and difficulty transferring knowledge from one task to another" (p. 117). Children classified as learning disabled sometimes display difficulty with specific thinking skills, such as visualizing imagery, organizing information, abstracting, or synthesizing (Adelman & Taylor, 1983).

Finally, most students in special education are described as being deficient in social skills, partially because they "seem to be lacking in self-control, ego strength, and social-personal adjustment, all of which are necessary for establishing positive interpersonal relationships" (Gearheart, DeRuiter, & Sileo, 1986, p. 245). By definition, children classified as emotionally disturbed have "an inability to build or maintain satisfactory interpersonal relationships with peers and teachers" (Public Law 94–142). Children classified as learning disabled often display antisocial or inappropriate social behavior, the result of receiving less positive and more negative reinforcement than most children; an impulsive cognitive style; hyperactivity; or visual-perceptual deficits that interfere with the ability to learn to read social cues (Bryan & Bryan, 1978).

Educators and researchers have used a variety of theoretical frameworks to understand these "deficiencies." The medical model assumes that the problems are caused by an organic defect, such as brain damage, chemical imbalance, or chromosomal abnormality. It attributes a child's problems to characteristics within the child and, with heightened frequency, prescription drugs such as Ritalin and Prozac are being used as remedies for diagnosed conditions. (For some handicapping conditions, such causes are clearly documented; for others they are not.) The behavioral model and the ecological model stress interaction between characteristics of the child and characteristics of the learning environment. Increasingly, these models are guiding special education research on intervention strategies. The behavioral model assumes that the child's problems are due to reinforcement for the wrong behaviors or a failure to have correct behaviors modeled and reinforced. The ecological model assumes that the child's problems are caused by a failure of multiple factors in the child's environment to support positive characteristics and learning behaviors of the child.

Although these models suggest that different factors are responsible for children's problems, they all see certain children as deficient in the various areas. The deficiency orientation suggests that these areas must be remediated to enable the students to function more successfully in the classroom and later on in society. For that reason, a substantial portion of the school day usually is spent on remediation.

Sexual Orientation

Because it is so often a taboo topic for discussion, many people regard homosexuality and bisexuality as deficiencies. For example, Sears (1993) describes a study of over 1,000 teenagers in which "three-fourths of the females and 84 percent of the males think that homosexual behavior is disgusting." With the recent AIDS hysteria and the gay rights movement, public attention is repeatedly directed toward homosexuality, but media often reinforce the notion that it is a deficiency. Van Gelder (1992) commented on the wave of recent movies depicting lesbian women as mentally deranged killers, arguing that such depictions appeal to deficiency images that are rampant. The "coming out" of Ellen on the television show "Ellen" is a rare exception to what is usually seen on televion, and since it was such an occasion it attracted a record number of viewers. Also, Ellen's picture made the cover of *Time* magazine.

Teachers very often do not think about sexual orientation as it relates to their students, and they usually are not encouraged to do so. As we will argue later, the failure to attend to this issue leaves students' needs and rights unaddressed. The general silence schools maintain about sexual orientation is reflective of the widespread belief that homosexuality is a disease. Frequently teachers prefer to think: No one who is gay is in my classroom or personal space. For students who are struggling with a gay, lesbian, or bisexual identity, the great stigma attached to their sexual orientation along with the general reluctance to discuss it leaves them in a very painful position that adversely affects the school achievement of many (Kissen, 1993). Sears (1991) found that 40% of the students in his study reported their academic work to be suffering as they struggled with their sexual identities, and he speculated that many of the remaining 60% also suffered academically but in less obvious ways (such as settling for mediocre rather than good academic performance). The deficiency orientation toward homosexuality does not provide a teacher with guidance about how to help. Later in this book, we will provide suggestions in the context of other approaches to multicultural education.

DIFFERENCE ORIENTATION

Advocates of the difference orientation to Teaching the Exceptional and the Culturally Different agree with advocates of the deficiency orientation that there is a standard body of knowledge and a set of values and skills that all American citizens need to acquire. However, the former believe that there are different models of healthy psychological development fostered by different cultural contexts or constitutional endowments. Rather than focusing on deficiencies that need to be remediated, advocates of the difference orientation focus on strengths to build on so as to help children assimilate into the American mainstream. As Table 2–1 shows, the school goal of this approach is to teach academic knowledge more effectively by building on the knowledge and skills students bring with them.

The academic expectations of adherents to the difference orientation are generally higher than the expectations of adherents to the deficiency orientation. The reason for this is that, although the deficiency orientation focuses on what students lack, the difference orientation focuses on what those same students bring to the teaching-learning situation, the knowledge and skills that can be built on to develop achievement. Those who subscribe to the difference orientation often argue that the main limitation to students' learning capacity is inappropriate teaching; if students are not learning well, we are not capitalizing on their strengths and resources. Learning to teach from the difference orientation requires expending time and effort in getting to know more about the background and strengths of students.

Cultural Difference

Many educators, particularly those of color, reacted strongly against the deficiency orientation. Their reaction prompted researchers to establish a research base documenting that cultural differences in language and learning style are not deficiencies and can be built on to facilitate learning. You probably have heard educators debate the pros and cons of using Black English to help teach African American, inner-city students or of providing bilingual education programs. You also may have heard educators refer to the importance of understanding the learning and communication styles of students—for example, recognizing that looking down instead of looking the teacher in the eye may be a sign of respect in the student's home culture.

A central idea behind the cultural difference orientation is *cultural continuity*. Anthropologists have documented that discontinuities between one set of cultural practices and another can be confusing to the individual who must make a rapid transition between the two different sets. One example is to think of how you feel when you are traveling in a foreign country and find yourself among people who are culturally different from yourself. You may feel confused, a bit frightened, unsure of yourself, and perhaps annoyed when you repeatedly find yourself doing or saying the wrong thing. After a period of time, you learn to function in the new culture, but initially the discontinuity jolts you.

The same thing happens with children whose home culture is different from the culture of the school. The discontinuity may be particularly aggravating for the child who is expected to function within the school's culture without being taught the culture and who must make the leap between cultures twice a day— once when arriving at school, then again when going home. Teachers who are not knowledgeable about the child's culture often interpret differences in behavior as deficiencies.

The main idea behind the Teaching the Culturally Different approach is to ensure as much cultural continuity as possible in order to teach mainstream academic content. There is no one right model of psychological development, and cultural context strongly influences how a child will develop. The psychological development of culturally different children may at times conflict with demands of the regular classroom, especially if the teacher is unaware of how children are interpreting and perceiving its demands. However, all cultural groups foster cognitive strengths that can be built on to facilitate classroom learning. As Trueba (1988) put it:

> At the heart of academic success, and regardless of the child's ethnicity or historical background, an effective learning environment must be constructed in which the child, especially the minority child, is assisted through meaningful and culturally appropriate relationships in the internalization of the mainstream cultural values embedded in our school system. (p. 282)

Considerable research on learning in diverse cultural contexts is based on neo-Vygotskian theory, which postulates that intellectual development takes place in natural interactive activities involving a child and an adult. Within a "zone of proximal development," which is the level of development for which a child is ready, a child can be assisted to learn new things. Effective learning requires that the child and adult share cultural values and patterns and that they communicate effectively (Trueba, 1988). Communication and cognitive style are two major areas of research on cultural difference. We will provide examples of some common differences between the cultural style of many children and that of teachers. The important point is that academic learning can be greatly enhanced when teachers learn the cultural style of the child well enough to connect effectively with the child within the child's zone of proximal development.

Shade (1989) distinguishes between two different cognitive styles: *analytical* and *synergetic*. Her main contention is that schools and mainstream individuals tend to function with an analytical style; African American students as well as many students from other minority groups tend to function with a synergetic style. Analytical learners are competitive and independent, and they focus well on impersonal tasks. They learn well through print, focus best on one task at a time, and work in a step-by-step sequence. Synergetic learners, on the other hand, prefer to work cooperatively rather than independently; they do not block out their peers, but rather attempt to integrate personal relationships into learning tasks. Synergetic learners are stimulated by multiple activities and become bored when only one thing is happening. They often prefer kinesthetic and tactile involvement as well as discussion. Shade argues that teachers who are analytical learners often misread the behavior of synergetic learners, viewing them, for example, as talking too much, being off task, or cheating rather than as building on their preference for cooperative work. When the teaching style of the classroom matches the learning style of students, students can achieve well; synergetic learners need not be low achievers. Stressing a similar appreciation for multiple cognitive styles, Markova (1992) developed a topology of learners on the basis of thinking patterns along auditory, kinesthetic, and visual channels and likewise called for greater educational sensitivity to such diversity.

Some educators shy away from discussions of learning and cognitive style, feeling that such discussions only promote stereotypes. It is important to recognize that within any cultural group, individuals vary greatly. However, groups share certain tendencies, which are the result of each group's historic culture as well as its experience with oppression in the United States (Shade, 1989). Sensitivity to group tendencies can enable a teacher to read students' behavior more accurately and to try more alternatives when teaching. It is also important to recognize that minority groups differ. For example, whereas African American students tend to prefer oral communication and kinesthetic activities for taking in new information (Shade, 1989), Native American students tend to have excellent visual skills (Gilliland, 1988).

Cultural groups also differ in communication style, sometimes to the detriment of student learning. Philips (1983), for example, studied communication patterns among Warm Springs Indians—documenting how much wait time there is between a person's utterances, how a person gains attention, how a person acknowledges that a message has been understood, and how people take turns in a conversation. She found that the patterns children learned in the community conflicted with the patterns used and expected by the Anglo teachers in school. As a result, the teacher and the students constantly responded to each other inappropriately, which fostered antagonism and lack of respect. For example, the children did not respond to the teacher's attempts to conduct recitation lessons, causing the teacher to view the children as slow and uncooperative and the children to view the teacher as rude and confusing. Philips suggested that teachers of Indian children could be much more successful if they learned to use the communication patterns of the local community.

Dialect is an important dimension of communication. Several different dialects are spoken within the United States; in addition to Standard English, dialects in current use include Appalachian, Hawaiian Creole, Tex-Mex, and Black English. Proponents of the cultural deficiency orientation view the speech of lower-class, African-American children (and other non-Standard English dialect speakers) as incorrect, poor, and "destitute" (Newton, 1966). Since the mid-1960s, however, considerable research has established dialects as linguistically sound, governed by their own rules of phonemics, syntax, morphology, and word meaning (Labov, 1969). This being the case, educators have wondered whether dialect interferes with teaching conducted in Standard English. Such concerns, for example, have shaped debates over the usage of Black English in school settings (e.g. Oakland, California).

In a review of debates about Black English, Smitherman (1981) argued that the attitudes of educators toward the "Blackness" of Black English is a larger problem than communication mismatch per se. Speakers of Black English come to school having mastered one dialect, and they are cognitively equipped to master a second one—Standard English—as well as the content encoded in it. Unfortunately, they are penalized by being required to take tests that assume competence in Standard English before they have been taught to use it, administered by teachers who assume that Black English is substandard or poorly learned language and that those who speak it are incapable of advanced learning.

African American students who exhibit competence in oral games, such as sounding, understand the use of figurative language better than White students. Teachers who incorporate these students' verbal skills in language arts instruction have a definite strength on which to build their achievement (DeLain, Pearson, & Anderson, 1985). During the late 1960s, before schools were desegregated, several bidialectal reading and language programs were developed to help Black-English-speaking children acquire Standard English language skills; upon desegregation such programs were dropped, and research on their effectiveness withered (Williams, 1991). And yet, there is evidence that building upon the community language practices of linguistically marginalized groups greatly enhances literacy and enriches the classroom environment (Maybin, 1994; Moss, 1994).

There is no question, however, that language difference interferes with instruction when teacher and student do not speak the same language. Historically, most U.S. schools actively maintained an English-only policy, often prohibiting the use of any language other than English for instruction, although European immigrants in the 1880s and early 1890s used bilingual programs (such as German-English) quite extensively. However, children of color whose native language was not English tended to be viewed as deficient and their home language and culture as inferior. Early strategies for dealing with linguistically and culturally different students included submersion in the English-language curriculum or placement in special English as a Second Language (ESL) classes. Neither approach successfully integrated the language-minority student into the mainstream. By the 1960s, spurred on by increased immigration from Cuba and the growing civil rights movement, education policy makers were desperately seeking another more promising approach. At the same time, parents, concerned teachers, and community activists began calling for the use of children's native languages in schools (Schneider, 1976).

From their inception with the passage of the Bilingual Education Act in 1968, bilingual education programs were pushed into a compensatory mold. Although there are bilingual programs that use all the approaches to multicultural education described in this book, the majority continue to use the Teaching the Culturally Different approach. Such programs use the child's native language as a medium of instruction in content areas until the child has learned enough English to get by in an English-only program. Of how much value is the child's native language? Heated debates between advocates of transitional models versus maintenance bilingual-education-program models have raged for years. In general, most programs in the United States follow the transitional approach, in which the child moves from native-language instruction to English-only instruction as soon as possible, with the average length of stay in such programs being 3 to 4 years. The less-practiced maintenance model strives to develop complete bilinguality in its students and to maintain it throughout the students' 12 years in public school.

Nevertheless, regardless of a particular program's structure, all bilingual education models assume that the language and culture a child learns at home can promote normal and healthy psychological development and communication competence. Moreover, evidence indicates that children with well-developed first-language skills acquire their second language with greater ease and success than children who are still learning their first language (Cummins, 1981; Skutnabb-Kangas, 1981). This phenomenon is explained by Cummins' "common underlying proficiency" model of language acquisition, which holds that many language skills and attitudes, once learned well, can be translated fairly easily into any language and that they are best learned in one's strongest language (Cummins, 1989). The language skills referred to include skills such as using verbs in different tenses, using language to describe objects or feelings, and connecting print with meaningful oral language.

If the school denigrates a child's native language, it may not only damage the child's self-concept (Kobrick, 1974) but also cut off normal communication development between the child and his or her parents. Many immigrant students, when enculturated with the Anglo, middle-class culture of the school, respond with shame and even hostility toward their parents, home language, and culture.

The degree of cultural continuity between home and school can vary; the larger the gap, the harder schools need to work to construct bridges. For example, Phelan, Davidson, and Cao (1991) distinguished among four patterns: (a) congruent worlds among home, school, and peer group, with smooth transitions from one setting to the next; (b) different worlds with boundary crossings from one to the next that are manageable; (c) different worlds with unbridged boundary crossings that are hazardous for the student; and (d) different worlds with insurmountable barriers. In their research, they found that students did reasonably well academically with teachers who tried to adapt their teaching to the students; when forced to choose between the peer group and the school, or between home and school, many students did not choose school and consequently failed.

When a student acts out behaviorally or drops out psychologically from the classroom, the student may be bored or may not see the relevance of what she or he is being asked to learn. Because minority students may not respond enthusiastically to many of the learning tasks they confront, lack of motivation is the attribute most often thought to be responsible. These misguided assumptions of lack of motivation combine with low expectations for academic achievement to form insurmountable obstacles for these groups (Brown, 1986, p. 13).

Acting out or dropping out may also indicate that the student is under stress because of a lack of cultural continuity between the child and the classroom. For example, Trueba (1989) described immigrant children who were unable to comprehend classroom instruction or who responded to the teacher in a way different from that which the teacher expected. Over time, the children's academic performance dropped, as did their effort. Although teachers viewed the students as exhibiting learning disabilities, Trueba argued that the students' learning abilities were normal, but that the culture of the classroom was sufficiently different from their home culture as to make it impossible for them to function well. Experiencing the stress of repeated failure, the students stopped trying.

Achievement can be enhanced when teachers attempt to make the culture of the school compatible with the child's culture and to work with the child within her or his zone of proximal development. For example, Jordan (1985) and her colleagues identified a few key practices that were interfering with native Hawaiian children's learning. Hawaiian children spend considerable time working with peers outside of school; if they are punished for interacting with peers in the classroom, and especially if punishment involves isolating them, they will put their energy into establishing illicit contact with peers. If a moderate level of peer interaction is allowed, they tend to stay on task.

Lucas, Henze, and Donato (1990) identified and studied high schools in which language-minority students were achieving; they found that teachers and school leaders in these schools expected high achievement of students and treated students' language and culture as a resource rather than as a handicap. For example, students were encouraged to develop skill in both English and their native language, and teachers tried to learn about students' past experiences in order to link academic content with what students know and find interesting.

James Comer (1988) helped several schools serving low-income, African American students to raise the achievement levels on standardized achievement tests to well above the district average. He helped the school staffs learn to use child development principles and build support systems for healthy development, rather than blaming children and their parents for problems. Parent teams were formed and parents began to work cooperatively with the teachers and administrators. This process of bridge building took several years, requiring teachers as well as parents to learn to change their behavior with each other; but the process paid off in terms of the children's achievement.

Deafness as a Language and Cultural Difference

Hearing people very often regard deafness as a deficiency, and they discuss people with deafness as lacking in normal language development and, as a result, full cognitive development. "The cultural view of the deaf community, on the other hand, views deaf people as a group that shares a common language and a common means of communication" (Stewart & Akamatsu, 1988, p. 238). American Sign Language (ASL) has been in existence since at least the early 1880s, and ASL and the difference orientation to educating deaf children have competed with the deficiency orientation for a long time. Oralism (teaching hearing impaired children to speech-read and to speak orally) and signed English systems (which put English grammar and morphology into signs) have been used heavily in schools to attempt to approximate the English language as well as possible.

Although both oralism and signed English systems provide access to spoken English for children who have some hearing, American Sign Language is an alternative language system that is more accessible to children with profound or total hearing loss. As linguists have gained interest in studying ASL, appreciation has developed for this language's sophistication and integrity as a language and for its broad acceptance in a community that uses it as the primary language of communication. As a language-minority community, the deaf community also has other cultural strengths and resources in which deaf children can learn to participate, such as a wide range of organizations, arts produced by the deaf community, and interpersonal networks. "It is not possible to understand deaf people until the language is acquired but it is not possible to achieve in the language until there is contact with the culture. One does not become deaf to do this anymore than one becomes French in France" (Kyle & Pullen, 1988, p. 57). Increasingly, the deaf community is asking to be regarded and taught as a language-minority group rather than as a disabled group.

Mental Difference

Children whose school performance is far below average are often considered mentally deficient. A teacher who views students such as those in classes for the learning disabled or educable mentally retarded as different rather than deficient is more likely to use an approach discussed later in this book than the approach discussed in this chapter. For example, imagine a ninth-grade teacher with some special education students who read on a fourth-grade level. The teacher who wishes to assimilate these students may not believe they are permanently deficient but may view the task of assimilating them into the classroom as virtually impossible if their reading deficiency is not corrected first. An alternative is to rethink the idea that there is a standard body of knowledge that all should learn and that this knowledge should be acquired through reading. Once a teacher examines this alternative, he or she is moving away from the Teaching the Exceptional and Culturally Different approach.

On the other hand, children who excel in certain areas and who may be classified as gifted and talented can be considered mentally different. Conceptions of what the word *gifted* means range widely, from narrow definitions that include only the top 1% to 5% in academic achievement (Terman et al., 1976) to broad definitions that view many people as having gifts or talents in a variety of areas. For example, Gardner (1983) describes seven intelligences: linguistic, local and mathematical, musical, spatial, bodily and kinesthetic, interpersonal, and intrapersonal. Many people believe that, regardless of how one defines giftedness, gifted children need educational experiences that are different from those of "normal" children and that these experiences should ultimately help them provide the leadership needed in our technological society.

Proponents of the Teaching the Exceptional approach for gifted students believe that failure to offer enriched or accelerated programming often results in the failure of abilities to develop, the development of frustration and sometimes psychological problems among the gifted, and the waste of a social resource. These educators condemn the belief that gifted children will make it on their own. For example, Robinson, Roedell, and Jackson (1981) concluded on the basis of two research studies that "superior abilities that are not nurtured will not develop" (p. 130). Proponents of this approach point to underachievers, dropouts, and even suicide victims, who have become frustrated with schooling and sometimes with life in general because their abilities were not being challenged or valued (Robbins, 1984). These educators point to medical, scientific, artistic, and social accomplishments that have been achieved for society by gifted people whose abilities were cultivated (Gallagher, 1979). For these reasons, these proponents argue, some sort of differential education needs to be provided for this different group of children, whether it be a program within the regular classroom, a pullout program, an accelerated program, a special class, or some type of extra enrichment program (Reis, 1994).

Gender Difference

Why do boys tend to outperform girls in mathematics and science? Why do boys tend to dominate in the area of leadership roles? Can girls be better assimilated into these areas through the use of any particular teaching approach? You may wonder why we have placed this discussion under the difference rather than the deficiency orientation, because by late adolescence the average performance of girls in these areas is below that of boys, although gender gaps have been steadily narrowing (Linn & Hyde, 1989). This issue is examined here because the "deficiency" among girls seems to result mainly from a sexist culture that allocates the sexes to different roles and fosters in them different strengths and dispositions. Girls do not bring to school less learning than boys, rather somewhat different learning. Nor are girls genetically inferior to boys for the tasks of learning mathematics and science (Crockett & Petersen, 1984).

According to Leder and Fennema (1990), "equal educational treatment does not necessarily result in equal opportunity to learn" (p. 190). Although teachers sometimes do treat girls and boys differently in math instruction, current research reveals that a much more important variable in differential achievement is what students believe about mathematics. Girls tend to have less confidence in their mathematical ability than boys and tend to attribute successes to luck or external causes and to attribute failure to a lack of ability (the reverse of boys' attributions). Both sexes also tend to see mathematics as a male domain; girls perceive it as less useful to their futures than do boys. Ironically, girls who are not helped excessively by the teacher tend to achieve better in mathematics, because they learn to work independently, which builds their confidence. This improved result suggests that what girls need is a boost in their self-confidence and a belief that mathematics achievement will be useful to them. In addition, girls simply need to take more upper-level math and science courses, because achievement is largely related to the courses taken (Linn & Hyde, 1989).

Male dominance in the use of computers is also becoming increasingly noticeable in schools. According to Campbell (1984), boys are encouraged much more than girls to work with computers from childhood on. For example, examine a few currently popular video games and determine to which sex they were made to appeal. Referring to a series of studies conducted by the Center for Children and Technology/Education Development Center on gender-related attitudes toward technology, Brunner (1997) explains that for boys, "technology is seen as a source of power" and as a means for "one-way communication" while girls tend to view technology "as a medium" which enables people to "communicate, connect, and share ideas" (p. 55). It is important, therefore, for teachers to develop approaches to computer instruction which are sensitive to the gendered ideas about technology that students bring to the classroom. As a result of differential socialization, the sexes bring to school different skill, interest, and confidence levels for mathematics, science, and computer-science learning which must be taken into account.

Leadership is another domain that men are better socialized to occupy. Although most people regard coeducational schooling as more "progressive" than single-sex schooling, some researchers find that girls develop more leadership skills and self-confidence in single-sex schools. In coeducational schools, boys are encouraged to experiment and seek solutions to problems on their own, whereas girls tend to be encouraged to develop social relationships at the expense of learning assertiveness and flexible, cognitive problem solving. Boys learn to dominate in leadership roles, and girls learn to let the boys dominate in order to maintain positive relationships with them (thus giving boys more practice in these areas at the girls' expense) (Block, 1984). In a study of the effects of single-sex schooling on general achievement, Riordan (1990) found that "minority females profit most from single-sex schooling, followed by minority males, and then by white females" (p. 147), largely because single-sex schools reduce the effect of the adolescent subculture that tends to disadvantage females.

No matter how similarly teachers may try to treat boys and girls in school, there needs to be some compensation for the differential socialization that the sexes experience outside of school. Interestingly, there is very little discussion about how to assimilate boys into traditional female domains—for example, evaluating techniques that might be successful in preparing boys to become secretaries. We think that this example gives some indication as to which sex has controlled the more interesting, prestigious, and well-paying work.

RECOMMENDED PRACTICES

No classroom is completely homogeneous. Teachers learn to expect differences among their students. Invariably, for any set of standards to which a class of students is expected to adhere, some students adhere better than others. The problem a teacher faces is what to make of those differences, and the more students vary from the standards the teacher values, the greater the problem. Teachers who see strong reasons for maintaining traditional conceptions of what students need to learn and who want to see all their students achieve these goals as well as possible will search for ways to teach their exceptional or culturally different students. Whatever methods or techniques teachers use, they usually expect them to be temporary adaptations until the students are able to swim on their own.

In this section, we will describe bridges teachers can build between the child and the curriculum to help the student achieve and assimilate. We have organized these bridges under content, instructional process, program structure, and parent involvement. Our discussion is based on the difference orientation rather than the deficiency orientation.

Curriculum Content

How academically difficult can the curriculum be for categories of students who traditionally have not achieved at grade level? We believe it can and should be as challenging as possible; unless students are genuinely mentally retarded, we do not believe the curriculum should be oriented toward remediation but rather toward academic excellence. Jaime Escalante has been one of the most visible advocates of a challenging curriculum for inner-city students. When asked whom he recruited for his Advanced Placement math program, he replied that he did not specifically recruit students identified as "gifted"; rather, he says, "I often chose the rascals and kids who were 'discipline problems' as well as those who simply liked math. I found that the 'class cut-ups' were often the most intelligent, yet they were extremely bored by poor teaching and disillusioned by the perceived dead end that school represented for them" (Escalante & Dirmann, 1990, p. 409). Escalante underscores the "effective schools" research, which found that inner-city students achieve when teachers have high academic expectations and frequently monitor their students' achievement for purposes of instructional improvement (Edmonds, 1979). Similarly, Ladson-Billings' (1994) study of teachers who are successful with African American students reports that these teachers academically challenged their students and received favorable results.

The Teaching the Exceptional and the Culturally Different approach does not take issue with what American students should be learning in school. However, as Table 2–1 shows, if students are not learning the standard curriculum satisfactorily, bridges need to be built between the student and the curriculum. We will discuss bridges that are designed to make the curriculum more relevant and meaningful, language bridges, and bridges that fill in gaps in the students' knowledge.

One important bridge is the effort made to relate the curriculum to the experiences and interests of students. Students sometimes do not try hard when they fail to see that what they are being taught is useful or personally interesting. In addition, students often need familiar concrete examples to help them acquire new concepts. For example, Moses, Kamii, Swap, and Howard (1989) described a successful program for teaching algebra to inner-city middle school students. Directionality was a concept students had not learned to attach to numbers, and many students were having difficulty with positive and negative numbers. So the teachers sent the students to the local subway and had them diagram the subway system in terms of directionality. The teachers then helped the students represent their experience with the subway numerically, in the process helping them to translate the familiar—subway routes—into the unfamiliar—positive and negative numbers. As another example, Moll (1992) helped teachers work with parents to construct a curriculum that built on what were, in his term, the *funds of knowledge* held by families in the community. Table 2–2 summarizes the funds of knowledge in the local community with which he worked. With practice, teachers became increasingly skilled at developing classroom lessons and homework assignments that tapped into community knowledge, creating more congruence between school knowledge and the students' lives.

To make the curriculum relevant to the lives of students, teachers need to ask two questions: (a) What is the academic concept I am trying to teach? and (b) What examples or experiences do my students have that connect to this concept? A science teacher in a low-income rural area thus seeks out everyday examples, such as plants or animal life familiar to students, to teach science concepts. A social studies teacher on an Indian reservation connects social studies concepts with the history of the tribe(s) of which the students are members. In so doing, the teacher attempts to broaden what students know—keeping mastery of a challenging academic curriculum as the goal but making the concepts taught "user friendly" and familiar to the students.

TABLE 2–2.
A Sample of Household Funds of Knowledge

Agriculture and Mining	Economics	Household Management	Material and Scientific Knowledge	Medicine	Region
Ranching and farming	Business	Budgets	Construction	Contemporary Medicine	Catechisms
Horsemanship (cowboys)	Market values	Childcare	Carpentry	Drugs	Baptisms
Animal husbandry	Appraising	Ccooking	Roofing	First aid procedures	Bible studies
Soil and irrigation systems	Renting and selling	Appliance repairs	Masonry	Anatomy	Moral knowledge and ethics
Crop planting	Loans		Painting	Midwifery	
Hunting, tracking, dressing	Labor laws		Design and architecture		
	Building codes			Folk medicine	
Mining	Consumer knowledge		Repair	Herbal knowledge	
Timbering	Accounting		Airplane	Folk cures	
Minerals	Sales		Autombile	Folk veterinary cures	
Blasting			Tractor		
Equipment operation and maintenance			House maintenance		

Source: Moll, L. C. (1992). Bilingual classroom studies and Community analysis. *Educational Researcher, 21*(2), 20–24.

A second bridge is language. How do teachers make academic content user friendly to students whose native language is not English? Students need to be provided with instruction in English, and they need plenty of opportunity to practice using the language in a nonthreatening context. Research on bilingual education documents the academic benefits of developing students' competence in their first language and using that competence as a basis for helping them acquire English (Crawford, 1989; Cummins, 1989; Garcia, 1988; Trueba, 1989). Educators tend to worry excessively about whether students whose native language is not English will learn English, and in the process these educators do not focus sufficiently on the students' overall academic development. Based on a review of research on bilingual education, Pease-Alvarez and Hakuta (1992) concluded: "Don't worry about English; they are learning it; instead, worry about the instructional content; if you are going to worry about language, worry about the lost potential in the attrition of the native language, for all of the languages of the world are represented in this country" (p. 6).

Academic content and skills must be meaningful for students to learn them; meaning should be conveyed in whatever language a student understands. Schools with curricula structured to promote academic achievement for language-minority students provide the most difficult content in a student's native language, content that uses many context clues (such as hands-on work) in sheltered English, and content in fluent, mainstream English as students become able to handle it. It requires 5 to 7 years to develop competence in learning new academic content in a second language (although it takes a much shorter time to achieve conversational fluency); it is important to recognize that the academic benefits of bilingual instruction may not show up for several years (Cummins, 1989).

When teaching reading and writing to students whose native language or dialect is not Standard English, teachers need to distinguish between mechanics and meaning. For example, Taylor (1989) described a process in which she taught Black-English-speaking students to write in Standard English. Her goal was to help students convey their own ideas and meanings as effectively as possible to particular audiences. She helped students learn to identify specific patterned differences between Black English and Standard English; students also analyzed writings by Black and White authors in order to understand writing style. However, most of all, she stressed the importance of what students have to say, helping them gradually learn to control the mechanics. In a study of reading instruction, Moll, Diaz, Estrada, and Lopes (1990) found that teachers equate Spanish-speaking students' skill in decoding English with their ability to comprehend meaning; as a result, instruction was too simple for the level of content that many students could comprehend and tended to bog down in the mechanics of decoding. The mechanics of language do need to be taught in isolation, but also with a meaningful use of language to convey the ideas being presented in the class.

A third kind of bridge is the use of various strategies to fill in important academic gaps. For example, to help female students catch up with male students in mathematics, computers, and science, some remedial or compensatory work may be necessary. Fennema (1984), for instance, described workshops to teach girls about opportunities in mathematics-related careers and the importance (and realism) of girls achieving in mathematics, which led girls to take more mathematics courses and view themselves as more capable in that subject. Campbell (1984) suggests that girls be given extra encouragement and instruction in school on using computers to duplicate what boys seem to be getting outside of school.

For mainstreamed special education students, Reynolds and Birch (1988) recommend that the curriculum be developmentally appropriate (e.g., do not teach long division before students have mastered addition and subtraction) and that teachers make sure students are taught what the authors call *cultural imperatives*: language skills, mathematics, health and safety, social skills, and career skills. They point out that mainstreamed special education students may not be able to learn everything that is in the standard curriculum; the teacher should decide what to emphasize, using these recommendations as guidelines.

Too often teachers become so overwhelmed with what students have not learned that they become bogged down in remediation. If the students' knowledge has large gaps, be selective about what they need to learn, focusing on the most important content for helping them catch up and start to excel.

Instruction

More attention has gone into modifying instruction than into modifying curriculum content for the Teaching the Exceptional and the Culturally Different approach. The classroom teacher usually feels fairly confident about what students should be learning but may be perplexed about how to help them learn it. It is generally recommended that teachers be familiar with a repertoire of instructional strategies, picking those that seem most fruitful for individual students.

Instruction should be adapted to the learning style of the students. For example, whole language learning is compatible with the style of Native American children because whole language emphasizes meaning and process over product, uses cooperative work, capitalizes on oral language, and integrates subject areas. These features are compatible with Native American students' preference for communal learning and personal meaning, use of time, and holistic world view (Kasten, 1992). Many African American students "tune in" more in a classroom that encourages interpersonal interaction, multiple activities, and multiple modality preferences than in quiet classrooms in which students are supposed to pay attention to tasks more than people, print more than sound, and only one thing at a time (Shade, 1989). Fennema and Peterson (1987) found that girls learn mathematics better through cooperative learning than through competitive learning.

There are many formal and informal methods available to assess students' learning styles, including both paper-pencil and computerized instruments. The important point is for teachers to find out which strategies hold their students' attention and engage their minds and then use those strategies, particularly when teaching material that is new or difficult.

Language-minority students' language skills tend to improve when they are encouraged to talk with peers in cooperative learning contexts. For example, Garcia (1988) found that language-minority students learn math and literacy skills most effectively when student-student discussions took up at least 50% of the instructional time.

Research on effective instruction is increasingly informing recommendations for teaching mainstreamed special education students, as well as all students. Reynolds and Birch (1988), for example, recommend that teachers of mainstreamed special education students use frequent monitoring of student work, with frequent feedback, reinforcement, and review. Although teachers usually give feedback and review to all students, students with learning problems profit from these practices when they are used frequently and when they are focused on specific learning objectives. In addition, students benefit from instruction in learning how to learn—using metacognitive strategies—and encouragement to follow appropriate behavioral models. Mainstreamed students also benefit from having choices to make in some of their work.

Students deemed exceptional and culturally different are often described as unmotivated or hard to motivate, and educators have suggested how to deal with this problem. One recommendation is to make sure these students experience immediate success by assigning tasks within their capability and rewarding them for successful performance. For example, special education students usually have a history of school failure, and teachers are told that those "who have faced failure may have developed low frustration tolerance, negative attitudes toward schoolwork, and possibly some compensatory behavior problems that make them socially unpopular … [Teachers should] organize a day-to-day program presenting the child with short-range as well as long-range tasks in which to succeed" (Kirk & Gallagher, 1979, p. 163). Teachers are advised to use as motivators the students' interests or prior experiences. Lovitt (1977) suggests that a teacher bring into the classroom a variety of things to find out what actually turns the kids on, then deliberately use their interests as motivators and reinforcers. The point is that students who have done poorly in or been turned off by school will need some sort of "carrot on the end of a stick" to lead them willingly into more traditional content and instruction.

Program Structure

Programs are structured to teach exceptional or culturally different students in four distinct ways, each distinguished by the degree to which it takes the child out of "normal" education. One way of structuring a program is to keep the child entirely within the normal program but to make sure that adaptations are offered that will enable the child to succeed. For example, students with low vision might be given large-print books and audio aids, or students from a different cultural background might be given culturally relevant materials and instruction based on their learning styles. Another example is team-taught bilingual programs, in which two languages are used. This is not just business as usual, provided the teacher is actively attempting to teach students and is using many of the recommended practices to facilitate learning. The teacher tries to keep the curriculum and instruction as normal as possible but, at the same time, offers whatever bridges are needed for students to learn successfully.

A second way of structuring a program is to keep the student in a full-day normal instructional program but to provide help at the preschool level or before or after school. Probably the best example of this type of program is Head Start, which attempts to provide school-readiness skills for low-income students before those students enter school. After-school enrichment programs for gifted students are additional examples of this method of structuring instruction.

A third kind of structure is a pull-out program, in which the child is in a normal classroom for much of the day but in a special program for part of the day. This use of support services, as Table 2–1 notes, is a common structural arrangement for compensatory education programs such as Chapter I, bilingual education, and special education. Pull-out programs should be temporary; if students become permanently trapped in remedial programs, more academic harm than good may result.

A fourth kind of structure offers an entirely different education program for the different or exceptional child. Students with severe retardation and multiple disabilities are frequently educated most of the day in a separate, self-contained class. Moreover, children who do not speak English may be in a separate program all day until they learn enough English to be mainstreamed. Block (1984) recommends a greater use of single-sex schools to free girls from competition against male students (which many girls find discouraging), allow more girls to assume leadership positions, lessen the conflict between achievement and peer acceptance, and provide greater exposure to female role models.

Recently, some large school districts have begun to implement African American immersion schools to attempt to raise the achievement and promote the overall development of African American students, especially males. The main idea is that most White students attend EuroAmerican immersion schools: They are staffed mainly or exclusively by White teachers, the curriculum is Eurocentric (see Chapter 4), and instructional practices connect with the culture of White homes. Minority students, especially in desegregated schools, do not have access to the same degree of cultural fit. In their description of two new African American immersion schools in Milwaukee, Leake and Leake (1992) explained that, "the goal of the African American immersion school proposal was to develop a setting that consciously and systematically connects the total schooling experience to African/African American heritage" (p. 27). Although it is too early to evaluate the effectiveness of such schools, historically Black colleges, which are similar, have a much higher success rate in graduating African American students than do White colleges (Farrell, 1992).

Working with Parents

Public schools are frequently a source of alienation for low-income and minority parents (Calabrese, 1990). For a wide variety of reasons, such parents often do not participate in schools the way teachers expect. Some parents feel it is the teacher's job to teach and that parents should stay out; some parents who were low achievers themselves in school feel uncomfortable dealing with teachers; and some parents, when they try to participate, are turned off by school personnel (Harry, 1992; Lareau, 1989; Soto, 1997). It is important for teachers not to lower their expectations for children's learning, whether parents participate or not. However, there are many recommended practices teachers can use in attempting to connect more effectively with parents. For example, teachers can try to meet parents on the parents' turf rather than in the school. Initial meetings with parents should focus on a child's strengths rather than problems. Problem solving should involve genuine two-way rather than one-way communication. Schools can encourage parents to network. Teachers can also collaborate with institutions and organizations in minority communities, such as the church (Billingsly & Caldwell, 1991; Cummins, 1989; Frase, 1994; Gilliland, 1988; Soto, 1997).

To illustrate the implementation of Teaching the Exceptional and the Culturally Different, we offer two vignettes.

MS. VANDERBILT

Ms. Vanderbilt has been teaching a Head Start class on Chicago's southwest side for 3 years. This teaching assignment was her first after acquiring her teaching certificate from a large university in the Midwest. The class this semester is typical of classes she has taught since she began. Her students are African American and Hispanic residents of a poor socioeconomic community. The community members, including the parents of Ms. Vanderbilt's students, respect the school and look on it as the main institution that will improve life chances for their children.

Of the 28 students in Ms. Vanderbilt's class, 16 are girls—10 Black and 6 Hispanic. Two of the Hispanic girls are Spanish speaking. Of the 12 boys, 8 are African American; of the 4 Hispanic boys, 1 is bilingual.

On entering Ms. Vanderbilt's classroom, you are struck by the richness and warmth of the environment. Colorful bulletin boards, colorful posters (mostly of nature), bushy plants in decorative pots, two aquariums, and two hamsters (in cages) capture your attention. Three learning centers, a library corner with the "big books," or the so-called classics, and Great Books for children, a rocking chair, and a large yellow carrel that students can climb up into are also prominent features of the room.

As you bring your gaze back from the room's artifacts to the teacher and students, you learn that the class is preparing for a field trip to the Art Institute, with a stop in nearby Grant Park for a picnic lunch. The class is discussing the lunch arrangements, and several of the students are calling out what they are planning to bring to eat. Ms. Vanderbilt calls their attention to the "basic four" food poster on the side wall and reminds them of the nutrition unit that concluded the previous week. She tells them that she expects their lunches to consist of the food categories that are pictured in the poster. She also tells them to review the worksheet on the three French painters—Monet, Manet, and Renoir—whose work they will see on the field trip. She has students pair up to review this information, explaining that her students work better cooperatively than alone. The recess bell rings, interrupting the discussion; Ms. Vanderbilt quickly gets the students ready for one of their favorite school activities and leads them out to the playground. She tells you as she leaves to meet her later for coffee in the teachers' lounge.

When the two of you meet, she tells you that this class is really super, and this field trip is their fourth time taking in a cultural event downtown. She adds that next week they are going to attend the youth symphony. She says that, given time and an active enrichment program, most of the students will have a good opportunity for academic success in school. Her curriculum is geared to exposing the students to a way of life they have not known; she points out that the information on the bulletin boards and posters is designed to help students learn about life on the other side of the tracks. In her classroom, every boy and girl learns the same things—academically and socially—that students in the suburbs learn. She makes active use of after-school tutoring programs to get students up to grade level in basic skills, and she works extensively with parents on homework-monitoring strategies.

MRS. STEPHENS

Mrs. Stephens is a high school learning disabilities teacher. She has been teaching for 5 years in a suburban high school. During the course of a day, she sees about 30 students, most of whom are boys. Her classroom is small; it is furnished with two round tables, several chairs, several carrels, three well-stocked bookshelves, and a teacher's desk. Student work is displayed prominently around the room.

Mrs. Stephens tells you that her main job is to teach the students whatever she can to help them make it in the regular classroom and survive in the outside world. She has informally divided her students into two categories: those who can probably be remediated well enough to handle regular classes and maybe even college, and those who are too far behind to catch up with regular classwork and who need real-world survival skills, such as vocational training, skill in handling a checkbook, skill in filling out job applications, and so forth. The class about to be described consists of 10 students who are preparing themselves for a more academic course of study.

As the bell rings, the students enter class, laughing and shoving each other on their way to their seats. Mrs. Stephens jokes with them in a friendly manner. The second bell rings and the students quiet down. Mrs. Stephens says, "Today we will continue with grammar. We will learn about the preposition." One boy jokes to a girl, "I'm gonna preposition you!" Mrs. Stephens says, "I'm gonna preposition you, too. Brian, come up here." She gives him a poster with a word written on it. She says, "You are a preposition. Hold this."

Mrs. Stephens calls up other students and gives them posters with other words on them. She has the students arrange themselves in various combinations to form various sentences, having them identify the subject and verb of each sentence. For each sentence, she has students explain what words go with *to* and why. Then she says, "You can all sit down. You are really getting the idea."

Dave raises his hand. "My friend Marc, in the regular English class, said they studied this stuff last month."

Mrs. Stephens nods her head. "Right. So far they have studied a lot more parts of speech than you have, but by the end of the semester you should have pretty well caught up." Joe asks, "Does that mean we won't need to be in here anymore?"

Mrs. Stephens replies, "Not yet. You still don't have the vocabulary and reading skills the English teachers require, although by next year some of you may be ready to handle Mr. Ross's class. Now, let's get back to these prepositions."

Mrs. Stephens gives the students a list of prepositions on a handout. She then writes several sentences on the board and asks the students to identify the parts of speech and explain which word is the preposition. The last 10 minutes are spent playing a game with prepositions.

After class, you ask how many of her students actually learn to make it in school on their own. She replies, "Not that many. A lot of this stuff I teach does stick—for a while at least—but they are so far behind; it's like running after a moving train. Most of them won't completely graduate from LD, but they will become more successful in their other classes, and some will need LD less and less. Reading-oriented work just isn't their thing, so every day it's a struggle."

You ask if the regular teachers assume any responsibility for teaching these students. She replies, "Oh, sure, a number of them do. They give me new vocabulary words to review with the students—study guides to help them with. Some let me give tests orally. Some make allowances on their written work—have them do stuff orally, have them work with a buddy. They don't change their whole approach to teaching, of course. But a lot of them make modifications here and there so my students can at least get something out of the class and experience some success. A lot of high school teaching is heavy reading and lecture. Sometimes I wonder if it has to be that way, but that's the way it is. I've got kids who would drop out before they'd endure another day of heavy reading and lecture in a regular class. I mean, I've got 11th and 12th graders who read on a 4th grade level. Without LD or something like it, they'd be on the streets, and most regular teachers aren't at all equipped to deal with them. But the teachers are very cooperative about trying to modify things for the students who are reading on maybe a junior high level."

CRITIQUE   Ms. Vanderbilt and Mrs. Stephens are both very concerned and caring teachers, and they give their best effort to implementing the approach described in this chapter. If they care about their students and do their jobs as well as they can, what criticisms can we have of what they, or others adopting this approach, are doing?

Let us first summarize the main criticisms of the cultural deficiency orientation, which were very cogently stated in 1970 by Baratz and Baratz. The notion of cultural deficiency was promoted by educators and social scientists who lacked an anthropological background and who took middle-class Anglo culture as their reference point for judging other cultures. Those people whose behavior, language, and cognition differed from this narrow standard were judged as "sick, pathological, deviant, and underdeveloped," with blame placed on their genes or their environment or both (Baratz & Baratz, 1970, p. 31). "Instead of explicating the strengths of African American [and other minority] youth, a number of educators, opinion shapers, and policy-makers have persisted over the years in characterizing these young people as culturally deprived, educationally disadvantaged, learning disabled, and (using a term in vogue nowadays) at risk" (Madhere, 1991, p. 59).

There is abundant anthropological and linguistic data, however, that amply demonstrate that lower-class people and people of color have very well developed cultures that are simply different in some ways from that of middle-class Whites. Low-income people do lack access to economic resources, but lacking that access is not the same thing as lacking knowledge and culture. School failure to support and develop the knowledge, skills, and language abilities that low-income and minority students do have disables these students, promoting academic failure rather than growth (Cummins, 1989). Thus, the cultural deficiency position is an ideological position that ignores a wealth of data. Educators who persist in thinking of their students as "culturally deprived" are really *choosing not to learn* a good deal that could help them teach more effectively.

The notion of mental deficiency is also flawed, especially the categories of educable mental retardation, emotional disturbance, and learning disabilities. It is very likely that you view these categories as real deficiencies that educators have discovered and are learning how to treat. Most nonspecial educators believe that special educators agree, for example, on what mental retardation is, how to identify a retarded child, and what to do about mental retardation. Actually, special educators do not agree on these issues, particularly as they apply to the largest special education category—learning disabilities. Ysseldyke and Algozzine (1982) distinguished between objective categories—blindness and deafness—which have an objective, sensory basis, and subjective categories—learning disabilities, emotional disturbance, and mental retardation—which are "completely subjectively derived" (p. 43). Objective categories are fairly clearly caused by a physiological defect, and it is not necessary to be a professional to recognize members of these categories. For example, blindness is caused by damage to the eye or optic nerve, and usually you do not need to give a series of complicated tests to determine whether someone is blind, although it may be necessary to give such tests to determine the visual limitations of a partially sighted person.

Subjective categories are different. How, for example, do you determine who is learning disabled and what causes learning disabilities? Although learning disabled individuals have been thought historically to be neurologically impaired, evidence of such impairment is questionable (Kavale & Forness, 1985). Professionals disagree among themselves on how the category should be defined and exactly which children should be in it. As another example, although most severely retarded children have identifiable organic impairments, about 90% of those classified as mildly retarded are not identified as having such impairments (Kneedler, 1984). A child may be classified as EMR (educable mentally retarded) in one school but not in another. Some professionals may see a certain child as emotionally disturbed even though others do not.

In a discussion of special education categories, Ysseldyke and Algozzine (1982) argued that "the definition is the basis for the *existence* of the condition" (p. 48, emphasis theirs). In other words, people are mildly retarded, for example, because educators have chosen to regard as defective certain behaviors that can be tested. Over the years, the education system has created "a narrowing of the definition of what is considered 'normal'" (Gartner & Lipsky, 1987, p. 382), resulting in an expansion of who is considered disabled. In fact, educators have tended to regard the same behaviors as both symptoms of mental or emotional defect as well as of cultural deficiencies. For example, Mercer (1973) found that African American and Hispanic children in California were being disproportionately classified as retarded because institutions, and especially schools, had race- and class-biased notions of what constitutes intelligence and how one measures it. By defining differences as mental deficiencies, educators ignore the strengths and capabilities that children have, doing so on the basis of ideology more than science. Ysseldyke and Algozzine (1982) warned "that an elaborate, psychometrically inadequate system of identifying and explaining the extent of presumed important differences among individuals has evolved … Educators are searching an empty field and expect to find solutions to problems they have created without recognizing the error of their omission." (p. 253)

The deficiency orientation is based on an additional fallacy. Imagine that you are forming a neighborhood basketball team and you decide that the main characteristic team members should have is substantial height. You round up your neighbors and discover you have more than enough people for a team. You line them up by height, and because you can afford to, you define the shortest 5% of the neighborhood as deficient. The neighborhood could treat shortness as a serious problem and expend considerable energy looking for a remedy. Perhaps some of the shortest neighbors could even be cured of their defect by eating well. Soon there is a concerted effort among the neighbors to see that their children are fed well enough to grow tall. A year passes and heights sprout up. The next season, you line everybody up again, choose the tallest people for your team and most of the rest for the bench, and again define the shortest 5% as deficient. Crazy? This process is exactly like using norm-referenced tests to determine who is mentally deficient. Norm-referenced tests are specifically constructed to rank-order people—to line them up by height, so to speak, except instead of according to height, we line people up according to reading level, skill in certain thinking processes, or general knowledge. We then decide where to draw the line between "normal" and "deficient." As long as we have enough workers for available jobs, we can afford to classify those on the lower end of our rank order as deficient.

To some extent, Mrs. Stephens in the case study recognizes these problems. She realizes that the content and skills taught in the regular classroom form a yardstick for judging the extent to which her students are normal. Some of what she teaches has functional value outside school, and some has value mainly in helping her students cope with the demands of the regular classroom. Hence, she spends considerable time teaching concepts such as prepositions, although she wonders if such time might be better spent helping her students develop their talents and interests more. She has sufficient sustained contact with her students so that she gets to know most of them as interesting people with a variety of abilities, and she sometimes wonders if it is accurate or fair to call them "handicapped." Nevertheless, she also knows that our society has little tolerance for people who lack functional literacy skills, and so she builds her instruction around attempting to remediate these so-called failings.

If mild mental deficiencies are socially constructed notions, what of physiological deficiencies, such as blindness and paralysis? We would be foolish to argue that a blind person is not impaired physiologically. Impairments to one's body do not usually prevent learning, although they may necessitate the development of skills and strategies that most people do not need. For example, manual communication lends itself better to a deaf person than does oral communication, but there is no evidence that deafness itself (or other physiological impairments, except clearly identifiable brain damage), manual communication, or the strategies that deaf people use to compensate for hearing loss retard their learning ability. Thus, although there may be differences in how some physiologically impaired people learn, these differences are not learning deficiencies.

In spite of objections to it, the deficiency orientation maintains considerable popularity, resurfacing periodically with new terminology. In the first edition to this book, we predicted that this orientation was waning, especially the notion of *cultural deprivation*. However, the concept then revived in the *children at risk* discourse. The notion of *children at risk*, like that of the *culturally deprived* or *socially maladjusted*, may direct our attention toward services that need to be provided; but more often such a term locates the source of a child's problems within the child, as if the problems were personal or biological characteristics, and directs our attention away from larger social problems such as poverty or racism that create barriers and problems for many children (Fine, 1990).

The difference orientation corrects many flaws in the deficiency orientation. It focuses on strengths, recognizes the legitimacy of various cultural experiences and routes to becoming a mature person, and does not advocate that a child be ashamed of or give up anything he or she is. Certainly the difference orientation also has its critics, although they are fewer in number. Valentine (1971) charged the difference orientation with a tendency to stereotype, to oversimplify, and to take an either-or position where none is needed. It tends to stereotype by implying that all members of a given group share the same cultural and behavioral patterns. Although researchers who developed the theory may recognize differences among individuals within a group, educators who use the theory often do not. Witness, for example, the teacher who comments, "Mark is probably doing well in math because Asians are so good in that area; he doesn't seem to talk much or have many friends, but then Asians are quiet." The teacher is turning group tendencies in achievement and style into a stereotype she is using to "explain" Mark, which leads her to refrain from actually critiquing Mark's math skills, wondering why Mark doesn't have many friends and what she can do about it. Positive stereotypes, such as those attributed to Asians, are almost as damaging as negative stereotypes because both deflect attention away from individual needs and characteristics (Pang, 1990).

Furthermore, the difference orientation tends to assume that minority-group people lack competence in the dominant culture. Valentine (1971) pointed out that much of this is erroneous. He noted that "members of all subgroups are thoroughly enculturated in dominant culture patterns by mainstream institutions, including most of the content of the mass media, most products and advertising for mass marketing," and so forth (p. 143). Most speakers of Black English, for example, comprehend Standard English very well, and a teacher who assumes they do not is underestimating people's ability to become bicultural. Indeed, such a teacher may be less bicultural than the students! Failing to recognize errors in these assumptions, many educators make needless adaptations—and excuses— for their culturally different students. Based on a review of research on learning styles, Kleinfeld and Nelson (1988) concluded that, although ample evidence documents that learning style preferences do vary cross-culturally, there is no demonstrable impact on achievement when teachers try to match specific teaching strategies to specific aspects of student learning style. Achievement does improve when teachers use variety but not necessarily when specific teaching and learning styles are matched.

The difference orientation to language-minority students has focused almost exclusively on the "language problem." One indication of the limits of this orientation is the continued high rate of school failure among groups of language-minority youth at the same time that bilingual education programs have been expanding. This phenomenon is partially due to the compensatory model mandated and followed in many bilingual programs as well as to the finding that what has passed for bilingual education has lacked such essential elements as qualified teachers and native-language instruction (Orfield, 1986). Cummins (1989) argues that bilingual education and compensatory education have been unsuccessful because they have not significantly altered the relationships between educators and minority students and between schools and minority communities. This condition has prompted one researcher on Hispanic education to state, "Programs that attempt to address the educational outcomes of Hispanic students without a consideration of the school-based variables which give rise to those problems will only scratch at the surface" (Arias, 1986, p. 55).

Now let us look more broadly at the entire approach that has been presented in this chapter. Some of you probably agree with the foregoing criticisms but still see the approach as sound. After all, many of the recommended practices seem like sensible, effective strategies that good teachers use. Further, both research and experiential evidence confirm the usefulness of these practices. For example, most teachers know that students become more interested in a concept that the teacher has tried to make relevant. Who would argue with the recommendation that the level of instruction be matched to a student's readiness level? What criticisms, then, have been directed toward this approach?

One of the main criticisms is that it is assimilationist, and, as such, it seeks to eliminate minority cultures and make everyone like White, middle-class people. Banks (1981) summarizes several problems that "Third World writers and researchers" have had with this approach (p. 66). One problem is that people of color have viewed assimilation as a "weapon of the oppressor that was designed to destroy the cultures of ethnic groups and to make their members personally ineffective and politically powerless" (p. 66). Another problem is that the melting-pot idea never worked for people of color, even when they wanted to melt. No matter how hard some people have tried to melt, White society is not color blind and still devalues people of color. Finally, the assimilationist ideology is a "racist ideology that justified damaging school and societal practices that victimized minority group children" (p. 66), for example, using culturally biased tests to classify minority children as mentally retarded. As Banks points out, "The assumption that all children can learn equally well from teaching materials that only reflect the cultural experiences of the majority group is also questionable and possibly detrimental to those minority group children who have strong ethnic identities and attachments" (p. 68).

By seeing the cultures of people of color, women, and lower-class people as problems, the approach deflects attention away from the majority group and how it perpetuates discrimination and inequality. So long as majority-group children are not seen as needing to learn another culture, implicitly they are being taught to accept "cultural elitism, meaning that minority groups are treated like second-class citizens, either in terms of a refusal to take their traditions and beliefs seriously or with a patronizing acceptance aimed at seducing or manipulating them" (Pratte, 1983, p. 23). Racism within the White culture, sexism within male institutions, homophobia, and the competitive individualism and Horatio Alger myth that uphold classism all remain unexamined. As Mukherjee (1983) puts it, this approach allows Whites to "externaliz[e] the issue" of race rather than "owning up to that racism" (p. 279).

For example, Ms. Vanderbilt sees her main task as teaching White, middle-class culture to African American and Hispanic children. She does not teach much about subjects such as Black or Hispanic artists or the racism encountered by artists of color who attempt to succeed in the mainstream of American society. She does not particularly think about these matters: She believes that the children will learn a smattering of such information at home and knows that this knowledge is not required for later school success. Implicitly, however, she is also teaching that Whites are the main group to have attained worthwhile accomplishments and that discrimination would disappear if children of color did a better job of learning White culture.

This approach also allows males to externalize problems related to sexism. As long as sex equity is seen only as helping women to compete in male-dominated domains, women are the only ones seen as needing to change. This viewpoint deflects attention away from the need for men to learn, for example, nurturing skills and attitudes that women normally learn in the process of their socialization. It also deflects attention away from examining the competitiveness, impersonality, and violence that often characterize the male-dominated world. Most female educators and researchers who study sexism, including most of those cited earlier in this chapter, do not subscribe wholly to the Teaching the Culturally Different approach for female students because of these limitations.

Finally, the approach completely ignores structural and institutional bases of oppression. It assumes that people do not succeed in life because they have not learned a certain repertoire of skills and knowledge. This assumption implies that success is open to as many people as will expend the time and energy necessary to earn it. The assumption ignores the fact that our economy sustains a certain level of unemployment and a stratum of low-paying jobs, regardless of people's qualifications. (Witness the last recession and ask yourself whether the unemployment and suffering that people faced was caused by a sudden lapse in the cultural competence of the recession's victims.) Also ignored is the fact that people develop culture around their life conditions and that cultural patterns tend not to change until the conditions supporting them change. Liebow (1967) illustrates the problem as follows:

> Many similarities between the lower-class Negro father and son (or mother and daughter) do not result from "cultural transmission," but from the fact that the son goes out and independently experiences the same failures, in the same areas, and for much the same reasons as his father. What appears as a dynamic, self-sustaining cultural process is, in part at least, a relatively simple piece of social machinery which turns out, in rather mechanical fashion, independently produced look-alikes. The problem is how to change the conditions which, by guaranteeing failure, cause the son to be made in the image of the father. (p. 223)

Most educators who study multicultural education, as well as most members of oppressed groups, do not subscribe exclusively to the Teaching the Exceptional and the Culturally Different approach for their own groups, although they do incorporate the approach's best features into other approaches. During the civil rights era in the United States, the approach gained some popularity and is still used by many. However, most of its acceptance has been by White, middle-class teachers who take their own background and culture for granted and are searching for a way to incorporate or deal with those backgrounds and cultures they view as different. The approach also tends to be accepted by those who see American society as the land of opportunity and as a good, technological society that is constantly improving itself. People who do not share this view of American society tend to subscribe to one of the approaches discussed later in this book.

Let us hasten to add that most of these educators would not wish to throw the baby out with the bath water. The approach does contain elements that are very useful in other approaches. Critics of this approach do not believe, for example, that all children should master one standard body of knowledge—which happens to be based primarily on the experience of White, middle-class males—but many do believe that there are some things, such as reading skills, that all citizens do need. The question is, How much of the existing curriculum should be retained and taught to everyone? Many critics who warm to the idea of making the curriculum relevant take issue with the idea that relevance should be a temporary bridge. This approach offers some useful concepts of instruction, such as building instruction around student learning styles. Nevertheless, critics become concerned when teachers are searching desperately for instructional techniques that will help them fit square pegs into round holes. If a body of information is not being accepted well or is not making sense to a class of Appalachian students, for example, perhaps the solution lies not in hitting upon the right teaching strategy but in examining possible biases or lack of relevance in the information itself. Students' problems in schools may reflect problems with schools, rather than merely technical problems revolving around the teacher selecting the best instructional strategy.

REFERENCES

Adelman, H., & Taylor, L. (1983). *Learning disabilities in perspective*. Glenview, IL: Scott, Foresman.

Arias, M. B. (1986). The context of education for Hispanic students: An overview. *American Journal of Education, 95*, 26–57.

Ausubel, D. P. (1966). Effects of cultural deprivation on learning patterns. In S. W. Webster (Ed.), *The disadvantaged learner: Knowing, understanding, educating* (pp. 251–257). San Francisco: Chandler.

Banks, J. A. (1981). *Multiethnic education: Theory and practice*. Boston: Allyn & Bacon.

Baratz, S. S., & Baratz, J. C. (1970). Early childhood intervention: The social science base of institutional racism. *Harvard Educational Review, 40*, 29–50.

Bernstein, B. (1964). Elaborated and restricted codes: Their social origins and some consequences. *American Anthropologist, 66*, 55–69.

Billingsly, A., & Caldwell, C. H. (1991). The church, the family, and the school in the African American community. *Journal of Negro Education, 60*(3), 437–440.

Block, J. H. (1984). *Sex role identity and ego development*. San Francisco: Jossey-Bass.

Brophy, J. (1983). Research on the self-fulfilling prophecy and teacher expectations. *Journal of Education Psychology, 75*(5), 631–661.

Brown, T. J. (1986). *Teaching minorities more effectively*. Lanham, MD: University Press of America.

Brunner, C. (1997). Opening technology to girls: The approach computer-using teachers take may make the difference. *Electronic Learning, 16*(3), 55.

Bryan, T. H., & Bryan, J. H. (1978). *Understanding learning disabilities* (2nd ed.). Sherman Oaks, CA: Alfred.

Calabrese, R. L. (1990). The public school: A source of alienation for minority parents. *Journal of Negro Education, 59*(2), 148–154.

Campbell, P. B. (1984). The computer revolution: Guess who's left out? *Interracial Books for Children Bulletin, 15*, 3–6.

Chasnoff, I. J., Marvey, J., Landress, A. C., & Barrett, M. E. (1990). The prevalence of illicit-drug or alcohol use during pregnancy and discrepancies in mandatory reporting in Pinellas County, Florida. *The New England Journal of Medicine, 322*(17), 1202–1206.

Comer, J. P. (1988). Educating poor minority children. *Scientific American, 259*(5), 42–48.

Contreras, A. R., & Delgado-Contreras, C. (1991). Teacher expectations in bilingual education classrooms. In J. J. Harris III, C. A. Heid, D. G. Carter, Sr., & F. Brown (Eds.), *Readings on the state of education in urban America* (pp. 75–96). Bloomington, IN: Indiana University Center for Urban and Multicultural Education.

Cooper, D. H., & Speece, D. L. (1990). Maintaining at-risk children in regular education settings: Initial effects of individual differences and classroom environments. *Exceptional Children, 57,* 117–126.

Crawford, J. (1989). *Bilingual education: History, politics, theory and practice.* Trenton, NJ: Crane.

Crockett, L. J., & Petersen, A. C. (1984). Biology: Its role in gender-related educational experiences. In E. Fennema & M. J. Ayer (Eds.), *Women and education* (pp. 89–116). Berkeley, CA: McCutchan.

Cummins, J. (1981). The role of primary language development in promoting educational success for language minority students. In *Schooling and language minority students: A theoretical framework* (pp. 3–49). Los Angeles: California State University Evaluation, Dissemination and Assessment Center.

Cummins, J. (1989). *Empowering minority students.* Sacramento: California Association for Bilingual Education.

DeLain, M. T., Pearson, T. D., & Anderson, R. C. (1985). Reading comprehension and creativity in black language use: You stand to gain by playing the sounding game! *American Journal of Educational Research, 22,* 155–174.

Deutsch, M. (1963). The disadvantaged child and the learning process. In A. H. Passow (Ed.), *Education in depressed areas* (pp. 163–180). New York: Teachers College Press.

Dunn, L. M. (1963). *Exceptional children in the schools.* New York: Holt, Rinehart & Winston.

Edmonds, R. (1979). Effective schools for the urban poor. *Educational Leadership, 37,* 15–24.

Escalante, J., & Dirmann, J. (1990). The Jaime Escalante math program. *Journal of Negro Education, 59*(3), 407–423.

Farrell, C. L. (1992). Black colleges still carrying their load—and then some. *Black Issues in Higher Education, 9*(5), 10–13.

Fennema, E. (1984). Girls, women, and mathematics. In E. Fennema & M. J. Ayer (Eds.), *Women and education* (pp. 137–164). Berkeley: McCutchan.

Fennema, E., & Peterson, P. L. (1987). Effective teaching for girls or boys: The same or different? In D. C. Berliner & B. V. Rosenshine (Eds.), *Talks to teachers* (pp. 111–125). New York: Random House.

Fine, M. (1990). Making controversy: Who is "at risk"? *Journal of Urban and Cultural Studies, 1*(1), 55–68.

Frase, L. (1994). Fostering school, community, and family partnerships. In L. Frase (Ed.), *Multiculturalism and TQE: Addressing cultural diversity in schools* (pp. 67–88). Thousand Oaks, CA: Corwin Press.

Gallagher, J. J. (1979). Issues in education for the gifted. In A. H. Passow (Ed.), *The gifted and the talented: Their education and development* (pp. 28–44). The 78th yearbook of the National Society for the Study of Education. Chicago: University of Chicago Press.

Garcia, E. E. (1988). Attributes of effective schools for language minority students. *Education and Urban Society, 20*(4), 387–398.

Gardner, H. (1983). *Frames of mind.* New York: Basic Books.

Gartner, A., & Lipsky, D. K. (1987). Beyond special education: Toward a quality system for all students. *Harvard Educational Review, 57*(4), 367–395.

Gearheart, B., DeRuiter, J., & Sileo, T. (1986). *Teaching mildly and moderately handicapped students.* Upper Saddle River, NJ: Prentice-Hall.

Gilliland, H. (1988). *Educating the Native American.* Dubuque, IA: Kendall-Hunt.

Goldberg, M. L. (1963). Factors affecting educational attainment in depressed urban areas. In A. H. Passow (Ed.), *Education in depressed areas* (pp. 68–100). New York: Teachers College Press.

Grant, C. A., & Sleeter, C. E. (1985). Equality, equity and excellence: A critique. In P. G. Alt-back, G. P. Kelly, & L. Weis (Eds.), *Excellence in education* (pp. 139–160). Buffalo, NY: Prometheus.

Gross, J. (1992, March 29). Collapse of inner-city families creates America's new orphans. *The New York Times National.* pp. 1, 616.

Hardman, M. L., Drew, C. J., & Egan, M. W. (1984). *Human exceptionality: Society, school, and family.* Boston: Allyn & Bacon.

Harry, B. (1992). *Cultural diversity, families, and the special education system.* New York: Teachers College Press.

Herrnstein, R., & Murray, C. (1994). *The bell curve.* New York: The Free Press.

Hirsch, E. D., Jr. (1996). *The schools we need and why we don't have them.* New York: Double-day.

Hunt, J. M. (1961). *Intelligence and experience.* New York: The Ronald Press.

Jensen, A. S. (1969). How much can we boost IQ and scholastic achievement? *Harvard Educational Review, 39,* 1–123.

Jordan, C. (1985). Translating culture: From ethnographic information to educational program. *Anthropology & Education Quarterly, 16,* 105–123.

Kasten, W. C. (1992). Bridging the horizon: American Indian beliefs and whole language learning. *Anthropology and Education Quarterly, 23*(2), 108–119.

Kavale, K. A., & Forness, S. R. (1985). *The science of learning disabilities.* San Diego: College Hill Press.

Kirk, S. A., & Gallagher, J. J. (1979). *Educating exceptional children.* Boston: Houghton Mifflin.

Kissen, R. (1993). Listening to gay and lesbian teenagers. *Teaching Education, 5*(2), 57–68.

Klaus, R., & Gray, S. (1968). The early training project for disadvantaged children: A report after five years. *Monographs of the Society for Research in Child Development, 33*(4).

Kleinfeld, J., & Nelson, P. (1988). Adapting instruction to Native Americans' learning style: An iconoclastic view. In W. J. Lonner & V. O. Tyler, Jr. (Eds.), *Cultural and ethnic factors in learning and motivation: Implications for education* (pp. 83–110). Bellingham, WA: Western Washington University Press.

Kneedler, R. D. (1984). *Special education for today.* Upper Saddle River, NJ: Prentice-Hall.

Kobrick, J. W. (1974). The compelling case for bilingual education. In F. Pialorsi (Ed.), *Teaching the bilingual* (pp. 169–178). Tucson: University of Arizona Press.

Kyle, J. G., & Pullen, G. (1988). Cultures in contact: Deaf and hearing people. *Disability, Handicap & Society, 3*(1), 49–62.

Labov, W. (1969). The logic of non-standard English. *Monograph Series on Languages and Linguistics,* 22. Washington, DC: Georgetown University School of Languages and Linguistics.

Ladson-Billings (1994) *The Dreamkeepers.* San Francisco: Jossey Bass

Lareau, A. (1989). *Home advantage: Social class and parental intervention in elementary education.* London: Falmer Press.

Leake, D. O., & Leake, B. L. (1992). Islands of hope: Milwaukee's African American immersion schools. *Journal of Negro Education, 61*(1), 24–29.

Leder, G. C., & Fennema, E. (1990). Gender differences in mathematics: A synthesis. In E. Fennema & G. C. Leder (Eds.), *Mathematics and gender* (pp. 188–200). New York: Teachers College Press.

Liebow, E. (1967). *Tally's corner: A study of Negro street-corner men.* Boston: Little, Brown.

Linn, M. C., & Hyde, J. S. (1989). Gender, mathematics and science. *Educational Researcher, 18*(8), 17–27.

Lovitt, T. C. (1977). *In spite of my resistance … I've learned from children.* New York: Merrill/ Macmillan.

Lucas, T., Henze, R., & Donato, R. (1990). Promoting the success of Latino language-minority students: An exploratory study of six high schools. *Harvard Educational Review*, *60*(3), 315–340.

Madhere, S. (1991). Self-esteem of African American preadolescents: Theoretical and practical considerations. *Journal of Negro Education*, *60*(1), 47–61.

Mandell, C. J., & Gold, V. (1984). *Teaching handicapped students*. St. Paul: West.

Markova, D. (1992). *How your child is smart: A life-changing approach to learning*. Berkeley, CA: Conari Press.

Maybin, J. (Ed.). (1994). *Language and literacy in social practice*. Philadelphia: Multilingual Matters.

Mercer, J. R. (1973). *Labeling the mentally retarded*. Berkeley: University of California Press.

Moll, L., Diaz, S., Estrada, E., & Lopes, L. M. (1990). Making contexts: The social construction of lessons in two languages. In M. Saravia-Shore & S. F. Arvizu (Eds.), *Cross-cultural literacy* (pp. 339–366), New York: Garland.

Moll, L. C. (1992). Bilingual classroom studies and community analysis. *Educational Researcher*, *21*(2), 20–24.

Moses, R. P., Kamii, M., Swap, S. M., & Howard, J. (1989). The algebra project: Organizing in the spirit of Ella. *Harvard Educational Review*, *59*(4), 423–443.

Moss, B. J. (Ed.). (1994). *Literacy across communities*. Cresskill, NJ: Hampton Press.

Mukherjee, T. (1983). Multicultural education: A black perspective. *Early Childhood Development and Care*, *10*, 275–282.

National Commission on Excellence in Education. (1983). *A nation at risk: The imperative for educational reform*. Washington, DC: U.S. Government Printing Office.

Newton, E. S. (1966). Verbal destitution: The pivotal barrier to learning. In S. W. Webster (Ed.), *The disadvantaged learner: Knowing, understanding, educating* (pp. 333–337). San Francisco: Chandler.

Orfield, G. (1986). Hispanic education: Challenges, research, and policies. *American Journal of Education*, *95*, 1–25.

Orr, E. W. (1987). *Twice as less: Black English and the performance of black students in mathematics and science*. New York: Norton.

Pallas, A., Natriello, G., & McDill, E. L. (1989). The changing nature of the disadvantaged population: Current dimensions and future trends. *Educational Researcher*, *18*(5), 16–22.

Pang, V. O. (1990). Asian-American children: A diverse population. *The Educational Forum*, *55*(1), 49–65.

Pease-Alvarez, L., & Hakuta, K. (1992). Enriching our views of bilingualism and bilingual education. *Educational Researcher*, *21*(2), 4–6.

Phelan, P., Davidson, A. L., & Cao, H. T. (1991). Students' multiple worlds: Negotiating the boundaries of family, peer, and school cultures. *Anthropology and Education Quarterly*, *22*(3), 224–250.

Philips, S. U. (1983). *The invisible culture*. New York: Longman.

Portes, P. R. (1996). Ethnicity and culture in educational psychology. In D. C. Berliner and R. C. Calsee (Eds.), *Handbook of educational psychology* (pp. 331–357). New York: Macmillan.

Pratte, R. (1983). Multicultural education: Four normative arguments. *Educational Theory*, *33*, 21–32.

Ralph, J. (1989). Improving education for the disadvantaged: Do we know whom to help? *Phi Delta Kappan*, 395–401.

Reis, S. M. (1994). How schools are shortchanging the gifted. *Technology Review*, *97*(3), 38–45.

Reynolds, M. C., & Birch, J. W. (1988). *Adaptive mainstreaming* (3rd ed.). New York: Longman.

Richardson, V., Casanova, U., Placier, P., & Guilfoyle, K. (1989). *School children at risk*. London: Falmer Press.

Riordan, C. (1990). *Girls and boys in school: Together or separate?* New York: Teachers College Press.

Robbins, W. (1984). Student's suicide stirs new interest in gifted. In C. A. Grant (Ed.), *Preparing for reflective teaching* (pp. 281–283). Boston: Allyn & Bacon.

Robinson, H. B., Roedell, W. C., & Jackson, N. E. (1981). Early identification and intervention. In W. B. Barbe & J. S. Renzulli (Eds.), *Psychology and education of the gifted* (3rd ed., pp. 128–141). New York: Irvington.

San Miguel, G., Jr. (1987). *"Let all of them take heed": Mexican Americans and the campaign for educational equality in Texas, 1910–1981.* Austin: University of Texas Press.

Schneider, S. G. (1976). *Revolution, reaction or reform: The 1974 Bilingual Education Act.* New York: Las Americas.

Schultz, T. W. (1977). Investment in human capital. In J. Karabel & A. H. Halsy (Eds.), *Power and ideology in education* (pp. 313–324). New York: Oxford University Press.

Sears, J. T. (1991). *Growing up gay in the South.* New York: Hayworth Press.

Sears, J. T. (1993). Responding to the sexual diversity of faculty and students: Sexual praxis and the critically reflective administrator. In C. Capper (Ed.), *Administration in a pluralistic society.* New York: SUNY Press.

Shade, B. J. R. (1989). *Culture, style and the educative process.* Springfield, IL: Charles C Thomas.

Sheets, R. H. (1995). From remedial to gifted: Effects of culturally centered pedagogy. *Theory into Practice, 34*(3), 186–193.

Silber, J. (1988). Education and national survival: The cycle of poverty. *Vital Speeches, 54,* 215–219.

Skutnabb-Kangas, T. (1981). *Billingualism or not? The education of minorities.* Clevedon, Avon, England: Multilingual Matters.

Sleeter, C. E. (1992). *Keepers of the American dream: A study of staff development and multicultural education.* London: Falmer Press.

Smitherman, G. (1981). What go round come round: King in perspective. *Harvard Educational Review, 51*(1), 40–56.

Soto, L. D. (1997) *Language, culture, and power.* New York: State University Press.

Stewart, D. A., & Akamatsu, C. T. (1988). The coming of age of American Sign Language. *Anthropology and Education Quarterly, 19*(3), 235–252.

Taylor, H. U. (1989). *Standard English, Black English, and bidialectalism.* New York: Peter Lang.

Terman, L. M., Baldwin, B. T., Bronson, E., DeVoss, J. C., Fuller, F., Goodenough, F. L., Kelley, T. L., Lima, M., Marshall, H., Moore, A. H., Raubenheimer, A. S., Ruch, G. M., Willoughby, R. L., Wyman, J. B., & Yates, D. H. (1976). *Genetic studies of genius: Mental and physical traits of a thousand gifted children.* Stanford: Stanford University Press.

Trueba, H. T. (1988). Culturally based explanations of minority students' academic achievement. *Anthropology and Education Quarterly, 19*(3), 270–287.

Trueba, H. T. (1989). *Raising silent voices: Educating the linguistic minorities for the 21st century.* New York: Newbury House.

Valentine, C. A. (1971). Deficit, difference, and bicultural models of Afro-American behavior. *Harvard Educational Review, 41,* 137–157.

Van Gelder, L. (1992). Attack of the "killer lesbians." MS: *The World of Women, 2*(4), 80–82.

Walker, C. L. (1987). Hispanic achievement: Old views and new perspectives. In H. Trueba (Ed.), *Success or failure? Learning and the language minority student* (pp. 15–32). Cambridge, MA: Newbury House.

Williams, S. (1991). Classroom use of African American language: Educational tool or social weapon? In C. E. Sleeter (Ed.), *Empowerment through multicultural education* (pp. 199–215). Albany, NY: SUNY Press.

Ysseldyke, J. E., & Algozzine, B. (1982). *Critical issues in special and remedial education.* Boston: Houghton Mifflin.

CHAPTER THREE

Human Relations

What comes to mind when you hear the term *human relations*? "Getting along," "tolerance," "interactions between individuals and groups," and "learning how to resolve differences between individuals and groups" were some of the responses our students gave to this question. Our students also said that *human relations* means trying to reduce prejudice and stereotypes among the races, helping men and women to eliminate their gender hang-ups, and helping all people to feel positive about themselves. Central to most definitions was the development of positive interactions between individuals or groups.

GOALS

Our students' statements were consistent with the goal statements of educators who advocate a Human Relations approach. As we note in Table 3–1, the goals of this approach are to promote positive feelings among students and reduce stereotyping, thus promoting unity and tolerance in a society composed of different people. Colangelo, Dustin, and Foxley (1985) explain, "Human relations is the act of engaging other people in our many interactions" (p. 1); in order to engage successfully with another person, we must develop skills that enable us to recognize our common humanity, as well as acknowledge and respect individual differences. Human relations training helps us learn these skills. Three components of human relations training can include (a) examining social groups of which one is a member and the views society has of these groups; (b) examining friendship groups, the meaning of group membership, and group skills; and (c) developing attitudes of acceptance and friendship between groups (Grambs, 1960, p. 19). In this chapter we will examine how advocates of the Human Relations approach suggest developing positive relationships among individuals or groups that differ from one another.

Some proponents of the Human Relations approach (often called intergroup education) relate it directly to the study of prejudice and intergroup hostility. These advocates claim that because so many complex factors, such as home background, social situations, health, income, intelligence, and aspirations affect human interaction and human relationships, intergroup education must take into account one's total personality. Examine Grambs's (1960) comment:

TABLE 3–1.
Human Relations

Societal goals:	Promote feelings of unity, tolerance, and acceptance within existing social structure
School goals:	Promote positive feelings among students, reduce stereotyping, promote students' self-concepts
Target students:	Everyone
Practices:	
Curriculum	Teach lessons about stereotyping, name-calling; teach lessons about individual differences and similarities; include in lessons contributions of groups of which students are members
Instruction	Use cooperative learning; use real or vicarious experiences with others
Other aspects of classroom	Decorate classroom to reflect uniqueness and accomplishments of students; decorate with "I'm OK, You're OK" themes
Other schoolwide concerns	Make sure activities and school policies and practices do not put down or leave out some groups of students; promote schoolwide activities, such as donating food to the poor, aimed at peace and unity

> Research workers now claim that intergroup relations cannot properly be understood in a narrow sense at all but must be considered in terms of the total personality, the interaction of persons in groups, the sources of group tension and conflict, and the cultural context within which people grow and learn. In fact, the field is now often defined as "human relations" rather than as intergroup relations. (p. 5)

The importance of this concept, argue Colangelo et al. (1985), is that it "encompasses a recognition of the humanness of people" (p. 1), which Wesley (1949) claims is "more important in a democratic society than land, sea or sky" (p. 30). Wesley believes this concept to be significant to our society because human relations will reduce prejudice and develop attitudes of racial tolerance:

> The teaching of facts about race will not solve race problems but it will develop attitudes of tolerance where hitherto there were emotional reactions in disintegrated personalities based upon lack of knowledge. Is there anything more tragic in human relations than to see the college graduate refuse association with another college graduate who happens to be of different religious faith or a different national origin or color? There is something wrong with an education which leads to such results. (p. 30)

We can synthesize these various goal statements by saying that the Human Relations approach is directed toward helping students communicate with, accept, and get along with people who are different from themselves; reducing or eliminating stereotypes that students have about people; and helping students feel good about themselves and about groups of which they are members, without putting others down in the process. This approach is aimed mainly at the affective level—at attitudes and feelings people have about themselves and others. It attempts to replace tension and hostility with acceptance and care. Advocates of human relations, or intergroup education, believe the approach needs to be fostered in everyone, and in all schools, to make our democracy work.

Systematic attention to intergroup-human relations education began during World War II and grew rapidly right after the war as the result of a number of different factors (Taba, Brady, & Robinson, 1952). Prior to the war, organizations such as the Anti-Defamation League of B'nai B'rith, the Urban League, the National Association for the Advancement of Colored People, and the National Conference of Christians and Jews had fought to eliminate discrimination and prejudice and were encouraging legislation that would help to accomplish their aims. World War II brought about some specific changes that fueled the efforts of these organizations to draw serious attention to their concerns. World War II created jobs, and people often had to move to other regions to take advantage of these opportunities. These relocations brought together people who were not used to being together, which sometimes resulted in intergroup conflicts—for example, when African Americans and Whites from the South moved to the North and West and had to interact under different rules. As poor people and people of color became integrated, they also began to experience a more fulfilling and enriched life and began to demand a larger slice of the American pie. War veterans, especially those of color, believed that they and their people deserved fair treatment because they had fought and died for democracy—democracy not just for some citizens, but for all citizens. Intergroup and human relations education was seen as a way to bring about harmony among these different groups.

During the war, the United States was especially concerned with maintaining and improving its relations with its neighbor countries, Canada and Mexico. Roosevelt's Good Neighbor policy had implications for educators in Texas. Pressure from the Mexican government was exerted to expose the poor treatment of Mexican American students in schools. In response, the Inter-American Education movement developed, holding conferences, developing curricula, and conducting studies aimed at improving relations between Anglos and Mexicans in the schools.

Another factor supporting intergroup education was the belief that America's concern about human interactions was being ignored while we invested the country's financial and human resources in the technological race. There was more interest in the atom than in relationships among people. Many believed that our role as free-world leader and as champion of the democratic way of life throughout the world was inconsistent with the way of life experienced by many U.S. citizens.

It was not enough to advocate justice and fair play abroad; we had to put these ideals into practice at home. Minority and majority group relations had to be improved. Finally, the war itself had produced some devastating consequences that pointed strongly to a need to promote better intergroup relations. The Holocaust demonstrated how inhumanely one group can treat another group, and the bombing of Hiroshima and Nagasaki revealed to the world a more terrible and destructive kind of weapon than had ever been used in human history.

These events and circumstances gave human relations and intergroup education a big push, and interest in this concept grew rapidly over just a few years. Many books, pamphlets, articles, and lectures and discussions at professional association meetings concentrated on this concept during a short period of time and thus provided the momentum for its growing acceptance. Another big push for human relations came a decade later with the school desegregation and civil rights movements. School desegregation meant that, in many cases, people of color and White people would have to share the same facility (school). Human relations and intergroup education programs were often put into place (and some still exist) to help promote harmony among racial groups.

During the late 1970s and 1980s, following the passage of PL 94–142, the human relations approach was viewed as useful in mainstreaming special education students. As students who previously had been kept segregated were increasingly placed into the regular classroom and school, educators became concerned about negative attitudes among both regular students and teachers, particularly because one reason for the mainstreaming movement was to encourage the acceptance of students with disabilities. By the early 1980s, books and articles began to appear with some frequency that discussed how to modify attitudes toward people with disabilities and increase their social integration.

The late 1980s and early 1990s witnessed a resurgence of name calling and racial hostility in schools, on college campuses, and in cities and suburbs, and the Ku Klux Klan engaged in cross burnings, an expression of hate that many Americans believed to be extinct. This period also saw a rise in attention to sexual harassment, particularly following television coverage of Anita Hill's testimony in Congress against Supreme Court nominee Clarence Thomas. As a result, educators and the general public became increasingly concerned about what is and what is not proper for members of different groups to say to each other, resulting in debates about what constitutes legitimate free speech. In addition, teachers who previously had not been concerned with Human Relations or any other approach to multicultural education began to ask themselves—especially if their own students were becoming more diverse—What can I do?

This same question was responsible, in fact, for the emergence of the first conflict resolution programs in the early 1970s programs which were "sparked by the increasing concern of educators and parents about violence in the schools" (Girard & Koch, 1996, p. 111). Growing out of these earlier efforts, the National Association for Mediation in Education was established in 1984, further contributing to this growing movement. Now known as the National Institute for Dispute Resolution (NIDR), the organization works toward the development and implementation of conflict resultion and peer mediation programs in the schools. As of 1995, NIDR estimated that over 6,000 of these programs operated in schools across the United States (Girard & Koch, 1996, p. 111). Thus, the 1990s have seen schools begin to dedicate more time and attention to conflict resolution, peer mediation, and the elimination of violence. Some school districts advocate beginning training as early as kindergarten and the primary grades where children would learn about resolving conflicts such as playground disputes over balls, use of swings, and so forth. Children are taught skills related to speaking, using "I messages" to identify feeling, needs, and desires. They are taught to listen, negotiate, mediate, apologize, postpone gratification, and compromise. In the middle grades and in secondary school, conflict resolution skills are also taught to help students better get along with one another and to deal with different people and perspectives they encounter throughout society. A variety of materials which deal with such issues as peer mediation, anger management, and violence prevention have been and continue to be published. (See, for example, publications from Conflict Resolution Media, Ellicott City, Maryland.) Particularly in the area of violence prevention, programs and materials have begun to proliferate; Creighton and Kivel (1992), for example, have developed a step-by-step program aimed at preventing violence in teen relationships (for other program examples, see Crawford & Bodine, 1996).

Peer mediation and conflict resolution have also become a very important curriculum topic in the 1990s for fostering better student–teacher interaction. In order to teach tolerance, Valentine (1997) suggests that eduators begin by examining their own cultural perspectives. This means that teachers need to examine who their friends are, who comes to their homes, and who attends their houses of worship. In schools, suggestions for teaching tolerance include examining instructional material for biases, modeling empathy and respect for others, addressing intolerance as it arises, and creating opportunities for people from different cultures to work with one another. In some states, such as Wisconsin, it is required that prospective teachers receive training in conflict resolution; in other states, programs now exist where students can obtain advanced degrees in conflict resolution itself.

THEORIES BEHIND HUMAN RELATIONS

The theoretical underpinnings for the Human Relations approach have come mainly from general psychology and social psychology. Human relations is a field that examines relationships among people, regardless of whether race, social class, gender, disability, or sexual orientation is involved. For example, there is a body of literature on human relations in formal organizations and a cadre of people who conduct human relations workshops for businesses. For this chapter, we will draw only on the research that develops human relations as an approach to multicultural education; nevertheless, it is important to remember that this approach is a subset of a larger body of thought and rests on many of the same theoretical foundations.

Some theorists have emphasized the development of prejudice and stereotyping within individuals. Others have emphasized the development of prejudice and hostility between groups. Still others pay more attention to individual self-concept. These ideas are not mutually exclusive; in fact, as Allport (1979) notes, no one theoretical formulation by itself can account for prejudice, although different people see different theories as being the most persuasive.

Development of Prejudice Within Individuals
Gordon Allport (1979) was probably the main theorist to write about the development of prejudice in individuals. He focused on individuals for two reasons: Not everybody in any given society is prejudiced, which raises the question of why

some people are much more prejudiced than others and why prejudice and discrimination are acted out by certain individuals. Allport drew mainly on cognitive development theory and psychoanalytic theory. We will explain these theories, incorporating examples (some used by Allport, some not) to show how they apply to race, gender, social class, disability, and sexual orientation. We will also provide elaborations of these ideas that have been offered by other theorists.

According to cognitive development theory, the mind has a need to relate, organize, and simplify phenomena in order for experiences to make sense. Thus, on the basis of concrete experience, people create categories to organize similar phenomena. As people mature and acquire an increasingly broad range of experience, they attempt to assimilate as many of their new experiences as possible into existing categories. Occasionally, people have to restructure (accommodate) categories to fit experience. How does this apply to prejudice?

By age 2 or 3, children are aware of visible differences among people, including skin color (Goodman, 1952; Katz, 1982), physical impairment (Weinberg, 1978), and gender (Kohlberg, 1966). Initially, these differences do not suggest stereotypes or evaluations, although Allport suggests that children often associate dark skin with dirt. At the same time, children are also learning language, and with it, labels for categories and the emotional overtones of those labels. In fact, children sometimes learn a label and its emotional overtone (e.g., *homosexuals*) before they have constructed a category to which the label applies or before they have connected the label with a category. Allport (1979) cites an example:

> One little boy was agreeing with his mother, who was warning him never to play with niggers. He said, "No, Mother, I never play with niggers. I only play with white and black children." This child was developing an aversion to the term "nigger" without having the slightest idea what the term meant. (p. 305)

Student teachers in preschool or kindergarten classes are sometimes struck by the degree to which children play together without seeming to notice differences among themselves. Student teachers sometimes comment that maybe the younger generation is growing up without prejudice, or that because children don't "see race" the teacher should not bring up the subject of differences. A more accurate interpretation is that the children have not yet learned the meanings society attaches to the differences the children do see. As they mature, they will be bombarded with interpretations of human characteristics: in the media, at school, at home, in jokes and stories, and from friends.

In fact, children are curious about what they see and often unabashedly ask questions adults consider impolite or taboo, such as: "Why is that man black?" "Why does that lady have only one arm?" "Is that a girl or a boy?" How adults respond to children's natural curiosity teaches children how to view differences. If adults adopt a color-blind position, refusing to take such questions seriously and answer them, children are taught that they should not try to learn about differences, and thus they are allowed to hold onto their own conclusions, however misinformed they may be (Derman-Sparks, 1989).

By late childhood, children tend to overcategorize and stereotype many things. Their categories will have acquired many descriptive attributes that they apply to whoever or whatever seems to fit the category. Thus, all dogs are large and brown, or all people in wheelchairs are friendly (or quiet, or stupid, or whatever the child has experienced with one or two members of that category). Finding their system of organizing experience useful, children overuse it, often without recognizing its limitations. Pogrebin (1981) gives an example of a girl who insisted that women could not be doctors, even though her own mother was a physician. Her experience with doctors told her that women were not doctors, and she dealt with exceptions by refusing to accept them as true.

As children mature, their categories modify by varying degrees to fit reality better. Allport describes people in general as operating under the "principle of least effort," which means that the mind will avoid restructuring its categories unless it has to. As one encounters people who do not fit a designated category, one tends to view them as exceptions to the rule. For example, upon meeting a man who is a homemaker, a person who sees homemakers as women will consider the man an exception, rather than restructure the category to make it genderless. Most people learn to allow for numerous exceptions and qualifications and do not see the boundaries of their categories as fixed and rigid. Thus, a person can say, "Some of my best friends are Jews," allowing the retention of a stereotypical image of "Jew" although admitting to many exceptions to the stereotype (Allport, 1979, p. 309). However, the more diverse examples of a category to which a person has been exposed, and the more that person examines the category itself, the less rigid and stereotypic the person's system of mental categories becomes. For example, a child who has been exposed to a wide range of Asian Americans has a good experiential basis to question stereotypes, such as "Asians are good at math."

Allport notes the important role that perception plays in this process. When the mind perceives, "it selects, accentuates, and interprets sensory data" (p. 166). To view a diverse group of people (such as the poor) as a category, we find it necessary to pay special attention to the attributes that members of the category are believed to have in common. In attending to these attributes, we tend to accentuate them unconsciously. For example, we look for skin color so we can identify a person's race; in the process, we exaggerate the importance of skin color and minimize the significance of attributes that people have in common. As another example, an adult viewing a young child searches for clues to the child's gender and unconsciously overemphasizes these clues in the process. Similarly, when teachers hear they are receiving a new student who is "at risk," certain images and personal characteristics of the students often rush forward. Research on stereotyping also finds people to be more accepting of individuals who fit a stereotype than individuals who do not. Stereotypes seem to give us a map of reality that suggests how to interpret and act toward people, and individuals who do not fit that map make us uncomfortable. Rather than questioning the stereotypes, however, we often avoid or put down the persons who do not fit.

You may be wondering whether, if the development of prejudice is so natural, prejudiced beliefs be changed? Yes, they can. Earlier we noted that answering children's questions accurately and providing them with multiple different examples of members of a category helps them to develop more accurate, complex interpretations of people. Beliefs can be changed or broadened by making use of dissonance theory. According to Watts (1984),

> Dissonance occurs whenever an individual simultaneously holds two cognitions (ideas, beliefs, opinions) which are psychologically inconsistent. Because dissonance is an unpleasant motivational state, people strive to reduce it through a cognitive reorganization that may involve adding consonant cognition or changing one set of opinions. (p. 44)

An example Watts provides is that of a person who believes that cigarette smoking is dangerous to one's health but who smokes nonetheless. All of us live with some degree of dissonance, especially if not forced to confront opposing beliefs. To reduce dissonance, if it were to become uncomfortable, the person could belittle the research on lung cancer or decide to quit smoking.

Consider the child who thinks retarded people are unpleasant but then begins to play with a neighbor with mental retardation. The child could reduce the dissonance between attitude and behavior either by clinging to the attitude and ceasing to play with the retarded child or by adopting a more positive attitude that would support their play relationship. Teachers can create planned dissonance. For example, a teacher with a class who regard women as unathletic can confront the students with multiple examples of excellent women athletes—including the disproportionate number of American women athletes who brought home gold medals from the 1992 Winter Olympics. Students can resolve their dissonance by treating women athletes as exceptions, but eventually the number and power of the exceptions will make the stereotype increasingly difficult to maintain.

Thinking in terms of categories and stereotypes is natural and does not necessarily, by itself, lead to prejudice and hostility. Why do some people hate groups unlike themselves, whereas other people are simply curious and accepting of others? For an answer to that question, Allport (1979)—and others—turned to psychodynamic theory. Essentially, psychodynamic theory holds that the mind has built-in urges and capacities that manifest themselves in feelings and needs. Only a portion of these urges and capacities reach the conscious level in any individual; a large portion remain at the unconscious level, where they nevertheless direct our thoughts and behaviors, but in ways of which we are unaware. Allport describes several needs or capacities that are built into the human mind: aggression, affiliation with others, fear of strangers, need for status, and need for a positive self-image. Early in life, children attempt to form relationships with others, build positive self-images, and acquire status, with some children experiencing more success than others. Lack of success leads to frustration. Many people learn to channel frustration productively (e.g., it becomes a motivation to try harder until success is achieved), whereas others allow the frustration to smolder inside. People who do not learn to handle frustration develop a free-floating hatred that can be directed against any convenient group or individual, and the hatred can turn into active aggression against that target.

Projection is the main process by which frustration becomes directed against a group. Allport defines projection as "the tendency to attribute falsely to other people motives or traits that are our own, or that in some way explain or justify our own" (p. 382). Projection is based on feelings of guilt, fear, or anxiety about traits or urges within ourselves or factors in our own lives. For example, many people develop feelings of guilt about their own homosexual thoughts, and because they are unable to deal with these feelings at a conscious level, they project fear of their own urges onto others who are openly homosexual. These others become a target for hate. People who fear losing their jobs, either because of their own inadequacies or because of economic conditions, may project this fear onto a group, often a minority group, that they can blame for stealing jobs from people who deserve them. Such a group becomes a scapegoat.

It is here that the content of stereotypes becomes important but hard to change. The categories in which we place people contain beliefs and attitudes about members of those categories. For example, take the category of *fat person*: What do you believe most fat people are like? How do you feel about fat people? Feelings cannot be tested to determine how true they are. Although beliefs can be tested, feelings strongly influence one's willingness to test the truth of one's beliefs. If one believes that fat people are greedy, for example, one could check the accuracy of that belief by observing a number of fat people. If one's attitudes about the group are not passionately negative, one would revise the belief upon observing fat people who are not greedy. If, however, one hates fat people because of an inability to deal constructively with one's own appetite, one may well resist altering the stereotype or may substitute another negative stereotype. ("Well, they may not be greedy, but they are certainly sloppy!") As Allport (1979) puts it, "We cannot help but strive to put flesh and clothes upon the skeleton of an attitude" (p. 317). In so doing, we construct and hang on to a stereotype that justifies a hostile attitude, regardless of its accuracy.

You may be thinking that although this makes some sense, many people do not externalize their problems and blame others. Why are some people prone to hate much more than others? Psychodynamically oriented research by Adorno, Frenkel-Brunswik, Levinson, and Sanford (1950), and by Harris, Gough, and Martin (1950), strongly suggests that certain child-rearing styles develop personality types that are prone to be either prejudiced or open. People who scored high on prejudice scales tended to come from homes that were authoritarian, where parents expected rules to be obeyed without question, where all rules were handed down by parents, and where parents punished broken rules or behavior that they saw as immoral. People who scored low on prejudice scales tended to come from homes in which love was given unconditionally and where matters of daily living were dealt with flexibly (but not chaotically). The authors suggest that children from authoritarian homes develop feelings of guilt regarding matters such as sex or develop resentments toward their parents, and these feelings smolder at the unconscious level until later directed against others. In addition, such children fail to develop self-confidence and self-reliance because they have been continually directed by someone else, and they adopt their parents' view of things as being black or white and rigid. Children from democratic homes, on the other hand, develop self-confidence because they are allowed to make some decisions and express themselves; they learn to accept others in spite of their perceived shortcomings because their parents allowed them to recognize shortcomings in family members without withdrawing love or approval. Allport argues that the tendency for prejudice becomes a core personality trait and is due in large part to family upbringing. A person with a prejudiced personality will direct hostility against virtually any available target group.

Psychodynamic theory suggests another process that can foster prejudice: identification. As Allport (1979) points out, most children identify with their parents and, in so doing, accept the parents' beliefs and actions as desirable. Children who identify with prejudiced parents thus tend to acquire their prejudices, often without being aware of this tendency. Children also tend to rely on their parents to tell them which social groups to belong to and how to behave toward others. Answers are usually accepted by young children without question and form the basis for attitudes and behavior patterns that will condition further learning about a group.

Social learning theory, as developed by Bandura and Walters (1963), expands on these ideas. Bandura and Walters explain that much social behavior is learned through imitation and reinforcement. Children learn behaviors and responses by watching others; they develop tendencies to copy what they see by having their actions reinforced by others. Parents provide particularly powerful models as well as reinforcers.

With respect to prejudice, parents model for children "whom they should hate and for what reasons, and how they should express their aggression toward the hated objects" (Bandura & Walters, 1963, p. 19). To reduce a child's prejudice, it is insufficient simply to teach the child that prejudice is unfounded or irrational, so long as the child is receiving positive reinforcement for prejudicial behavior from loved ones. Instead, positive behavioral patterns need to be modeled and their use reinforced by some means that the child finds genuinely rewarding. For example, children who attack weaker and unattractive peers need to learn not only why this behavior is inappropriate, but what behaviors would be preferable and what positive consequences would follow the use of the more acceptable behaviors.

Children may not identify with teachers as strongly as with their parents or value a teacher's reward as much as one offered by a parent, but teachers should not regard as nonexistent the possibility of having an influence on students. We have observed many teachers and student teachers who feel powerless to change beliefs and attitudes children bring from home, and consequently they do not try. We have, however, also interviewed young people who overtly rejected some of their parents' beliefs, including their parents' racism (Grant & Sleeter, 1996). Although teachers may not affect children as strongly as parents do, teachers nonetheless are among the most important adults in young peoples' lives. Teachers who are "real" with students—who talk honestly with them about real issues—can serve as influential role models and can prod students to think about their beliefs.

Development of Prejudice and Hostility Between Groups

Many social psychologists see the preceding theories as inadequate for understanding prejudice and discrimination. For example, can we say that the Germans constructed death camps for the Jews in the 1930s because, for some reason, most Germans experienced levels of frustration they could not handle and so projected their individual guilts and failings on the same target group? Although to some extent this theory may have some validity, it does not account very well for groups mobilizing against groups. To understand intergroup relations, we turn to reference group theory, developed by Sherif and Sherif (1966).

The Sherifs conducted numerous observations and some experiments with small groups to understand how groups form interactions with other groups. One notable set of experiments took place in a number of boys' summer camps at which situations were constructed in order to encourage groups to form; these groups were then studied in isolation from one another as well as in contact with one another. Those of you who have attended camp yourself may well remember the sense of "we-ness" that can develop among tent-mates or cabin-mates and the friendly rivalry that often develops between cabins.

According to reference group theory, people derive much of their identity from association with others. All people belong to a set of in-groups, beginning with one's family during early childhood. As one matures, the number of groups to which one belongs expands. People identify with some groups more than others; in fact, one can identify with a group to which one does not even belong. For example, an aspiring basketball star might initially identify with the neighborhood basketball team with whom he or she plays, but that individual might shift identification to the Bulls as a changing perception of his or her own potential as a great basketball player develops. Similarly, with the establishment of the Women's National Basketball Association, female basketball players who could only dream of playing at the college level can now envision themselves playing with a pro team. A reference group is any group with which one identifies. We all have reference groups, and they are a central regulator of our identities.

We all willingly conform to groups with which we identify, and we may deliberately behave in ways that distinguish us from other groups. For example, the Sherifs found that each group of boys in camp adopted a color as its own; having chosen a color, each group then avoided wearing the colors of other groups. During the late 1970s, many girls adopted the "preppie" look, which identified them with conservative, upper-class or upper-middle-class, White girls. One visible badge of group membership was a string of real pearls; particularly if the rest of one's garb on a given day was ordinary, the pearls would indicate that one had the money to sport expensive jewelry, even with jeans.

During the 1980s many African American young people wore Malcolm X caps and T-shirts; these signify that the wearer regards race as a significant social division and identifies with Black power strategies to strengthen the African-American community, rather than with White-controlled strategies. Presently, gang members can be identified by the colors they wear. The wearing of these colors symbolizes a form of status and belonging. However, the wearing of color in school has led to so much tension and violence related to "group belonging" that school policy now often outlaws the wearing of colors. In and of itself, group formation does not necessarily cause prejudice and discrimination. However, the

Sherifs noted that when groups come in contact, they begin to make a concerted effort to define and maintain group boundaries. To encourage all group members to stay within the group and to remain loyal to the group, individual group members begin to depict the group as superior to out-groups and try to convince one another in the group of this superiority. Hostility develops as soon as groups perceive themselves to be in competition with one another. Sherif and Sherif noted that groups need not even really be competing; as long as group members believe another group is competing for something they want, hostility and rejection of the out-group can result.

This theory can easily be applied to ethnic, gender, social class, and disability group relationships, as well as to relationships among other kinds of groups. In applying the theory, one can combine it with psychological theories described earlier. For example, take gender. According to cognitive development theory, children learn early that sex is an important way to categorize people. Children also learn early to which category they belong. Once they know, most children actively strive to conform to that category as part of constructing a self-identity. If a little girl believes that girls wear only dresses, she will not wear anything but dresses. In early childhood, there is some sex segregation and rejection between the sexes as each group seeks to maintain its boundaries and to conform to its image of its own sex. "Fags" and "tomboys," as they are disdainfully called, threaten the integrity of group boundaries, group norms, and personal understanding of what the terms *male* and *female* mean. As children grow up, the opposite sex becomes a target group for individuals with the psychological problems described in psychoanalytic theory; hence, rape and wife beating take place. When people perceive the sexes to be competing over such matters as jobs, stereotyping and hostility develop: Males are seen as "chauvinist or sexist" and females as "aggressive" people who are failing to provide a secure home for their children.

When victimized, according to Allport (1979), most individuals and groups react, and some reactions further intensify the problem. Reactions that intensify the problem include becoming obsessively concerned with prejudice (e.g., reading anti-Semitism into remarks that are not intended as discriminatory); withdrawing or becoming passive (thus, for example, reinforcing stereotypes that characterize people with disabilities or Asian Americans as unassertive); covering up hurt by clowning; strengthening in-group ties (which can make outsiders see the group as too clannish or too different); rejecting one's own group; striving extra hard to succeed in spite of discrimination (which reaffirms stereotypes that the group is cunning or works too hard); acting militant (which reaffirms the idea that the group is hostile); and allowing the prophecy to be self-fulfilling. Such reactions can unwittingly intensify prejudice and stereotyping, but they are normal reactions to victimization.

Think, for example, about a time you were treated unfairly, picked on, or put down. How did you react? The reactions of a group should direct our attention to the unfair treatment that prompted the reactions. However, when we expect to see stereotyped behavior (such as passivity, violence, or lack of effort), the appearance of such behavior may cause us to conclude, "That's just how they are," rather than forcing us to pay attention to how the group was mistreated in the first place.

Self-Concept Theory

Human Relations deals with self-concept as well as intergroup relationships. Purkey and Novak (1984) defined self-concept as "our view of who we are and how we fit into the world" (p. 25). Advocates of the Human Relations approach are particularly concerned about how members of different sociocultural groups view themselves and see their place in the world. Intergroup and interpersonal relationships can be thought of as attitudes toward other people, self-concept and self-esteem as attitudes toward oneself and toward groups of which one is a member.

Self-concept and self-esteem are very complex phenomena that educators frequently oversimplify, especially when considering children who are members of other sociocultural groups. In *Why Are Black Kids Sitting Together in the Cafeteria?*, Tatum (1997) offers a more complex portrait of the formation of self-concept. She emphasizes, for example, the importance of understanding why students, as members of cultural groups, cohere in school settings. Forming social groups with peers "like oneself" facilitates the formation of a positive identity as well as a sense of belonging. At times, too, group formation serves to protect students whose identities are devalued by the school setting and curriculum. Discussing the formation of racial identity, Tatum stresses the need for appreciating the development of self-concept and engaging in conversations across currently existing racial and ethnic divides. The narrow manner in which teachers frequently address issues of self-concept is illustrated by the following observations: We heard a teacher remark that a particular Mexican American child who frequently comes to the teacher for a hug must have a poor self-concept because he is not getting much love at home and comes to school hungry for attention. Similarly, we have heard teachers describe African American children from low-income families as not trying very hard on assignments because they bring low self-esteem from home. To attempt to build up their students' self-esteem, some teachers insert lessons into the curriculum about heroes or heroines of the children's cultural group, often without considering the genuine complexities involved in the development of self.

We must caution educators against assuming that children from low-status groups develop poor self-concepts at home, especially if they are not behaving as the teacher expects. Often the assumptions of these educators are not true. For example, considerable research has been done on various dimensions of the self-concepts and self-esteem of African American and White children; a review of this research concludes that "it is repeatedly found that young African Americans express above-average levels of self-esteem often higher than those of White youngsters of the same age" (Madhere, 1991, p. 47). Knowing the social hostility their children will have to face, many African American parents and other parents of color deliberately build up their children's sense of self and sense of belonging to a strong group, so that they enter school feeling good about themselves, their personal abilities, and their racial or ethnic group. Further, children who seek hugs from teachers often are used to being hugged by adults—at home as well as in school.

Beane and Lipka (1986) list four common dimensions to the self-concept of a young person: self as a member of a family, self as a peer, self as a student, and self as a person with attributes. Each dimension can be further broken out; for example, "self as a student" can refer to self as a learner, a participant in school activities, or an academic achiever; one may further differentiate, say, between self as a math achiever versus self as a music achiever. Beane and Lipka also distinguish between self-concept and self-esteem: Self-concept is "the description an individual attaches to himself or herself," and self-esteem "refers to the evaluation one makes of the self-concept description" (pp. 5–6). Self-concept and self-esteem are complex; one cannot make sweeping statements about a child's self-concept based on how the child behaves in one setting. Further, although the child's behavior in a particular setting, such as a classroom, may reflect the child's self-esteem developed in other contexts, it may also reflect a direct response to that setting itself.

Children develop their self-concepts through interactions with other people in various contexts. The home and neighborhood provide contexts, as does the school. Schools, however, to the degree that they reflect institutionalized inequalities, support the self-concepts of students differentially. Beginning with kindergarten, children gain feedback regarding their ability to perform school tasks, in the form of verbal praise or criticism, grades, test scores, and assignment to an ability group. Some children learn to view themselves as capable in school, and some learn very early to view themselves as incapable. Children also gain feedback from teachers and peers regarding their likability. In addition, schools transmit images of various sociocultural groups—images that can act like mirrors in which children view people like themselves. For example, if the accomplishments of males are celebrated repeatedly in the curriculum, children learn which sex is capable of doing interesting things, and children often do notice. A teacher we know remarked that one of her fifth-grade girls commented one day about their reading text, "Oh, good, this story is about fish! The girls in this book never do anything interesting." Upon reviewing the text, the teacher agreed; the student had noticed a pattern the teacher had not noticed.

By late elementary school and middle school, the self-esteem of some categories of students begins to drop. Madhere (1991), for example, found the self-esteem of African Americans, and particularly boys, to drop in seventh grade. A study by the American Association of University Women (1992) found that the self-esteem of girls dropped more than that of boys in secondary school. Gay and lesbian students first experience homoerotic feelings around the age of 9, on the average, and by adolescence are struggling with feelings they have learned are socially unacceptable, which takes a toll on their self-esteem (Sears, 1993). As children gain exposure to the wider society and its evaluation of themselves and people like themselves, their self-esteem and esteem for their reference group is affected.

The school is a part of that wider society and may be transmitting damaging messages to which children then react. Many children of color react negatively to the celebration of White people that most curricula embody. Low-income people are generally looked down upon by the broader society, including most schools; many students from low-income families learn to regard the school as an alien institution. Many Spanish-speaking students learn in school that speaking Spanish is regarded as a problem rather than as an asset, and so these students eventually refuse to speak Spanish.

Some homes do not support the development of healthy self-esteem, but teachers often misread the home. Rather than blaming the home for a child's behavior, it is more fruitful to examine the kind of context one's own classroom may be providing for children's self-concepts. Are some categories of children reprimanded, ignored, or praised disproportionately? Does the curriculum celebrate the importance of some sociocultural groups more than others? Does every child have a regular opportunity to succeed and appear talented and capable at something? What kind of interpersonal relationship do you have with each child? These kinds of questions direct teachers toward factors they can control. The classroom is only one context of several within which self-concept and self-esteem develop, but it is an important context.

Many teachers react to these kinds of questions by saying, "I don't see color; I just see children." We must point out that nobody, literally, does not "see" color or other differences. If we only associate negative images with color or other human characteristics, we may try not to see those characteristics so that our negative associations do not come into play. However, as we noted earlier, children do see visible differences, and they are curious about what those differences mean. Teachers using the Human Relations approach try to construct classrooms that celebrate individual differences. Race, language, personal talents, body size, hair color, physical abilities, interests, and so forth, are presented to children as characteristics that we all have but that differ among us; and the differences are not only normal, but they are interesting and worthwhile. Further, such teachers try to provide a range of experiences in which different children are successful and to develop the self-esteem of diverse children—an approach based on the philosophy that everyone has something to offer and that no one is perfect.

Some Thoughts on Theory

We believe that reference group theory and cognitive development theory provide the strongest explanations for the development of prejudice and discrimination, primarily because both theories deal with groups of people. Cognitive development theory helps us understand how individuals learn to categorize people into groups and apply stereotypical descriptions to those groups. In a society that is already somewhat segregated and stratified on the basis of race, sex, family background, and disability, cognitive development theory explains how individuals construct sense out of the social world they encounter. Reference group theory helps explain why racial, gender, social class, and disability prejudice are group phenomena rather than isolated individual problems. This theory helps us understand why people tend to hold tenaciously to certain values and perceptions and reject people they see as nonmembers of their group and why tension can exist between groups even when individuals have no personal reason to dislike those who belong to the out-group.

Psychodynamic theory and social learning theory help explain why some people are more prone than others to reject out-group members, but their focus on the individual does not help explain intergroup relations on a large scale. In fact, viewing prejudice and discrimination as emotional disturbances overlooks the advantages that social stratification confers on the dominant group. By acting in ways that help maintain racism, Whites preserve certain economic and political benefits for themselves. By maintaining sexism, males preserve benefits for themselves. Acting on the basis of self-interest may at times be morally questionable, but it is not necessarily the product of emotional instability.

For example, take the wealthy White neighborhood in which families hire women of color as "cleaning ladies." The White employers may harbor positive attitudes toward their employees, may have learned positive behaviors for interacting with them, and may manifest great emotional stability in their own lives and in their acceptance of people. Yet, at the same time, they may accept as natural that only women do housework and that women of color do other people's housework for minimum wages. They may accept stereotypes about this category of person and see the category as an out-group, albeit a group having a useful function. It is possible that individual members of the neighborhood may harbor negative feelings about women of color; some in the neighborhood may dislike these women intensely. On the other hand, others may feel they treat their cleaning ladies well and like them personally. At the same time, they still see them as different, perceive them in terms of stereotypes about women of color, and accord them a lower status.

The strategies that follow are based mainly on reference group, cognitive development, social learning, dissonance, and self-concept theories.

STRATEGIES

Human Relations strategies for classrooms are based on the theories we have just discussed, with the major exception being psychoanalytic theory. Allport (1979) and Cook and Cook (1954) have recommended individual counseling and therapy to help people who have unusually hostile attitudes toward others. Counselors and therapists have at their disposal psychotherapeutic techniques for helping people resolve their inner frustrations and conflicts and develop more positive attitudes toward others. This therapy is not normally done in classrooms, nor is it recommended for classrooms.

Advocates of the Human Relations approach have developed several strategies for classroom use; these strategies are summarized in Table 3–1. These advocates have also developed four underlying principles that teachers should consider before selecting specific strategies. We will present these principles first.

General Principles
First, the Human Relations program should be comprehensive. This means that it should be infused into several subject areas, and it should be school-wide to avoid giving children mixed messages. For example, a school attempting to promote social acceptance of students with mental retardation is working at cross-purposes if lessons in social studies are aimed at prejudice reduction, but language arts and mathematics classes are ability grouped, with retarded students composing the lowest group, and school clubs are dominated by the most academically successful students.

Second, diverse strategies should be used. We will present a variety of strategies that can be considered for implementation. Different strategies accomplish different things, and no single strategy has been found to be the one best strategy for promoting positive human relations. However, strategies actively involving children tend to be most effective. Although there is value in presenting information or in demonstrating, those strategies that place children in a passive role have less impact than those that place them in an active role.

Third, the program should start with the children's real-life experiences. Educators recommend, for example, starting with interpersonal relationships in the classroom or intergroup hostilities in the school. These familiar experiences enable the children to more easily grasp the point of developing human relations involving more distant and abstract groups.

Finally, each child should be able to experience academic and social success in the classroom, and the success of some students should not be contingent on the failure of others. Often in classrooms children compete for grades or rewards. This competition teaches a child to devalue the feelings and accomplishments of others, because others must do poorly in order for the child to look good. Those students who consistently come out at or near the bottom tend to suffer some rejection by others and may develop feelings of personal inadequacy. These feelings run counter to the goals of the Human Relations approach.

These principles govern the use of a number of strategies: providing accurate information, using group process, using vicarious experience and role playing, involving students in community action projects, and teaching social skills. A discussion of each of these principles follows.

Providing Accurate Cognitive Information

Ignorance supports prejudice; accurate information can help to reduce prejudice. Young children are naturally curious about what they see, and they want information. Derman-Sparks (1989) provides an example of a young child's question and an appropriate response:

> "How do people get their color?" asks 3-year-old Heather. "What are your ideas?" her teacher responds. "Well, I was wondering about pens. You know, the pens you can put red or blue or brown on your skin if you want to." Teacher: "I'm glad you are trying to figure things out, but that's not how people get their skin color. We get our skin color from our mommies and daddies. Your skin is the same color as mine. Marizza's skin color is like her mommy and daddy's. Denise's skin is lighter brown because she is a mixture of her mommy's white skin and her Daddy's black skin." (p. 33)

The information the teacher provided is accurate and about as conceptually sophisticated as a 3-year-old can grasp. Older children could learn about melanin, how melanin protects the skin, and why people who developed in geographical areas near the equator developed more melanin than those nearer the North Pole. Providing such information is much more constructive than ignoring the issue or telling students not to ask about such matters.

In multicultural education programs, providing accurate cognitive information means providing accurate information about various racial, ethnic, disability, gender, or social class groups. At the very least, it means making sure that class-room materials do not contain overt stereotypes and biases. Most educators advo-cate going beyond the removal of stereotypical materials by presenting accurate and comprehensive information. This strategy is important because, as noted ear-lier, people learn stereotypes, and they focus attention on attributes of categories of people (such as skin color) that exaggerate traits, oversimplify, and in many cases misrepresent people. Accurate cognitive information seeks to replace stereo-types and misconceptions that children may already have.

Human Relations educators agree that this information should stress "the *commonality* of people as well as their *individuality*" (Colangelo et al. 1985, p. 1, em-phasis theirs). For example, Taba et al. (1952) recommended that teachers teach chil-dren about cultural differences by stressing ways in which culture is a reasonable response people make to their particular life conditions in an effort to resolve com-mon human problems. These educators give an example regarding teaching about the Chinese diet. Anglo children may view the preponderance of rice in the Chinese diet as peculiar until they are made aware of the preponderance of wheat in the An-glo diet and until they learn why all people need a grain product in their diet. Sim-ilarly, Turnbull and Schulz (1979) recommend that teachers of students with dis-abilities stress the similarities among all students so that differences are placed in perspective, rather than allowing them to assume exaggerated importance. How-ever, teachers should also provide information about specific disability characteris-tics or equipment; for example, children will very likely wonder what a wheel-chair is like or how Braille works, and they should be taught about these matters.

As noted earlier, young children ask questions freely before they learn that some kinds of questions are impolite. Questions about human differences are of-ten treated by adults as rude, so children stop asking them. Instead, they learn to verbalize differences in the form of jokes, snide remarks, and name calling. Sears (1992), for example, notes, "Too many school children remain ignorant of the di-versity of human sexuality, and too many teachers and students fear discussing sexuality beyond whispered conversations, cruel jokes, or sexual innuendo" (p. 147). By late elementary or junior high age, students may be very uncomfortable engaging in initial lessons about differences they have learned not to discuss openly.

One of us witnessed a junior high teacher trying to discuss ethnic back-ground with a group of students who apparently had never talked openly about this issue; her invitation for students to share their ethnic background was met with silence, then embarrassed giggles, then joking behavior (such as African American students saying that they were Chinese). Unprepared for the students' reaction, the teacher stopped the lesson and moved on to something else. With older students, teachers may wish to begin instruction by acknowledging that this subject may be one students have never discussed, reflecting on the teacher's ear-lier discomfort in discussing the subject (such as racial differences). Then the dis-cussion proceeds to the highly interesting information the teacher learned and wishes to teach (giving an example). As the teacher provides correct terminology and accurate information, modeling comfort while discussing a human difference or characteristic, students soon open up and begin asking questions that have been suppressed, often since early childhood.

Grambs (1968) recommends that representatives of minority groups be invited to school as classroom speakers because "using the 'real thing'—the live representation of the thing we wish to demonstrate—speaks far louder than the words we say" (p. 34). Donaldson and Martinson (1977) have made a similar recommendation regarding people with disabilities: Speakers who are themselves members of disability groups have more impact on students than information out of a book.

However, the teacher should not rely exclusively on members of other groups to teach about themselves; if the teacher does not have enough information to get started, there are excellent teaching resources to use. For example, numerous books provide insightful vignettes and focus activities which may help teachers to construct meaningful lessons (e.g. Grant, 1995; Tiedt & Tiedt, 1995). Additionally, children's literature books can be an excellent source of information about diverse groups.

Teachers also need to educate themselves about what is worth teaching. When teachers first begin to teach about differences, they often construct what Derman-Sparks (1989) refers to as a "tourist curriculum," which focuses on artifacts of other countries, such as food, traditional clothing, folk tales, and household items (p. 7). For example, on Cinco de Mayo (a Mexican American holiday in May), children eat tacos and learn to count to ten in Spanish; or to study Native Americans, children make headdresses or totem poles, eat fry bread, and listen to a folk tale. Derman-Sparks criticizes the "tourist curriculum":

> Tourist curriculum is both patronizing, emphasizing the "exotic" differences between cultures, and trivializing, dealing not with the real-life daily problems and experiences of different peoples, but with surface aspects of their celebrations and modes of entertainment. Children "visit" non-White cultures and then "go home" to the daily classroom, which reflects only the dominant culture. The focus on holidays, although it provides drama and delight for both children and adults, gives the impression that that is all "other" people—usually people of color—do. What it fails to communicate is real understanding. (p. 7)

Instead, she recommends starting with a variety of differences—cultural, physical, and gender—that students actually see and experience, here and now. Rather than treating differences as exotic, teachers should treat differences in the community as normal. Teachers should also discuss stereotyping and prejudice, so that students comprehend how people react to differences they do not understand.

How much impact can the teaching of cognitive information have? Banks (1991) reviewed numerous research studies on the impact of content about race and gender on students. He found that, although results of the studies are inconsistent, curriculum interventions can have a positive impact on students' racial and gender attitudes. The studies he reviewed were conducted in a variety of ways, using a variety of measures of impact. However, many of them reported a positive change in students' attitudes; none reported a negative impact. Most of the interventions were short-term; the impact of a long-term course of study has not been investigated to nay appreciable extent.

Educators see limitations to presenting information as a primary teaching strategy: By itself, presenting information does not necessarily change behavior or attitudes. For example, Watts (1984) reviewed research studies on the impact of persuasive information on attitudes. He found that information is most likely to change attitudes when a person is not already committed to the target attitudes or when the attitudes are not directly connected to core beliefs. Attitudes that help anchor a person's core beliefs are resistant to change, and the information presented may simply be ignored. Teachers who couple the presentation of information with additional strategies are likely to create a stronger impact on students. In discussing teacher education, for instance, King (1991) discourages the isolated presentation of factual information about social inequality; rather, she stresses the need students have for "an alternative context in which to think critically about and reconstruct their social knowledge and self-identities" (p. 143). Likewise, Berlak (1996) emphasizes the possibilities of narrative in challenging student perspectives and raising awareness.

However, presenting children with positive information about their own group can be very helpful, especially if it counters negative perceptions. People want to feel good about themselves and look for information that will validate their self-worth. School curricula tend not to include much positive, substantive information about many groups, such as women of color, contemporary American Indians, or people with disabilities. This lack of information sends the message to members of these groups that they are relatively unimportant, which can be detrimental to their self-concepts. For example, when an Indian child is taught about his or her tribe's accomplishments, this information is embraced with more enthusiasm than information that suggests that Indians in the 1980s are an artifact of U.S. history. The strategies that follow involve students actively. They are very useful when coupled with information presentation.

Group Process
Group process can be defined as the "use of the group to educate its members" (Cook & Cook, 1954, p. 243). Human Relations educators usually advocate the use of heterogeneous groups (i.e., racially mixed, sex mixed, or containing both special education and regular students); cooperative learning in particular has become very popular. Group process strategies make use of two of the theories discussed earlier. One is cognitive development theory. As a result of direct contact with members of another group during carefully structured situations, students should be able to gain accurate information that will probably challenge stereotypes about members of that group. For example, if a student believes that hearing-impaired people are unsociable but then works on a class project with one who is gregarious, that stereotype might be weakened or eliminated. The other theory that group process builds on is reference group theory. By building groups of heterogeneous students, teachers attempt to construct in-groups with students who had previously regarded each other as out-group members. For example, in a sex-segregated classroom, cross-sex team members begin to identify with teammates of

both sexes, in addition to identifying with members of the same sex who are on other teams. Also, the peer group within the entire class develops a norm against sex discrimination (or race or disability discrimination) as students on each team see the value of interacting with teammates of the opposite sex.

Depending on how a teacher structures group work, it can be either very successful or disastrous. Some teachers mistakenly believe that contact by itself among members of different groups is beneficial. Actually, contact by itself can encourage stereotyping, prejudice, and social rejection. For example, imagine a teacher in a desegregated school who has White, middle-class students, who have attended suburban schools with good teaching, and African American, low-income students, who have previously attended schools with inferior teaching. Suppose that this teacher establishes racially mixed groups that are assigned to complete a library research project on the Industrial Revolution. It is quite possible that the African American students would not be as well prepared for this task as the White students. Consequently, if the White students believe that African Americans are inferior, the contact experience might reaffirm that belief. Conversely, if the African American students believe that Whites are arrogant, this belief too might be reaffirmed.

Allport (1979) has specified conditions under which cross-group contact can be beneficial:

> Prejudice (unless deeply rooted in the character structure of the individual) may be reduced by *equal status* contact between majority and minority groups in the pursuit of *common goals*. The effect is greatly enhanced if this contact is sanctioned by institutional supports ... and provided it is of the sort that leads to the perception of common interests, and common humanity between members of the two groups. (p. 281, emphasis ours)

Cooperative learning is a form of group work that is currently receiving considerable attention. Johnson, Johnson, and Holubec (1988) differentiate cooperative learning from traditional grouping on the basis of several factors. In cooperative learning groups, students must work together to complete the task successfully; the work is structured to promote their interdependence. Cooperative learning should involve individual as well as group accountability; the teacher should give both individual and group feedback. In cooperative learning groups, students share responsibility for leadership functions; they also share responsibility for each other's achievement; the teacher makes sure students are rewarded for sharing these tasks. Teachers of cooperative learning groups help students develop group process skills, such as conflict management and listening. Considerable evidence points to the use of cooperative learning in classrooms as a successful strategy for reducing stereotyping and social rejection across disability, race, and gender lines (e.g., Johnson & Johnson, 1987; Johnson, Johnson, & Maruyama, 1983; Sharan, 1980; Slavin & Madden, 1979).

There are various models of cooperative learning and several handbooks to help teachers implement these models. The *group investigation* model involves students working in small heterogeneous groups to create a product that requires diverse talents, skills, or viewpoints (see Johnson, Johnson, & Holubec, 1991). The product may be something as elaborate as a multimedia production in which students synthesize information they have gathered about a topic; or it can be as small as a list of ideas generated during a short discussion. Group investigation assignments require considerable advance planning by the teacher, because the tasks must draw on the strengths or abilities of each student in the group; no group should be assigned a task that sets up some of its members to fail. For example, creating a newspaper as a way of investigating a topic requires different skills, such as preparing articles that have diverse writing styles, creating drawings, doing interviews, and designing layouts. By contrast, sending groups of students to the library to do a research paper usually sets up some students for failure, unless all of them are skilled in doing library research or unless the teacher has identified in advance those materials that are of interest to and within the skill levels of all the students.

The *jigsaw* model uses two groupings to complete an assignment. In the first grouping, each group studies a different but related piece of a topic, and group members work together to make sure they all understand the material and become "experts" on it. The students are then regrouped so that each new group has one or two "experts" on each piece. A task is then given requiring students to pool their expertise. For example, suppose students in an English class are studying sonnets. The teacher divides the class into groups and gives each group a different sonnet to study; each group member is given a copy of the sonnet, and the group is given questions to use as a guide in discussion. Students are then regrouped with others who have read different sonnets, so that each new group is composed of "experts" on one sonnet. Their task could be to determine the essential characteristics of a sonnet by comparing the different sonnets studied. Many teachers like this particular model of cooperative learning because when students get to their second group, everyone has an important piece to contribute that the rest of the group members need. Even the lowest academic achievers have some expertise to share.

In the *team games* model, students are divided into heterogeneous groups. All the students are expected to master a body of skills or knowledge, but they compete as a team against other teams in some form of tournament. The main way for teams to succeed is for group members to tutor each other before the competition. Teachers can use team games in a wide variety of ways, ranging from giving fairly short and simple quizzes on the material (in which, say, the group with the best average score wins) to conducting very elaborate tournaments (Slavin, 1986).

Some teachers use cooperative learning activities occasionally, as a break from traditional teaching methods; others structure much of their teaching program around cooperative learning. For example, the Tribes Program involves groups of "five or six children who work together throughout each day throughout the school year" (Gibbs, 1987). The teacher plans group process activities to help the students learn to work together and uses the models of cooperative learning described above; students are also encouraged to help each other, even when they are not required to provide such help.

An important part of group process is teaching students the skills and attitudes needed for working together; the benefits of cooperative learning come from students actually learning to work together well. Several curriculum guides are full of activities that are specifically designed to teach students how to cooperate, such as how to listen to each other, how to resolve differences, or how to encourage each other to participate (e.g., Johnson, Johnson, & Holubec, 1991; Prutzman, Stern, Burger, & Bodenhamer, 1988).

Teachers who are interested in group process strategies will find many useful books and workshops available to help them. It does take practice to learn to use cooperative learning well. Sometimes teachers try it out and then give up because what they intended did not work automatically. Failures with cooperative learning are usually due not to the concept but to one's skill in using the concept.

Vicarious Experience and Role Playing

Cook and Cook (1954) described vicarious experience as "an experience in, a contact *with*, rather than reading *about*" (p. 291, emphasis theirs). Group dynamics, described earlier, foster direct, face-to-face contact; vicarious experiences promote contact through the use of symbols of reality. Vicarious experiences include contact through role playing, sociodrama, literature, and film, in which the student takes the perspective of a member of another group.

Vicarious experiences are rooted in different theories, depending on how the experiences are structured. These experiences may be structured primarily to reduce stereotyping. For example, if some students who believe that all Japanese Americans are quiet view a film depicting a realistic story involving Japanese Americans who do not conform to that stereotype, the stereotype may be weakened (depending on the believability of the film).

Vicarious experiences can also reduce social distance and develop feelings of empathy. For example, a boy who plays the role of a woman trying to raise a family single-handedly on a secretary's salary may reevaluate his stereotypes about working women as well as discovering the problems such women face and feeling more concern for their situation. According to dissonance theory, the boy would experience a discrepancy between his previous negative attitude and his feelings while playing the role. The experience could lead to a change in attitude, provided the role playing is realistic. Simulations of disabilities are currently popular for preparing regular education students for the inclusion of mainstreamed special education students in their classes. Research has found role playing and simulation to be a helpful approach to improving attitudes toward people with disabilities (Kitano, Stiehl, & Cole, 1978). Simulations, of course, may facilitate sensitization across a variety of domains. For examples, Sylvester (1994) transformed his elementary classroom in a way which reflected economic problems in the surrounding community and society; by having to confront issues such as unemployment, wage structures, and taxation, students gained a deeper understanding of the struggles encountered by social groups. However, simulations can also greatly oversimplify a situation, leading students to view another group's problems as easily resolvable; teachers who use simulations need to be aware of this possible outcome.

Skits are useful for helping students examine group behavior. For example, Prutzman and colleagues (1988) suggest that a teacher can have students stage a skit involving interpersonal conflict. As students act out what they would do or what they have seen others do, the skit can be interrupted periodically for discussion of alternative courses of action. Skits are useful in teaching conflict resolution: "When children encounter a problem similar to one they have already resolved, they are better prepared to meet it with a creative solution" (Prutzman et al., 1988, p. 60).

Community Action Projects

Community action projects, another form of direct contact experience, move the students out of the classroom and place them in contact with members of a target group in the community to do some sort of service project. Cook and Cook (1954) explain that the idea is to provide learners with direct, perceptual experience in area life, issues, and affairs. This approach is seldom easy and it is never safe, yet it is hard to find any better way by which abstractions can take on meaning and be acted upon (p. 249).

Like group dynamics, this strategy provides contact in an effort to reduce stereotyping. For the strategy to be most effective, students performing community service must behave in a constructive and positive manner. Like role playing, this strategy can create dissonance between behavior and prejudiced attitudes.

Watts (1984) discussed community action projects, using the term *counterattitudinal behavior*. He argued that research supports the effectiveness of community action in changing negative attitudes and reducing prejudice as long as several interrelated conditions are present: The student must commit himself or herself to the task voluntarily; the student must feel personally responsible for the negative consequence of any negative behavior he or she displays; and the student must not justify acting in a negative manner in the situation. For example, suppose that a student is assigned to do volunteer work in a welfare office as a way of dealing with prejudice against the poor. The student should not be coerced to perform the service, as the coercion in itself could engender increased hostility.

The work situation should be structured so that the student feels personally responsible for his or her own actions; if the student talks to a client in a condescending manner and the client becomes angry, the student should realize, after observing that other clients do not become angry when being helped, that his or her behavior has triggered the client's anger. Furthermore, there should be a supervisor who can help the student realize that the condescending behavior was inappropriate. If the student behaves in a positive and helpful manner over a period of time, he or she will probably develop positive relationships with some clients as well as see firsthand the sorts of problems clients face, which may lead to a change in attitude.

Social Skills Training

Teaching social skills to someone who does not interact positively with members of another group can facilitate cross-group relationships and positive attitudes. This strategy has two rather different kinds of applications. One application is primarily for members of dominant groups who behave toward others in a manner that breeds hostility or simply indifference. Johnson (1972) provides examples of the sorts of skills one could teach: self-disclosure, developing and maintaining trust, listening, responding, sending clear messages, expressing feelings both verbally and nonverbally, and confronting others constructively. Some educators have trained teachers and students to use these skills in interracial situations to facilitate positive and constructive communication (Banks & Benavidez, 1981).

A particular problem teachers often must deal with is harassment and name calling. Sexual harassment is one form of harassment that has received considerable attention recently. To what degree does harassment occur in most schools? The problem occurs probably to a greater degree than most adults are aware or admit. For example, in a review of literature on sexual harassment in schools, Linn, Stein, Young, and Davis (1992) note that there is a high occurrence among students, with young women being victims much more often than young men; and, "more often than not, nothing is done with this information [about allegations of sexual harassment], and the problem and conditions fester" (p. 115). Adults may be unaware of harassment among students for a variety of reasons: it often occurs when adults are not around, students are often embarrassed to report it, and adults often trivialize it when it is reported (for example, replying that "boys will be boys," or tacitly agreeing that a particular student is a "fag").

How do Human Relations advocates recommend that harassment and name calling be handled? Teachers must establish rules and explain to students the reasons for the rules. Young children are often unaware of the hurtfulness of name calling or other exclusionary behaviors; older children may well be aware that such behavior hurts others, but they try to get away with it. Teachers should intervene immediately, comfort or support the target, and enforce the rule prohibiting the behavior. Teachers should then consider the underlying reason for the behavior. Sometimes harassment or name calling results from peer pressure or prejudice; harassment is also often a power play, in which dominant group members try to keep subordinant group members "in their place." For example, sexual harassment is frequently a way of reminding females of their vulnerability, especially if they try to succeed in "male" areas such as sports.

Reactive solutions (i.e., stopping the behavior) have limited long-term effects; teachers who approach harassment proactively assume that the potential for harassment exists and continuously use the strategies described in this chapter and in subsequent chapters to build more positive relationships among students *before* problems occur (Derman-Sparks, 1989).

A second application of social skills training has been for special education students or socially unpopular students; such students are taught skills to facilitate their social relationships with regular education students. For example, Oden and Asher (1977) studied the effects of teaching the following skills to socially unpopular children:

> Participation (e.g., getting started, paying attention); cooperation (e.g., taking turns, sharing materials); communication (e.g., talking with the other person, listening); and validation support, referred to as being friendly, fun, and nice (e.g., looking at the other person, giving a smile, offering help or encouragement). (p. 499)

In a control-group design study, the researchers found that children who were taught these skills rose in popularity, with the results persisting in a one-year follow-up study.

Social skills are usually taught using a variety of techniques, including modeling, coaching, and role playing. Positive reinforcement is given consistently, immediately following a child's use of a desired positive social behavior. Students need to be helped with skills development until they are able to use the skills appropriately in real-life situations. Many guides, in fact, have been published which provide exercises for fostering students' abilities to respect differences, communicate, and resolve conflict (Drew, 1987; Duvall, 1994).

How does a Human Relations approach get into a school? What kinds of considerations and problems make such an approach seem useful? The following vignette describes one morning in a typical middle school, where problems with human relationships suddenly assumed great importance.

A BLUE MONDAY MORNING

Mr. Mack, a middle-school social studies teacher, was not feeling his best this morning as he sped along the expressway to Hemingway School, located in the suburbs. He was annoyed with himself for arguing with his wife about where to spend spring vacation. She wanted to go to San Francisco to see their just-born niece and then rent a car and drive along the California coast for a second honeymoon. He wanted to go to Boston to see a few Celtics games and spend some time in the Harvard library doing research on his thesis. Not only was he annoyed for having lost the argument that had occupied most of their attention over the weekend, but he had spent too much time this morning making a final plea for his position (it being the last day for Super Saver fares) and was now in danger of being late for school. He was well aware that the nonverbal communication conveyed by his principal, Mrs. Wilson, hung staff members by their thumbs, so to speak, when they arrived late; and his anxiety was compounded by having been late Thursday of last week.

When he pulled his car into the first open space in the school parking lot, a glance at his Swatch informed him that he had 1½ minutes before being late. He figured that if he walked fast across the playground, he could make it and not have to endure the scowls of Mrs. Wilson. He was halfway across the playground and beginning to feel like he just might get in under the wire when he suddenly saw three boys from his class—Ernest, Ken, and Harold—yelling and chasing Victor Cheng, the new boy in school. He wondered if he had correctly heard what they were shouting. He called the boys over to him. As they arrived—28 seconds left before the scowl—he told Ernest, Ken, and Harold to meet him in his classroom. He then took Victor Cheng gently by the arm and continued his trek to the office. On the way, he asked Victor why the boys were chasing him and what they were calling him.

He scribbled his name and time of arrival on the time sheet just as the bell sounded, alerting all faculty that the workday had officially begun (and telling any teacher who hadn't yet signed in that he or she was late). Victor told him then what the boys had said—that they didn't like wormy Chinese food or people who try to act smart in class. He said that they had told him that if he didn't bring some fortune cookies to school, they would do him in; he hadn't brought the cookies to school.

Mrs. Wilson overheard this conversation from her vantage point near the sign-in sheets, and she moved closer to listen until Victor finished his story. Then she asked Mr. Mack to have Victor wait in the library. She wanted to talk privately with Mr. Mack.

Mrs. Wilson told Mr. Mack that this was the ninth name-calling and fighting incident that had come to her attention in the last few days. She said, "We have had basically a peaceful integration of students of color into the school, but the name calling, fighting, and writing of graffiti—words like Nigger and Chink—on the boys' bathroom wall suggest that the students need to have some human relations orientation. They also need to learn what sexual harassment is and that it is illegal. Just yesterday a father came in very angry because his daughter said some boys had been trying to touch her where they shouldn't." She suggested that Mr. Mack organize a committee of three other teachers to recommend some school-wide and classroom human relations activities that would help reduce the prejudice, elimi- nate the stereotyping and name calling, and put a stop to any sexual harassment. She suggested that they consider bulletin boards that would point out the similar- ity of people, the importance of brotherhood and sisterhood, the obligation to re- spect others, and the need for appropriate behavior between members of the op- posite sex. She also suggested that they establish policies for reporting and dealing with name calling and sexual harassment when these practices occur.

Mr. Mack said, "Okay, I'll get back to you this afternoon with the names of the other committee members. I've become increasingly interested in learning more about these matters anyway. Besides, I've heard that getting students to work on these issues in cooperative groups can help."

Mrs. Wilson remarked that she had heard the same thing, although she cau- tioned that the faculty should not just leap onto one possible solution before in- vestigating an array of strategies.

As he left Mrs. Wilson and headed to pick up Victor Cheng, Mr. Mack thought, "Human relations are important on the job and off!"

CRITIQUE   The Human Relations approach seems to be the one that is most popular with teachers, particularly White elementary teachers. For example, in a study of 30 teachers participating in a long-term, staff-development program in multicultural education, one of us found that teachers define multicultural education as the Hu- man Relations approach more frequently than any other approach (Haberman & Post, 1990; Sleeter, 1992). However, this is not the approach preferred by most peo- ple who have studied discrimination or multicultural education in depth. Why is there this discrepancy?

One can criticize the Human Relations approach, not for what it aims to do, but for what it does not aim to do. Few can quarrel with the desirability of reduc- ing prejudice, stereotyping, tension, and hostility among groups. The approach itself, however, is limited in its analysis of why discrimination and inequality exist and in its simplistic conception of culture and identity.

Advocates of the Teaching the Exceptional and Culturally Different approach see the Human Relations approach as too soft and ineffective in addressing academic achievement. The approach they advocate directly addresses how to teach the curriculum better, which the Human Relations approach does not. For example, in the vignette the teachers were probably ignoring Victor Cheng's ethnic background, as well as that of other students, until a social problem erupted. They were probably teaching students as if they were all alike and as if the school were predominantly White, as if all the students were White. Student diversity became an object of concern only when it threatened harmony within the school. However, as we have noted earlier, in most schools the chances are great that, on the average, students of color, students from low-income homes, students struggling with their sexual identity, and students with disabilities are not achieving on a par with the White, suburban students with whom they will be competing to get into college. Advocates of Teaching the Exceptional and Culturally Different (as well as advocates of approaches we will discuss later) view student achievement as one of the most fundamentally important issues to address. If we simply accept low achievement levels as natural and focus only on how students are getting along, we are not doing our job as teachers.

Actually, the two approaches we have examined thus far—Teaching the Exceptional and Culturally Different, and Human Relations—can be used simultaneously. Nevertheless, teachers who try to do so usually emphasize one or the other—teaching the existing curriculum well or improving feelings in the classroom—simply because there is not time to do everything exceptionally well.

The three approaches to multicultural education that we will discuss next view discrimination, inequality, culture, and cultural identity as much more complex than does the Human Relations approach. Ask yourself, for example, why substantially larger proportions of children of color live in poverty than White children. When asked this question, most White people at first draw a blank, then name things that families of color must lack (such as ambition or education) and sometimes make vague references to discrimination, such as mentioning a relative who will not hire employees of color. Or ask yourself why the poverty rate among women is growing despite the fact that some career opportunities have opened to women. Does stereotyping and sexual harassment fully explain the impoverization of women? Without having investigated these kinds of questions, most people simply don't know the answers. Therefore, in the classroom when symptoms of inequalities are acted out, teachers treat the symptoms only—the name calling, stereotyping, and prejudice.

For example, imagine two children, a lower-income Puerto Rican and a middle-class Anglo, fighting at school. One can teach them to play together rather than to fight, and one can teach that Puerto Ricans are not violent (contrary to the Anglo child's stereotype) or that Anglos are not arrogant (contrary to the Puerto Rican child's stereotype). Unfortunately, these teachings do almost nothing to change the fact that this Puerto Rican child, like many Hispanic children, is living in poverty; that middle-class Anglos tend to accept another's poverty and see it as the other person's fault; and that the Anglo child will have doors of opportunity open to him or her that will be closed to the lower-income Puerto Rican child and, in many cases, even the middle-class Puerto Rican child, especially if her or his skin is dark. Perhaps this particular Anglo child will deal more humanely with people of color as a result of human relations teaching, but kind treatment by individuals does not of itself eliminate poverty, powerlessness, social stratification, or institutional discrimination. As in the vignette, the other students may learn to interact pleasantly with Victor and to enjoy Chinese food, but this accommodation is no guarantee that they will learn about issues such as the poverty in Chinatown or the psychological devastation many Asian immigrants face when they realize they must surrender much of their identity to assimilate into American society. McCarthy (1993) has been quite critical of approaches to multicultural education which emphasize the changing of individual attitudes and the need for more positive relationships while failing to address the structural nature of inequality.

McCarthy's critique is both significant and valid as Human Relations curricula do not address these issues in much depth, if at all. For example, we reviewed *Multicultural Teaching: A Handbook of Activities, Information and Resources* (Tiedt & Tiedt, 1995), which contains a variety of human relations lessons for grades K–8. The lessons are in categories which include supporting individual self-esteem, achieving empathy for others, and recognizing and providing equity for all people living in the U.S. Written objectives inform the user that the lessons aim to teach children that diversity is something to be valued, that people of different colors have contributed to America and that the "range of diversity to be represented in a multicultural curriculum includes young and old, male and female, the physically able and disabled, as well as those who can be grouped by language, national origin, race, or religious belief" (pp. xiii–xiv). Included in the goals for the lessons are also the ideas that there is diversity within ethnic groups, that individual uniqueness should be cherished, that no cultural group is better or worse than any other, and that everyone has feelings. These are worthwhile purposes, and the lessons are creatively and skillfully written to accomplish them. However, though the authors state that multicultural education should include conversations about "controversial issues," the lessons and the goals for the lessons do not include teaching about injustices that have happened in the past or are now occurring. They do not teach that groups in real life compete for wealth and power, that power positions in America are dominated by White males of wealth, that unemployment is high in central cities partly because businesses do not find it profitable to locate there, and that many businesses are set up to value personal profit more than sharing with others. Such lessons do not teach that many women who head households and need jobs often lack child care facilities for their children and are forced to choose between holding a job but having to leave their children unsupervised or staying home with their children but having to live on welfare.

These are problems that are not resolved by teaching individuals only to get along better and value diversity. In fact, it is possible to interpret valuing diversity to mean believing, for example, that Mexican Americans should eat beans rather than steak because beans are "more Mexican." Such thinking ignores the fact that beans are also cheaper, and it can glorify the way people have adapted to poverty and powerlessness without acknowledging that many people who eat beans do so because they cannot afford steak.

In a very real sense, the Human Relations approach can be assimilationist. Some educators who adopt a Human Relations approach often do not address issues of assimilation versus pluralism; often, cultural differences are addressed only as much as needed to improve feelings toward self and others. Other Human Relations educators do address cultural diversity, stressing mainly the acceptance of differences without necessarily examining critically which differences are of most value and which are artifacts of historic or present injustices. In addition, by failing to focus adequately on social problems and structural inequalities, the approach implicitly accepts the status quo. It asks people to get along within the status quo rather than educating them to change the status quo.

Cooperative learning, as we have mentioned earlier, is currently very popular. Often teachers use it to improve relationships among students in the classroom, but otherwise the teachers maintain business as usual. For example, it is quite possible to use cooperative learning to process textbook assignments that teach about the conquest of Native American nations without ever critiquing the relations between Native Americans and Whites today—relations which for many tribes are not cooperative. Sapon-Shevin and Schniedewind (1989/1990) point out that

> Learning about and implementing cooperative learning can provide schools an opportunity to examine *all* aspects of school policy, philosophy, and practice, making these consistent with a belief in the value and educability of all students and a sense of the mutual responsibility that creates communities. (p. 65)

Strategies such as cooperative learning open up larger questions about how groups relate to each other, and advocates of the three approaches to multicultural education that will be discussed next hope that educators will pursue these larger questions.

Because of what the Human Relations approach does not address, it has not been adopted by most educators interested in fighting sexism, heterosexism, or classism, and many people of color who adopted the approach at one time have since shifted to one of the approaches examined later in this book. The Human Relations approach can be incorporated into other approaches, so one need not give up a fight against prejudice and stereotyping to adopt another approach.

The Human Relations approach currently is popular with those who work with special education students, probably because most people who write about and teach students with disabilities do not themselves have disabilities. Educators see human relations problems in schools, but they tend to view people with disabilities from a deficiency or difference perspective rather than an oppressed minority perspective. Therefore, many teachers believe that it is sufficient if children learn to get along and accept other physical or mental characteristics. An oppressed minority perspective, adopted by advocates of the three approaches this book will treat next and by disability rights advocates, focuses on issues such as access to a wide range of institutions, the cultures of disability communities, and "ablism" within the dominant society.

Early childhood and primary grade teachers feel that we are terribly off base if this critique implies that teachers should teach young children about issues such as job discrimination. Actually, at the early childhood level, good Human Relations teaching can provide a basis for more sophisticated approaches to multicultural education later. The key word here is *good* Human Relations rather than "tourist curricula." For example, we have made reference in this chapter to the *Anti-Bias Curriculum* (Derman-Sparks, 1989) and *Multicultural Teaching: A Handbook of Activities, Information, and Resources* (Tiedt & Tiedt, 1995). The *Anti-Bias Curriculum* is explicitly designed to provide children with a basis for learning that is consistent with the three approaches to multicultural education that we will explore next. *Multicultural Teaching*, although not explicitly so designed, also lays a very good foundation for young children on which it is possible to build the same three approaches. Similarly, King (1990) suggests many activities to help young children explore ethnic and gender differences in their immediate environment. Tourist curricula, teaching about the food and folk customs of other countries, do not lay such a foundation. Early childhood and primary grade teachers should become familiar with all five approaches to multicultural education, but they may find that much of their work is most consistent with the Human Relations approach.

REFERENCES

Adorno, T. W., Frenkel-Brunswik, E., Levinson, D. J., & Sanford, R. N. (1950). *The authoritarian personality*. New York: Harper & Row.

Allport, G. W. (1979). *The nature of prejudice* (25th anniversary ed.). Reading, MA: Addison-Wesley.

American Association of University Women (1992). *The AAUW report: How schools shortchange girls*. AAUW and the National Education Association.

Bandura, A., & Walters, R. H. (1963). *Social learning and personality development*. New York: Holt, Rinehart, & Winston.

Banks, G. P., & Benavidez, P. L. (1981). Interpersonal skills training in multicultural education. In H. P. Baptiste, Jr., M. L. Baptiste, & D. M. Gollnick (Eds.), *Multicultural teacher education: Preparing educators to provide educational equity* (pp. 177–201). Washington, DC: Association of Colleges & Teacher Education.

Banks, J. A. (1991). Multicultural education: Its effects on students' racial and gender role attitudes. In J. P. Shaver (Ed.), *Handbook of research on social studies teaching and learning* (pp. 459–469). New York: Macmillan.

Beane, J. A., & Lipka, R. P. (1986). *Self-concept, self-esteem, and the curriculum*. New York: Teachers College Press.

Berlak, A. C. (1996). Teaching stories: Viewing a cultural diversity course through the lens of narrative. *Theory into Practice, 35*(2), 93–101.

Clark, K. B. (1963). *Prejudice and your child* (2nd ed.). Boston: Beacon Press.

Colangelo, N., Dustin, D., & Foxley, C. H. (1985). *Multicultural nonsexist education: A human relations approach* (2nd ed.). Dubuque, IA: Kendall/Hunt.

Cook, L. A., & Cook, E. (1954). *Intergroup education*. New York: McGraw-Hill.

Crawford, D., & Bodine, R. (1996). *Conflict resolution education: A guide to implementing programs in schools, youth-service organizations, and community and juvenile justice settings*. Washington, DC: U.S. Department of Justice.

Creighton, A., & Kivel, P. (1992). *Helping teens stop violence: A practical guide for counselors, educators, and parents*. Alameda, CA: Hunter House.

Cummings, H. H. (Ed.). (1949). *Improving human relations*. Washington, DC: National Council for the Social Studies.

Derman-Sparks, L. (1989). *Anti-bias curriculum: Tools for empowering young children*. Washington, DC: National Association for the Education of Young Children.

Donaldson, J., & Martinson, M. (1977). Modifying attitudes toward physically disabled persons. *Exceptional Children, 43*, 337–341.

Drew, N. (1987). *Learning the skills of peacemaking: An activity guide for elementary-age children on communicating, cooperating, and resolving conflict*. California: Jalmar Press.

Duvall, L. (1994). *Respecting our differences: A guide to getting along in a changing world*. Minneapolis, MN: Free Spirit.

Gibbs, J. (1987). *Tribes: A process for social development and cooperative learning*. Santa Rosa, CA: Center Source.

Girard, K., & Koch, S. (1996). *Conflict resolution in the schools: A manual for educators*. San Francisco: Jossey-Bass.

Goodman, M. E. (1952). *Race awareness in young children*. Cambridge, MA: Addison-Wesley.

Grambs, J. D. (1960). *Understanding intergroup relations*. Washington, DC: National Education Association.

Grambs, J. D. (1968). *Intergroup education: Methods and materials*. Upper Saddle River, NJ: Prentice-Hall.

Grant, C. A. (Ed.). (1995). *Educating for diversity: An anthology of multicultural voices*. Boston: Allyn & Bacon.

Grant, C. A., & Sleeter, C. E. (1996). *After the school bell rings*. London: Falmer Press.

Haberman, M., & Post, L. (1990). Cooperating teachers' perceptions of the goals of multicultural education. *Action in Teacher Education, 12*(3), 31–35.

Harris, D. B., Gough, H. B., & Martin, W. E. (1950). Children's ethnic attitudes: II, Relationship to parental beliefs concerning child training. *Child Development, 21*, 169–181.

Johnson, D. W. (1972). *Reaching out: Interpersonal effectiveness and self-actualization*. Upper Saddle River, NJ: Prentice-Hall.

Johnson, D. W., & Johnson, R. (1984). Classroom learning structure and attitudes toward handicapped students in mainstream settings: A theoretical model and research evidence. In R. L. Jones (Ed.), *Attitudes and attitude change in special education: Theory and practice* (pp. 118–142). Reston, VA: Council for Exceptional Children.

Johnson, D. W., & Johnson, R. (1987). Research shows the benefits of adult cooperation. *Educational Leadership, 45*(3), 27–30.

Johnson, D. W., Johnson, R. T., & Holubec, E. J. (1991). *Cooperation in the classroom*. Edina, MN: Interaction Book Co.

Johnson, D. W., Johnson, R., & Maruyama, G. (1983). Interdependence and interpersonal attraction among heterogeneous and homogeneous individuals: A theoretical formulation and meta-analysis of the research. *Review of Educational Research, 53*, 51–54.

Katz, P. (1982). Development of children's racial awareness and intergroup attitudes. In L. G. Katz (Ed.), *Current topics in early childhood education* (Vol. 4, pp. 17–54). Norwood, NJ: Ablex.

King, E. W. (1990). *Teaching ethnic and gender awareness*. Dubuque, IA: Kendall/Hunt.

King, J. E. (1991). Dysconscious racism: Ideology, identity, and the miseducation of teachers. *Journal of Negro Education, 60*(2), 133–146.

Kitano, M., Stiehl, J., & Cole, J. (1978). Role-taking: Implications for special education. *Journal of Special Education, 12*, 59–74.

Kohlberg, L. (1966). A cognitive-developmental analysis of children's sex-role concepts and attitudes. In E. E. Maccoby (Ed.), *The development of sex differences* (pp. 82–173). Stanford, CA: Stanford University Press.

Linn, E., Stein, N. D., Young, J., & Davis, S. (1992). Bitter lessons for all: Sexual harassment in schools. In J. T. Sears (Ed.), *Sexuality and the curriculum* (pp. 106–123). New York: Teachers College Press.

Madhere, S. (1991). Self-esteem of African American adolescents: Theoretical and practical considerations. *Journal of Negro Education, 60*(1), 47–61.

McCarthy, C. (1993). After the canon: Knowledge and ideological representation in the multicultural discourse on curriculum reform. In C. McCarthy & W. Crichlow (Eds.), *Race, identity, and representation in education* (pp. 289–305). New York: Routledge.

Oden, S., & Asher, S. R. (1977). Coaching children in social skills for friendship making. *Child Development, 48*, 495–506.

Pogrebin, L. C. (1981). *Growing up free*. New York: Bantam.

Prutzman, P., Stern, L., Burger, M. L., & Bodenhamer, G. (1988). *The friendly classroom for a small planet*. Santa Cruz, CA: New Society.

Purkey, W. W., & Novak, J. M., (1984). *Inviting school success* (2nd ed.). Belmont, CA: Wadsworth.

Sapon-Shevin, M., & Schniedewind, N. (1989/1990). Selling cooperative learning without selling it short. *Educational Leadership*, 63–65.

Sears, J. T. (1992). The impact of culture and ideology on the construction of gender and sexual identities: Developing a critically based sexuality curriculum. In J. T. Sears (Ed.), *Sexuality and the curriculum* (pp. 139–156). New York: Teachers College Press.

Sears, J. T. (1993). Responding to the sexual diversity of faculty and students: Sexual praxis and the critically reflective administrator. In C. Capper (Ed.), *Administration in a pluralistic society*. Albany: SUNY Press.

Sharan, S. (1980). Cooperative learning in small groups: Recent methods and effects on achievements, attitudes, and ethnic relations. *Review of Educational Research, 50*, 241–271.

Sherif, M., & Sherif, C. W. (1966). *Groups in harmony and tension*. New York: Octagon.

Slavin, R. E. (1986). *Using student team learning*. Baltimore: The Johns Hopkins Team Learning Project.

Slavin, R. E., & Madden, N. A. (1979). School practices that improve race relations. *American Educational Research Journal, 16*, 169–180.

Sleeter, C. E. (1992). *Keepers of the American dream*. London: Falmer Press.

Sylvester, P. S. (1994). Elementary school curricula and urban transformation. *Harvard Educational Review, 64*(3), 309–331.

Taba, H., Brady, E. H., & Robinson, J. T. (1952). *Intergroup education in public schools*. Washington, DC: American Council on Education.

Tatum, B. D. (1997). *Why are all the black kids sitting together in the cafeteria?* New York: HarperCollins.

Tiedt, P. L. & Tiedt, I. M. (1995). *Multicultural teaching: A handbook of activities, information, and resources* (4th ed.). Boston: Allyn & Bacon.

Turnbull, A. P., & Schulz, J. B. (1979). *Mainstreaming handicapped students: A guide for the classroom teacher*. Boston: Allyn & Bacon.

Valentine, G. (1997). Get real! Teaching tolerance strategies that work. *NEA Today, 15*(5), 4–6. Washington, DC: National Education Association

Watts, W. A. (1984). Attitude change: Theories and methods. In R. L. Jones (Ed.), *Attitudes and attitude change in special education: Theory and practice* (pp. 41–69). Reston, VA: Council for Exceptional Children.

Weinberg, N. (1978). Examination of pre-school attitudes toward the physically handicapped. *Rehabilitation Counseling Bulletin, 22*, 183–188.

Wesley, C. H. (1949). Education and democracy. In H. H. Cummings (Ed.), *Improving human relations* (pp. 27–31). Washington, DC: National Council for the Social Studies.

CHAPTER FOUR

Single-Group Studies

Y ou probably have not heard the term *Single-Group Studies* before. You are correct in assuming that we made it up. It refers to an approach to multicultural education that is characterized by attention to a single group—for example, women, Asian Americans, African Americans, Hispanics, Native Americans, Appalachians, people with disabilities, gay people, or people of the working class. To refer to this approach as ethnic studies, women's studies, or African American studies would not correctly identify the various populations that can be addressed.

GOALS

Most advocates of the Single-Group Studies approach to multicultural education hope to reduce social stratification and raise the status of the group with which they are concerned. In Chapter 1, we described current differences among groups in the United States in terms of their power and access to various resources. The two previously discussed approaches to multicultural education—Teaching the Exceptional and Culturally Different, and Human Relations—do not directly confront the persistent inequalities that exist among groups. Advocates of Single-Group Studies each want their group to have greater power and control over economic and cultural resources. Table 4–1 shows as their main goal the promoting of social equality for and recognition of the group being studied. They hope to broaden what is included in American culture so that the group in which they are interested is an important part, no longer invisible or marginal. Essentially, the Single-Group Studies approach attempts to provide a basis for social action by providing information (in this case through schooling) about the group and the effects of past and present discrimination on the group. In the school, this approach is often implemented through a unit or a course of study, although it can constitute an entire educational program.

Goal statements vary, but the main idea of the Single-Group Studies approach is to empower oppressed groups. For example, Suzuki (1980) noted that ethnic studies should give students of color a sense of their history and identity in American society, increase their awareness and self-confidence, and provide a greater sense of direction and purpose in their lives. Programs should present a more accurate version of American history by including groups that have been left out, and they should meet economic, political and cultural demands by people of

TABLE 4–1.
Single-Group Studies

Societal goals:	Promote special structural equality for an immediate recognition of the identified group.
School goals:	Promote willingness and knowledge among students to work toward social change that would benefit the identified group.
Target students:	Everyone.
Practices:	
Curriculum	Teach units or courses about the culture of a group, how the group has been victimized, current social issues facing the group—from the perspective of that group.
Instruction	Build on students' learning style, especially the learning style of that group.
Other aspects of classroom	Use decorations reflecting culture and classroom contributions of the group; have representatives of the group involved in class activities (e.g., appearing as guest speakers).
Other schoolwide concerns	Employ faculty who are members of the group being studied.

color from both within and without local communities (Giles, 1974). They should support intellectual inquiries into the political, economic, and historical forces affecting the group, and they should help eliminate or reduce White racism (Nakanishi & Leong, 1978). Women's studies "rose as a critique to the traditional disciplines" (Rutenberg, 1983), with the goal "to change the sexist world" (Westkott, 1983). Gay and lesbian studies tried to "form an intellectual community for students and faculty that is ethnically diverse and committed to gender parity" ("A National Survey," 1990/91, p. 53). In discussing the goals of ethnic studies, Banks (1997) stresses that the curriculum "should help students develop the ability to make reflective decisions on issues related to ethnicity and to take personal, social, and civic actions to help solve the racial and ethnic problems in our national and world societies" (pp. 25–26). It may be said, then, that the ability to think through issues from a critical perspective and to act upon one's insights in an effort to transform unjust social conditions related to gender or race, for example, is central to the mission of any group-study program.

Single-Group Studies became popular, particularly on college campuses, during the civil rights struggle of the late 1960s. It is an intellectual approach to education, but it is also directly connected with political struggle. As Lauter (1991) put it,

> The movements for change after the postwar political and intellectual ice age reconstituted a vision of possibility and developed concrete efforts to achieve justice and peace. The meaning of these efforts has more to do with Montgomery and the bus boycott than with the demand a decade later for black studies programs. (p. 19)

Advocates of Single-Group Studies have usually instituted the approach to counterbalance the study of White, middle-class males, which the traditional curriculum emphasizes. A common argument for the study of diverse groups is that the United States is a pluralistic country—racially, ethnically, and culturally. The portrayal of a dominant national, cultural group that controls daily institutional and cultural processes is inconsistent with reality. Guerra (1973), for example, discussing the need for bilingual education, argues as follows:

> Monolingual and monocultural education in America has traditionally ignored the cultural pluralism of American society. We acknowledge ethnic and racial differences, religious variances, and a cultural heterogeneity of our cities, but the criteria of our value judgments, our value system, and our social consciousness remain predominantly White Anglo-Saxon Protestant—that is, representative of the monolingual, monocultural predominant society. The dichotomy between this cultural pluralism of America on the one hand, and the imposing conformity of the monolingual and monocultural predominant society on the other, is something that has never been reconciled. (pp. 27–28)

You may wonder at whom the Single-Group Studies programs should be aimed. For example, are African American studies for African Americans or for everyone? Are women's studies for women or for both sexes? We can find goals directed mainly toward the target group as well as goals directed toward students who are not necessarily members of that group. Both kinds of goals usually go into the establishment of a Single-Group Studies program, and this kind of basis, as we will see later, can create something of a problem.

Elementary, secondary, and university administrators (who are not necessarily true advocates of Single-Group Studies) often institute these programs to keep peace. In a review of Black studies programs in public schools, Giles (1974) comments that "black studies programs seem to have been implemented in response to demands from the local community and political pressures outside the community to which school administrators feel compelled to respond" (p. 11).

Since the late 1960s and early 1970s, scholars in Single-Group Studies programs at the university level have generated an enormous amount of research and theorizing. Not only has much information about diverse groups been compiled, but scholars have been mapping out new conceptual frameworks within various disciplines and challenging established ideas. Reflecting upon the way the work of feminist and ethnic-studies scholars has challenged the canon, Maher and Tetreault (1994) explain, "They have created new accounts, new theoretical frameworks, and new bodies of knowledge in every discipline, based on the lives of the marginalized" (p. 4). Educators who are new to multicultural education usually greatly underestimate the complexity and sophistication of this knowledge. To an important extent, the two approaches to multicultural education presented in Chapters 5 and 6—in addition to the approach discussed in this chapter—depend on this scholarship.

PHILOSOPHICAL FRAMEWORK

The Single-Group Studies approach has its roots in educational, philosophical orientations that argue that education is not a neutral process but is used by government and significant others (e.g., labor and business) for social and political purposes. Because of the social and political nature of education, Single-Group Studies advocates argue that study of their group should be included in schooling. This approach also has roots in the philosophical arguments that schooling should encourage individuals to become critical thinkers who are able to reflect on and guide their own behavior and that schooling should teach and encourage cultural analysis, evaluation, and a critical consciousness.

Whether one examines writings about African-American studies, women's studies, or Asian-American studies, for example, one will find similar philosophical tenets considering issues such as the nature of knowledge, the nature of society, and the purposes of schooling. We invite you to consider the issues raised by Single-Group Studies advocates.

Myth of the Neutrality of Education

Is knowledge neutral? Are the processes by which it is taught neutral? Although most of us can point to particular biases held by particular teachers, when the entire experience of education is considered in its totality, is it ideologically neutral?

Many see education as essentially a neutral process. In other words, many see education as not promoting a particular ideology or point of view. For example, we asked an undergraduate class of 36 beginning education students if education (schooling) was neutral, or if their schooling—kindergarten through high school—had a particular message. About half of these college juniors said that education was neutral and that their schooling did not argue a particular point of view or present one group's point of view over another. Several students who took this position pointed out that they could remember their teachers making a point of being neutral, but many others were quick to argue that their peers were naive. These students offered examples of how education serves as a socialization process to help the young buy into and fit into a particular conception of the American way of life. For example, some pointed out that until very recently women were for the most part omitted from textbooks, causing the young to accept male domination of society.

By the time the 2-hour discussion was over, the majority of the class had concluded that schooling was not neutral. Schooling, they argued, must be regarded as a social process: It is related to the country's political structure (often its present political scene), to its political and social history, and to its beliefs and ideals. Indeed, what counts as knowledge in schools is the result of complex struggles and cultural politics between identifiable groups and is shaped by the distribution of power within society (Apple, 1993, 1996).

However, the two approaches to multicultural education previously discussed—the Human Relations approach and the Teaching the Exceptional and the Culturally Different approach—view schooling as politically neutral. The Human Relations approach concerns itself with what schools teach only insofar as the schools help alleviate stereotyping by providing more information about groups that people frequently stereotype and more positive portrayals of groups to which all students belong. The Teaching the Culturally Different approach advocates modifying what schools teach only as needed to make the curriculum more relevant to students who might have trouble catching on. However, both approaches see most of the content and processes of schools as essentially fair and desirable and as politically neutral—not biased in favor of any particular group.

A central issue undergirding Single-Group Studies is the attempt to explain why a particular group has disproportionately less than its share of resources. For example, why do full-time working women earn about 71 cents for every dollar men earn? Why are most people with disabilities either unemployed or employed only part time? Why does the poverty level of African Americans and Latinos remain far higher than it is for Whites, in spite of the narrowing of an education gap between groups? Single-Group Studies offer a different way to approach this issue than the dominant school curriculum or the dominant perspective.

For example, artist Linda Nochlin (1971) has often been asked to explain why there are so few great women artists; she uses responses to this question to illustrate naive, then more sophisticated, attempts to answer. One reaction to this question is to refute the claim that there are few great women artists and to dig up as many as possible. An art curriculum, then, would have "famous women artists" uncritically added into it. In this response, one is asserting that there have always been plenty of women artists; we simply have not studied them. Nevertheless, the artists people recognize as "famous" are mostly men, and this phenomenon needs to be examined and questioned. So, another reaction one might have is to critique the prevailing standards for success as male rather than female, assuming that women have always created art (which is true) and that the problem is not the exclusion of women but the definition of art. However, as one probes the issue, one cannot escape the fact that numerically, men really have outnumbered women in producing art. Although both reactions do help address the question, the main problem is that art itself occurs in a social situation, is an integral element of the social structure, and is mediated and determined by specific and definable social institutions, be they art academies, systems of patronage, mythologies of the divine creator and artists as he-man or social outcast … By stressing the *institutional*—that is, the public—rather than the *individual* or private preconditions for achievement in the arts, we have provided a model for the investigation of other areas in the field. (Lauter, 1991, p. 167)

This discussion illustrates a framework for thinking that is depicted in Figure 4–1, which shows two quite different frameworks for understanding why inequality exists. The figure focuses on two elements: the nature of society and the nature of nondominant groups. Down the left column of the figure are listed those perspectives that the dominant groups in society usually accept. With respect to the nature of society, most of us have been taught repeatedly that the United States offers a fair and open system to all, and that everyone can achieve "the American dream" if one works hard enough. Further, those of us who are White, male, heterosexual, and economically secure generally experience a direct relationship between our efforts and our success. The system must be open for everyone because not only is that what we have learned, but we see that the system has also worked fairly for us. Then why have some groups disproportionately not succeeded? Most of us explain this result in terms of the characteristics of such groups, focusing

	Dominant groups	Oppressed groups
Nature of society	Fair, open	Unfair, rigged
Nature of "have-not" groups	Lack ambition, effort, culture, language, skills education	Strong, resourceful, work to advance

FIGURE 4–1.
Perspectives about Inequality

mainly on what they lack: education, culture, ambition, language, modern values, and so forth.

The perspectives that oppressed groups advance are listed down the right column of Figure 4–1. Society as it currently and historically has existed is not open and fair to all groups, in spite of what the dominant rhetoric says. Rather, dominant groups erect barriers to the advancement of people who are identifiably unlike themselves. Oppressed groups do not lack culture or capability; rather they have rich legacies of intellectual and artistic creativity that attest to their potential to achieve success, if society were open. This perspective is one that schools generally do not teach.

Thus, Single-Group Studies advocates argue that education is not neutral. Newton (1939) tells us that any form of neutrality, paradoxical though it may seem, becomes a form of positive social action. To allow for and encourage diverse viewpoints is to encourage the value of diversity and open debate. Schooling in the United States has an explicit purpose: to promote democracy or "the American way." In discussing schooling and democracy, Newton states:

> If democracy is to be conserved and fully realized, the American people must understand the meaning of democracy, both in its historical development and in its social bearings and implications for the world of today. ... *The first responsibility of organized education is, then, to enable children, youth, and adults to acquire this understanding of democracy and its problems. Every part of the educational system and every area of education is involved, the university no less than the high school, the arts and the sciences as well as the social studies.* (p. 94, emphasis ours)

However, for many groups in society democracy has been more an ideal to strive toward rather than a reality. The teaching of a particular point of view in our schools can be traced back through U.S. history. For example, Ellwood Patterson Cubberley (1909), a recognized educational leader in the early 1900s, stated:

> Everywhere these people [immigrants] tend to settle in groups or settlements, and to set up here their national manners, customs, and observances. Our task is to break up these groups or settlements, to assimilate and amalgamate these people as part of our American race, and to implant in their children, as far as can be done, the Anglo Saxon conception of righteousness, law and order, and popular government, and to awaken in them a reverence for our democratic institutions and for

those things in our national life which we as a people hold to be of abiding worth. (pp. 15–16)

Tyack (1966) points out that to some degree Thomas Jefferson, Noah Webster, and Benjamin Rush all saw as the function of public school the teaching of a balance between order and liberty. Tyack writes:

> Not content with unconscious and haphazard socialization provided by family, political meeting, press, and informal associations, not trusting in the "giveness" of political beliefs and institutions, these men sought to instruct Americans deliberately in schools. Having fought a war to free the United States from one centralized authority, they attempted to create a new unity, a common citizenship and culture, and an appeal to a common future. In this quest for a balance between order and liberty, for the proper transaction between the individual and society, Jefferson, Rush, and Webster encountered a conflict still inherent in the education of the citizen and expressed still in the injunction to teachers to train students to think critically but to be patriotic above all. (p. 31)

In other words, schools paradoxically teach Americans to believe in democratic participation, but also in allegiance to a culture and social structure defined primarily by Anglo-Saxon men of at least moderate wealth. Spring (1997) has discussed in great detail the manner in which schools have historically functioned to suppress cultural diversity, often marginalizing, disrespecting, rendering invisible, or aiming to "civilize" particular groups of students (e.g. Irish, Native Americans, Puerto Ricans)—frequently through assimilationist practices. This teaching is the concern of advocates of Single-Group Studies: Whereas democracy should be fostered in schools, democracy is a sham if it incorporates only the concerns and perspectives of those who already dominate politically and economically. For true democracy, the points of view of oppressed people must also be given full expression, and the concerns they have and experience must be addressed.

The curriculum is a central concern of Single-Group Studies advocates, because "knowledge is power. Those who have it are more powerful than those who do not. Those who define what counts as knowledge are the most powerful" (Pagano, 1990, p. xvi). Further, "reading is a vital way to gain power in a literate society. That is why marginalized groups have always had to struggle … to obtain access to the power of literacy—or, having obtained it, to get a hearing for their literary productions" (Lauter, 1991, p. 161).

In the 1960s, textbooks clearly presented the experiences and viewpoints of White, middle-class people only—mainly men. However, textbooks today appear to be more pluralistic; if you thumb through almost any textbook published over the past 10 years, it may look well integrated. Where is this bias that advocates of Single-Group Studies see in the curriculum?

In Chapter 1 we summarized the results of an examination we did of 47 textbooks used in Grades 1 through 8 in reading, science, mathematics, and social studies, all published since 1980 (Sleeter & Grant, 1991). The instrument we used, which we developed, involves tallying the representations of diverse groups in pictures and text references, describing the roles in which members of groups are depicted, examining characterization in readers, and examining the story line or

The United States is the land of wealth and opportunity; it is open to all who try; anyone can get what he works for.

American history flowed from Europe to the east coast of North America; from there it flowed westward.

American culture is of European origin; Europe is the main source of worthwhile cultural achievements.

National ideals are (and should be) individual advancement, private accumulation, rule by the majority as well as by market demand, loyalty to the U.S. government, and freedom of speech.

Some social problems existed in the past, but they have been solved.

Most problems society faces have technical solutions, for which science and math offer the best keys.

Americans share consensus about most things; differences are individual and can be talked out (usually in one story).

Other places in the world may have poverty and problems, but the United States does not; we tend to solve other nations' problems.

America is basically White, middle-class, and heterosexual; wealthy White men are the world's best thinkers and problem solvers, and they usually act in the best interests of everyone.

FIGURE 4–2.
Themes in a Eurocentric, Patriarchal Curriculum

focus of attention in history books and novels. After collecting data, we compiled it group by group in order to gain a sense of how individual groups are actually depicted. Our conclusions were summarized earlier, but in essence we found that groups other than White men have been added into the curriculum, but only in a fragmented fashion. One would learn quite little, for example, about Mexican Americans or Puerto Ricans by reading most textbooks; one may see representatives of these groups in pictures and mentioned occasionally in the text, but one would encounter very little substantive information. If one counts representation, in most texts White males still receive much more attention than any other group.

Curricula are not merely a collection of facts; they tell a story, present a picture. Some taken-for-granted themes undergird the content of most curricula. We have summarized these themes in Figure 4–2. They are rarely stated directly; rather they emerge from what is and what is not in textbooks and are reaffirmed in the life experience of students (and teachers) who are White, middle- or upper-class, and male. For example, few textbooks state that most of society's problems have been solved, but few examine current social problems, even though they may allude to problems such as slavery or the Great Depression that existed in the past. Textbooks never directly state that wealthy White men are the world's greatest problem solvers; the books simply present more members of this group than any other.

Garcia (1982) pointed out that every ethnic group has a unique history set within a definable geographic region and should therefore be studied in an ongoing, in-depth fashion rather than piecemeal, with bits and pieces of its history tacked onto Anglo studies. Note the following statement about the treatment of African Americans, given to undergraduates at the University of Wisconsin–Madison in the *Afro-American Studies Department Curriculum* (1970):

> Although the Afro-American community has had a unique historical experience, has evolved a distinct culture, and faces a special set of problems in American society, scholars have tended either to greatly distort or to completely dismiss the African American experience as an unpleasant footnote to the larger American experience. (p. 31)

As another example, consider Pagano's description of how women appear in art and literature curricula:

> One easily spends four years in college classrooms meeting mostly harlots, courtesans, fishwives, and bourgeois consumers who in the act of consumption consume themselves along with their husbands, children, and best friends. (1990, p. 110)

Even the teacher who refuses to take a position when presenting an issue makes numerous decisions throughout the school day about what and how to teach—decisions that could suggest a particular point of view. For example, a teacher who decides to teach the American novel could be teaching points of view that have race, gender, and class implications. If the teacher decides to use *The Adventures of Huckleberry Finn* (Mark Twain), *The Catcher in the Rye* (J. D. Salinger), *Deliverance* (James Dickey), and *The Grapes of Wrath* (John Steinbeck), then this teacher is also deciding to omit (at least so far) *Manchild in the Promised Land* (Claude Brown), *Woman Warrior* (Maxine Hong Kingston), *Forever* (Judy Blume), and *The Color Purple* (Alice Walker). The points of view given to the students in the two sets of novels are very different, because the second set includes novels by three women and three persons of color. If used over an extended period of time, neither set of materials is politically neutral. The question is, what political implications are there in any given set of decisions that teachers make about what to teach, whether those decisions are conscious or unconscious?

How a teacher teaches is also important and could suggest or influence a point of view. For example, if a teacher of an American authors class, in which only one or two African American students are enrolled, chooses to begin the semester with *Native Son* (Richard Wright) instead of *The Autobiography of Malcolm X* (Malcolm X, with Alex Haley), the African American students may be caused to feel powerless and vulnerable because the major character is powerless—a murderer and a servant. On the other hand, *The Autobiography of Malcolm X* usually inspires African American students, promoting a sense of pride and respect. How the curriculum is presented—particularly the order, timing, and presentation of examples—can have political implications and imply a position the teacher has taken, although it may be taken unconsciously.

Social Purpose of Schooling

Schools are society's agencies (or institutions) of socialization. Years ago Newton (1939) correctly characterized education, when he argued:

> Education is a form of socialization. The purpose of education is to modify behavior, to make the individual a different person from what he would otherwise be. It is for this reason that educational policy is always social policy and that, in the modern world, the school is employed, deliberately, for the achievement of definite social purposes, becomes, in fact, a crucial element in national policy. (p. 203)

Schools have a daily impact on students and serve to prepare them for the roles they will have as adults. Besides being used to teach about democracy, schooling is used as a form of social control by influencing attitudes and modifying behavior. For example, historically, schools were charged with teaching self-discipline and the literary skills required for reading the Bible. Throughout the 20th century schools have increasingly prepared a mass citizenry for an industrial labor market. Spring (1973), describing the school as an instrument of social control during the 20th century, observes:

> By the beginning of the twentieth century, industrialization and urbanization had severely eroded the influence of family, church, and community on individual behavior. As the power of these institutions waned, the school became increasingly important as a primary instrument for social control. It became the agency charged with the responsibility of maintaining social order and cohesion and of instilling individuals with codes of conduct and social values that would insure the stability of existing social relationships. Although a preserving institution, the school was viewed as a form of internal control—and therefore more in the "democratic" tradition than such external forms as law, government, and police. (p. 30)

Advocates of Single-Group Studies would explicitly describe the "codes of conduct" and "social values" that Spring (1973) discusses as having been prescribed mainly by White, middle-class males. For example, proper conduct for middle-class women included deferring to men, serving men, and running an orderly home; schooling reinforced this way of life. Children of color were taught to value and respect the culture and language of Whites and to devalue that of their families.

The school carries out its control through a process referred to as socialization. Socialization is a lifelong process, basic to human activity and occurring in the classroom as well as in the family and religious institutions. Schools contribute to the process of socialization by helping the student to fit into an established cultural or social tradition and by aiding in the student's development of personality or individual identity. Through participation in various social experiences in the school, the student becomes familiar with or learns knowledge, attitudes, behavior, and values. Schools are considered by many as society's instrument for inculcating the "right" values and social attitudes into the young. For example, some educators claim that in school, habits such as obedience, industriousness, neatness, and punctuality are taught as important social values that will help students grow to adulthood and become useful and productive members of society.

As already noted, the social control that schools orchestrate in this democratic society is not neutral or unbiased. According to Bowles and Gintis (1976), it is biased along race, social class, and gender lines:

> Schools foster legitimate inequality through the ostensibly meritocratic manner by which they reward and promote students, and allocate them to distinct positions in the occupational hierarchy. They create and reinforce patterns of social class, racial and sexual identification among students which allow them to relate "properly" to their eventual standing in the hierarchy of authority and status in the production process. Schools foster types of personal development compatible with the relationships of dominance and subordinance in the economic sphere. (p. 11)

For example, lower-class students tend to be sorted into lower-ability and remedial classes, whereas upper-class students tend to be sorted into college-bound classes. On the surface, this process appears fair because it uses objective testing and professional guidance. Once sorted, students learn to view their own status as acceptable and learn to relate to each other in a leader-follower fashion. The status quo is reproduced but in a manner that appears natural.

What does this mean specifically for children who are members of different social groups in society? Research on racial identity development helps us understand how schools shape student self-concept and maintain social control (Banks, 1981; Cross, 1991; Helms, 1990; Tatum, 1992). This research describes stages of identity development that differ between Whites and groups of color. We will apply these stages to other forms of diversity as well, distinguishing between how dominant group members (i.e., Whites, males, middle- and upper-income people, heterosexual people, people without disabilities) view their identity with a collective and how oppressed group members view their identity. Figure 4–3 summarizes the stages.

Students (and teachers) who are members of dominant groups are usually in the stage of Encapsulation. They have been taught that people like themselves have run this country since its earliest history and have contributed its greatest achievements. This message is one of arrogance, teaching those in control that they have rightfully earned that control and have little need to understand oppression or the experiences of the oppressed. In fact, the idea of "oppression" is foreign to them; they regard the United States as free and open to all. This stage is reinforced by "business as usual" schooling.

Advocates of Single-Group Studies wish to help students move to a higher stage. The next stage, Disintegration, occurs when students encounter evidence of discrimination, which Single-Group Studies attempt to provide. Typically, students who are members of dominant groups find such information very uncomfortable and often try to escape having to deal with it. Our students have commented, for example, that class sessions revealing powerful information about discrimination "turned their world upside-down." The easiest way for students to deal with their discomfort is to return to the first stage when the course or unit is over (which one can do fairly easily if the course or unit is short). If the student sticks with the study of another group, eventually she or he may achieve the stage of Autonomy.

Dominant Group Members

A. *Encapsulation:* Comfortable with status quo; have never really thought about other groups' experiences or perspectives; accept society's stereotypes of groups

B. *Disintegration:* Faced with evidence of discrimination that clashes with previous perspective—feel guilt, anger

C. *Reintegration:* One way of resolving discomfort of Disintegration stage; return as nearly as possible to first stage (Encapsulation)

D. *Pseudo-independence:* Other way of resolving discomfort of Disintegration stage; actively seek information about other group by contacting or hanging around its members; identify more with other group than with own

E. *Autonomy:* Work actively to end discrimination against oppressed group; have positive identity with own group but are not accepting of group's superior status

Oppressed Group Members

A. *Conformity:* Identify with dominant group and its version of society; accept negative images of own group

B. *Dissonance:* Faced with evidence of discrimination that clashes with previous perspective—feel confusion, want to know more

C. *Resistance and immersion:* Actively reject dominant society and its beliefs; thirst for knowledge about own group

D. *Internalization:* Have strong sense of positive identity with own group; willing to reconnect with dominant group but not with subordinate status

E. *Commitment:* Committed to long-term work on anti-discrimination strategies; have positive identity with own group and with members of dominant group who are in state of autonomy

FIGURE 4–3.
Stages of Identity Development

For an oppressed-group member, the lowest stage is Conformity, in which the individual accepts the status quo and negative images of her or his own group. Members of minority groups, females, the poor, gays, and people with disabilities are often socialized, in schools as well as in other social institutions, to occupy this stage. Taught that members of their group rarely make notable achievements, contributions, or political decisions, children of oppressed groups often see themselves and their group as powerless and worthless. This feeling may be aggravated when they are simultaneously taught that we live in a free democracy in which everyone can do as he or she chooses and people get what they work for. If an African American female child sees few African American women who seem to have contributed anything of social value, implicitly she is being taught that African American females—herself included—must not have much to contribute. This message is one of powerlessness and hopelessness. However, members of the dominant group are often most comfortable with oppressed-group members who are at this stage, because members of oppressed groups tend to be accepting. For example, White teachers tend to be most comfortable with minority group students who accept the teachers' authority and a White-dominant curriculum; the teachers often become uncomfortable with students who assert their racial identity.

The stage of Dissonance is usually triggered by something, either a personal experience (such as being obviously discriminated against on the basis of sex) or new information that contradicts what one has learned (such as new information about the accomplishments of people with physical impairments). This experience or information often leads the person to want to know more, a need that Single-Group Studies fill. At the stage of Resistance and Immersion, an individual tries to learn as much as possible about his or her group; at this stage, anger emanating from years of experiencing oppression is often expressed. Members of the dominant group, especially those who are themselves at the stage of Encapsulation, are often threatened by a person at the Resistance and Immersion stage. For example, a young woman experiencing Resistance and Immersion becomes angry about sexism and angry with the behavior of men around her that she views now as sexist. Her male friends (as well as female friends at the Conformity stage) may respond that she is "too much into that women's lib garbage" and shun her or make fun of her. If both the woman and her friends are experiencing women's studies together, they are at least being exposed to the same information and can battle out their differences together, helping each other to grow. Too often, however, the young woman (or minority-group member, etc.) is the only one in Single-Group Studies (if it is elective), resulting in a large gap in the awareness level between her and her friends. Eventually the anger of Resistance and Immersion can turn into a long-term commitment to work for change and an ability to recognize and trust members of the dominant group who themselves have achieved Pseudo-Independence or Autonomy.

Advocates of Single-Group Studies take a critical view of the nature of society but an optimistic view of human nature. Is human nature essentially active or passive? Do children by nature want to learn, or do they need to be coaxed? Is learning essentially a process of meaning-making or a process of imprinting a body of information on blank minds? The Single-Group Studies approach sees the student as willing and eager to learn, capable of making decisions, and committed to reflection about his or her learning. Education is consistent with Newton's (1939) observations:

> Education must aim, first of all, at the building of minds that are sensitive to the social realities of the world in which they live, that are free, that have acquired the capacity for thinking for themselves, because they have had opportunity to think for themselves. (p. 213)

From the perspective of Single-Group Studies, thus, schools should develop in students what Freire (1970) calls a "critical consciousness." When students learn about their heritage and contributions to society, they participate in a process of self-discovery and growth in social consciousness. This development results in the realization that, contrary to the myth of their inferiority, their actions can be a transforming process in the United States and in the world. In other words, as the students learn about their group, they grow in pride and knowledge about themselves; and as others learn about their group, they, too, will change in relationship to their new knowledge. Dominant groups will learn that their dominance has usually been seized rather than earned and that their use of power more often than not has been biased and unfair. The preamble of the Constitution of the National Women's Studies Association (Graber, 1997) directly addresses the point of consciousness-raising when it states: "Women's studies is the educational strategy of a breakthrough in consciousness and knowledge" (p. 6).

Examples of students who have had to be coaxed into learning probably spring readily to your mind. Yet students need to be coaxed only to learn material that has no personal meaning. Schooling for many young people is alienating when it is not about themselves; it is highly motivating when it is.

In summary, the Single-Group Studies approach is aimed toward social change. It attacks primarily the knowledge normally taught in schools, arguing that that knowledge reinforces control by wealthy White men over everyone else. "Business as usual" attempts to socialize the young into accepting the status quo as "right," at the same time alienating from social institutions children of color, children of the poor, and female children. Schooling needs to offer an in-depth study of all major social groups for the purpose of empowering group members, developing in them a sense of pride and group consciousness, and helping members of dominant groups appreciate the experiences of others and recognize how their own groups have oppressed others.

RESTRUCTURING KNOWLEDGE AND "THE CANON"

Since the late 1980s we have witnessed a heated debate in higher education over "the canon." Lauter (1991) provides a definition:

> By "canon" I mean the set of literary works, the grouping of significant philosophical, political, and religious texts, the particular accounts of history generally accorded cultural weight within a society. How one defines a cultural canon obviously shapes collegiate curricula and research priorities, but it also helps to determine precisely whose experiences and ideas become central to academic study. (p. ix)

Earlier we noted that Single-Group Studies had begun to be instituted in higher education during the 1960s: Black studies programs were quickly followed by women's studies, Chicano studies, and Asian studies; then disability studies and gay and lesbian studies programs were created, and a Center of Appalachian Studies was established at Appalachian State University in North Carolina. At first, such programs had a wide array of focuses, allowing faculty and students mainly to examine the history and literature of a particular group. Speaking of early Chicano studies programs, for example, Muñoz (1984) explains, "Ideologically, the spectrum ran from those who defined Chicano Studies as curricula that would emphasize the contributions of Americans of Mexican descent to American culture and society to those who defined it as curricula that would focus attention on racism and the structure of class oppression" (p. 9). Like Nochlin's (1971) first answer to the question of why there are so few great women artists, early programs tended to reply that there are plenty of people and events of a particular group whose contributions we can study.

Over time, scholars focused increasingly on questions regarding the nature of the persistent oppression of the group and why the mainstream curriculum (and society) so staunchly resists full incorporation of the group. For example, African American women have a long and rich literary tradition, from Frances E. W. Harper through Toni Morrison. Yet, mainstream literature courses usually add only selective pieces (if any), treated not as examples of great literature, but as examples of an add-on category of "minority literature," to be studied only after the "important" literature. Such biased and peripheral treatment sheds light on why, for example, the recent publication of *The Norton Anthology of African American Literature* (Gates & McKay, 1997) represents such an important and powerful challenge to the status of traditional bodies of knowledge.

As scholars synthesized the main ideas emerging in the study of their group and battled growing resistance on the part of the wider education system to incorporate their work, the debates came to be known as the battle over the canon: What and whose criteria define what knowledge is worth teaching? The most heated debates took place around Afrocentrism, which many African American scholars juxtaposed to the Eurocentric curriculum.

It is important for teachers to have a sense of the main themes that undergird Single-Group Studies today, because these themes should guide the creation of a curriculum about a group. We will briefly outline major common themes, although one must recognize they play out differently for different groups. It is important to remember that these are intellectual themes about how knowledge is constructed. Earlier, in Figure 4–2, we outlined themes that permeate traditional, White, male-dominant curricula; Single-Group Studies attempt to redefine the canon and disciplinary scholarship by organizing knowledge around different themes that emerge when a group other than White men is the center of attention. Figures 4–4 and 4–5 list the themes that undergird the study of two groups: respectively, Latinas and Latinos, and women.

Centering: Significance of the Starting Place

In one of our classes, a discussion with a history student illustrated the importance of the starting point in shaping an entire story. This student was attempting to explain why Mexican Americans are not in the curriculum prior to the Mexican War; one might study what happened in Mexico before the United States colonized half of it, but what one learns is not U.S. history. He went on to explain that U.S. history concerns what happened within the political borders of the United States and, prior to its founding, the European events that shaped it. The professor tried to explain that from a Mexican American (and Indian) perspective, the history worth studying goes back to the ancient Mayas and Aztecs, and the U.S. colonization is a relatively recent event in a long history. In this case, the student's starting point was the founding of the political system of the United States; the professor's starting point was the establishment of civilization in a land now known as Mexico, dating back to ancient times. According to the latter view, just as U.S. history tells us about the life in England that led to the Pilgrims setting sail, and the potato

Ancient Central and South American civilizations (especially Mayan, Aztec, and Incan) were highly developed.

Blending the cultures of indigenous Americans, Africans, and Europeans was often a violent process, but it yielded vibrant cultures.

U.S. conquest of Northern Mexico and Puerto Rico; how the process of colonization worked.

The Catholic Church: An institution of colonialism or liberation?

Latino/Latina labor in the U.S.: Resisting institutionalized impoverization by American agribusiness.

Language, literature, and philosophy; how the Spanish language encodes meaning, identity, and world view.

La familia y el barrio: Social organization; personal identity as inseparable from group membership.

Puerto Rico: Statehood or independence?

Immigration in the 1980s and 1990s from Central and South America; how U.S. immigration policies silence Latinos/Latinas.

Current political and cultural issues of Latinos/Latinas.

FIGURE 4–4.
Themes Central to Latina/Latino Studies

famine and political unrest that led to massive Irish immigration, U.S. history should also tell about Mexican American historical events.

Afrocentrism has redefined the starting point of African American history from the time of slavery in the United States to the time when early civilizations lived in ancient Africa, consciously articulating the importance of starting place. Asante (1990), one of the founders of Afrocentrism, explains, "All knowledge results from an occasion of encounter in place. But the place remains a rightly shaped perspective that allows the Afrocentrist to put African ideals and values at the center of inquiry" (p. 5). Figure 4–6 outlines topics one could study in an Afrocentric history course, beginning with Africa in ancient times. Afrocentrists have become involved in a tug of war with EuroAmericans over ancient Egypt: Is it best understood as basically European or African? The answer is important, because Egypt has historically been regarded as highly sophisticated in many areas, including philosophy and mathematics. In addition, Bernal (1981) amassed considerable evidence to argue that European civilization has strong Egyptian and Semitic roots, with ancient Greece having been colonized by Egypt and Phoenicia prior to the Golden Age. Thus, not only has Afrocentric scholarship reconceptualized the starting place of African-American history, it also questions the starting place of European and EuroAmerican history.

For racial and ethnic groups who have roots in a particular place in the world, defining the starting place shapes the rest of the story. A group's story may

Gender differences and gender inequality: What is actually fair and what isn't?

How biology is used as a control mechanism; to what extent are the sexes innately different, and to what extent does biology determine destiny? Physically, what are women capable of?

The private sphere (the home—dominated by women) versus the public sphere (dominated by men): How does the private sphere limit women's access to the public sphere, and why is the private sphere regarded as "out of bounds" for critique?

Impoverization of women; physical and psychological violence against women; processes used to exclude and devalue women from economic and political activity in the public sphere.

Gender as a cultural construct; how each sex, and how sex itself, is represented in the media, arts, etc.

Creative capacities of women and expressions of women's voices in the arts and domestic arts.

Work women do in producing and educating the next generation.

Women as racially, ethnically, and culturally diverse.

Women as social activists.

FIGURE 4–5.
Themes Central to Women's Studies

begin in Asia and move east, or South or Central America and move north, or Europe and move west, or right here on the North American continent thousands of years ago. Further, the story is different if one views the group as having started from a position of strength (for example, African civilizations), then having been subjugated, and now attempting to rebuild its original strength, rather than starting in a position of weakness (such as slavery) and now attempting to rise.

Social Creation of "Natural" Categories
Most of us take for granted distinctions among categories of people that we have learned to view as natural. For example, there are two mutually exclusive, biologically defined sexes. Racial groups are biologically defined and fixed; everyone knows, for example, how to distinguish White from Black people. People with disabilities are also biologically defined, having a deficiency of some sort. One is either a citizen of the United States, or not a citizen.

The "obvious" and assumed fixed nature of such categories has tended to work against oppressed groups, who are now examining how such categories are socially created and reinforced. For example, European and EuroAmerican people created the Negro, enslaving people of varying physical characteristics and from a variety of tribes in Africa, specifically because their dark skin color would brand them recognizable to anyone as slaves. Before slavery, tribal Africans did not think of themselves as African or Negro; the concept of race evolved later, in interaction with Caucasians. Despite what people today often say, no one is color blind; we

> ### *People of African Descent: Creators, Thinkers, and Builders*
>
> Ancient Egypt, the cradle of civilization
> Other precolonial African kingdoms
> Colonization and enslavement
> Building the church: the emergence of African American institutions
> Resisting the yoke of slavery
> Reconstruction
> The Harlem Renaissance
> The Civil Rights movement
> Black nationalism in Africa, the Caribbean, and South America
> Creators, thinkers, and builders today

FIGURE 4–6.
History Topics from an Afrocentric Perspective

still pay attention to color. How, then, do people use color to construct different categories of people?

Further, do people of African descent around the world have something in common that transcends their current country of citizenship? Pan-African studies answers in the affirmative. Latino studies does also; many Latinos regard U.S. boundaries as somewhat arbitrary. The term *la raza de Aztlan*, for example, describes the "race" of Mexican people. The U.S. border cuts Aztlan in half; the border was imposed on people indigenous to Mexico. More and more, the "diaspora" of people who have cultural and ethnic ties but have been scattered across modern countries (such as Jewish people, people of African descent, or people of Middle Eastern descent) are being studied based on the importance of their "peoplehood" that transcends their current nation of citizenship (Heller, 1992).

Gender is a concern of women's studies as well as gay and lesbian studies. To what degree does biology determine sex roles? To examine this question, women's studies focuses on the biology and psychology of gender. To what degree do two distinct sexes actually exist? Gay and lesbian scholars argue that male control of society is supported by the reinforcement of a clear distinction between the sexes; people who do not conform to traditional gender identities threaten "ideological beliefs and cultural values [that] prop up existing relations of power and control within society" (Sears, 1992, p. 145).

Social Construct of All Social Theories
A social theory is derived from the theorist's starting place. Even something as "factual" and neutral as a documentary reflects the values and perspectives of the creator: the film-maker chooses what to film, at what angle and depth, for what audience (Trinh, 1991). This theme is important, and it is one that provides a basis for critique and re-theorizing. For example, in his analysis of the AfroAsiatic roots of Greek culture, Bernal (1981) contrasts two theories: the Ancient theory (commonly believed until the 18th century), which traces Greek cultural roots to Egypt, and

the Aryan theory (constructed in Europe in the 18th century), which holds that Greece emerged from no significant roots. Bernal argues that the Aryan theory was advanced when Europeans were colonizing people of color around the world; it would not do to colonize and enslave people who had contributed significantly to Western culture, so non-Western cultural roots were "disproved" by limiting evidence to that which was archeologically verifiable and excluding evidence from linguistic analysis, mythology and legend, and analysis of literary texts.

Special education and the helping professions base their theories about people with disabilities on a medical framework. Questioning the medical model, Woodward and Elliott (1992) argue that the mainstreaming movement set people with disabilities back because it was predicated on the notion that "people with disabilities need Experts to tell them how to live" (p. 15): to define who can be mainstreamed and who cannot and to define the "needs" of children with disabilities.

Consider also the observation by Spender (1981) as she addresses male dominance in theoretical frameworks for educational research:

> From a feminist perspective one of the dominant theoretical frameworks of education is that of male dominance, but it is a framework which goes unquestioned and which has not been made the substance of educational enquiry. Unless and until education begins to examine male dominance as a fundamental issue in the entire educational process, the impact of feminism will be minimal. (p. 157)

By critiquing theories that rationalize the way things are, Single-Group Studies uncover vested interests that inform prevailing theories and propose alternative theories that suggest social change.

The Strength of Oppressed Groups

Mainstream curricula portray oppressed groups as passive and usually as victims: slaves, Indians who were killed off, people with disabilities who need help, Asians who were discriminated against, women who stayed at home. Contrast, for example, the way African Americans are portrayed in most history texts with the portrayal in Figure 4–6, where they are described as creators, thinkers, and builders.

Most traditional textbooks place Native Americans in history and in museums. However, Allen (1986) points out that one of the strongest themes that emerges in American Indian studies is that the American Indian people endure. After 500 years of systematic policies of genocide (by disease, murder, forced sterilization, severe impoverization), the American Indian people are still here and still creating. Women, when they have access to athletic opportunities, are now breaking Olympic records that men set years ago (Linn & Hyde, 1989). If one can convince an oppressed group that its members are weak and passive, they are more likely to accept their fate. The theme of activity and endurance is important to mobilize group members to act against their oppression.

Group Identity in Literature and the Arts

The dominant society constantly creates images of oppressed groups through various media: movies, TV, scholarly articles, stories and proverbs, literature, and art.

These identities usually rationalize the group's position in society. For example, Mazumdar (1989) lists identities the dominant society has constructed of Asian American women: "the depraved prostitute in nineteenth-century San Francisco; the quiet, courteous and efficient Asian female office worker today. Asian women in America have emerged not as individuals but as nameless and faceless members of an alien community" (p. 1). Churchill (1992) describes the dominant society's construction of Native American identities as *Fantasies of the Master Race*. The dominant society has defined the working class as "middle class," with interests aligned to capital and private gain. The poor have been given negative identities—criminals, welfare queens, the homeless—that validate the status quo and blame the lower class for their condition (Aronowitz, 1992).

Authentic identities of groups—how group members actually see and define themselves—are a major theme of the literature and artistic products created by group members. For example, consider the difference between the identities of women in most popular movies versus those in the film *Thelma and Louise*. Most movies construct women as the love interests, seductresses, office workers, mothers, and wives; even if women hold other roles, such as lawyer, their sexuality and relationships with men usually predominate. In contrast, the characters Thelma and Louise, whose identities were constructed by women, actively rejected sexual control. Boneparth (1978) argues that "the justification for women's studies is based upon the need to provide meaningful educational experiences for female students to search out their own identities. Knowledge for women is as important as knowledge of women" (p. 22).

People without disabilities tend to regard people with disabilities in one of two ways: as deficient people who need help or, as euphemisms such as "differently abled" suggest, as people who are just like nondisabled people with the exception of doing some things differently. In contrast, articles in *The Disability Rag*, which is created by people with disabilities, regularly discuss identity in ways that both acknowledge and deal with the limitations associated with disabilities as well as project an image of people with disabilities as complex human beings. When one reads or views literary and artistic creations by a group, one encounters a rich array of diverse identities that are usually quite different from those the dominant society projects. The video productions of Sadie Benning, a young woman struggling with her lesbian identity in a homophobic culture, and the photographs taken by homeless children participating in Shooting Back, an expanding artistic and social project which began in 1990, are just two more examples of the potential of the arts to bring to the foreground knowledge and experience generally excluded as legitimate (for more detail, see Paley, 1995). Again, such examples call into question the canon's designation of some artistic creations as "universal" and others as group specific.

A Collective Sense

Social changes to improve the conditions of life for an oppressed group usually come about because the group has collectively pressed for change. The civil rights movement, for example, resulted in legal changes and came about primarily because of the work of people of color, particularly African Americans. A sense of the collective is also psychologically strengthening for people who are battling discrimination and alienation every day. However, creating and maintaining this sense of the collective is problematic for groups, although the difficulties differ across groups.

For example, women, although identifiable by sight, usually live in family relationships with men. It is often difficult to get women to see gender issues they have in common and to develop a sense of sisterhood. This change in allegiance can conflict with family loyalties; many women resist viewing their husbands, fathers, and sons as part of a controlling group. People with disabilities experience a similar kind of isolation, only to a much more pronounced degree, because one disabled individual may not even have contact with other similarly disabled people. Gay people are not visibly identifiable unless they choose to project symbols of their sexual orientation, and coming "out of the closet" carries great risks because the heterosexual world still strongly rejects homosexuality.

Labor studies attempt to develop a sense of class consciousness in a society that persistently denies that social class has much to do with life chances. The main focus of labor studies has shifted as the political and economic context has changed (Dwyer, 1977). During the 1920s, workers' education existed primarily as a political movement concerned with reconstructing the social order; it was allied with the Socialist political agenda as much as it was with trade unionism. After the Depression and the passage of the National Labor Relations Act, labor education was much more pragmatic: Its primary purpose was to train labor union members in the day-to-day aspects of collective bargaining (Douty, 1950). Labor studies today attempt to provide "working men and women students with a theoretical background of their life experiences as well as equipping them with an understanding of the practical tools utilized by workers and trade unions to improve working conditions" (Dwyer, 1977, p. 202). However the issue of collectivity plays out for a given group, this theme is one that is regularly encountered in Single-Group Studies, and it runs counter to the dominant society's stress on individuality.

Attention to labor issues and working class culture, however, has received attention predominantly at the university level. In elementary and secondary schools, it has been less frequently focused upon. The authors (Sleeter & Grant, 1991), reviewing elementary school textbooks, found that discussions of class were largely absent. It appears, then, that knowledge produced by labor studies scholars does not constitute a major part of the curriculum. Teachers who wish to include a focus upon labor as a group that has profoundly shaped American history and culture may, despite the paucity of information found in the present school curriculum, refer to other texts which specifically emphasize working class experience. For example, *Labor's Heritage*, a publication of the George Meany Center for Labor Studies, includes a whole range of relevant materials. Kaufman, founder of this labor publication, described its contributions as follows: "Historians share their latest research; archivists write about the insights and angles to be found in their labor collections; museum curators conduct written and photographic tours through labor exhibits that many would never have the chance to see in person; musicians, artists, and folklorists share their insights into the world of work" (Palladino, 1997, p. 12).

Group Liberation

Oppressed groups that view themselves as having been subjugated wish to regain control over the telling of their own stories in order to create the basis for group liberation. For example, Adrienne Rich states,

> It is nothing new to say that history is the version of events told by the conqueror, the dominator. Even the dominators acknowledge this. What has more feelingly and pragmatically been said by people of color, by white women, by lesbians and gay men, by people with roots in the industrial or rural working class is that without our own history we are unable to imagine a future because we are deprived of the precious resource of knowing where we came from: the valor and the waverings, the visions and defeats of those who went before us. (cited by Gaard, 1992, p. 31)

Single-Group Studies should provide the intellectual offensive for the social and political struggle for liberation and cultural integrity (Cortada, 1974) and provide leadership for the group in escaping from physical and psychological bondage (Pentony, 1971, p. 62). Labor studies, for example, envision a world in which the organization of work does not place large segments of society under the control of a wealthy elite. Traditional curricula usually portray business and corporate leaders as acting in the best interests of everyone, based on a philosophy such as that expressed in the following company slogan: "What's good for General Motors is good for the nation." If people generally believe this philosophy and have little or no sense of the history of labor, they will tend to acquiesce to the "needs" of business and the corporate world. Labor history, however, chronicles activism on behalf of the working class—battles that have been both won and lost in order to visualize a future in which "common" people and poor people exercise more control over their lives.

Native American studies attempt to build the future by reclaiming the past. As Dupris (1981) explains, the U.S. government declared Indians its "wards"; having done so, "the value of the American Indians' culture was designated as 'dysfunctional' and was, therefore, to be eliminated" (p. 70). The elimination of Indian culture began when the task of education was turned over to the White-controlled Bureau of Indian Affairs, in which policies were overtly assimilationist. The results were disastrous. According to Dupris, Cherokees had 90% literacy rates 100 years ago; 70 years of White-controlled schooling has resulted in a Cherokee dropout rate of 75% and a literacy rate of only 60%. Similarly, Deyhle (1995) discusses the cultural conflicts experienced by young Navajo students in the midst of Anglo dominance. The rationale for American Indian education controlled by American Indians is to restore a language and culture that have been partially lost as well as to strengthen the identity and improve the achievement of Indian children.

Although these themes have emerged in university scholarship, they resonate with the everyday experiences of ordinary members of the target group. Members may enter a Single-Group Studies program after being exposed to only a traditional curriculum, but often they very quickly experience a surge of enthusiasm for an education that finally hits home and really makes sense. However, these themes have as yet not penetrated very far, with some exceptions, in the curriculum for K–12 education. There, Single-Group Studies often reproduce the themes of the dominant society, such as units featuring a string of famous people who have "made it," the implication being that society is open to anyone who tries. We urge teachers to listen carefully to what oppressed groups say about themselves and their own experience before plunging into the creation of Single-Group Studies curricula. One can learn to teach about another group very successfully, but not without work.

RECOMMENDED PRACTICES

The main goal of Single-Group Studies programs is to promote willingness and knowledge among students to work toward social change that would benefit a specific group, as stated in Table 4–1. Single-Group Studies programs have been developed most comprehensively at the university level, where courses of study lead to majors and minors at both the undergraduate and graduate levels. At the high school level, such courses have been added to the curriculum, usually within departments but sometimes across departments. At the elementary and middle school levels, one finds units or lessons about specific groups, which are usually more simplistic. Regardless of the level of schooling, however, and regardless of the group with which one is concerned, advocates recommend fairly similar practices.

Curriculum

We will sketch features common to Single-Group Studies curricula; the main commonalities are summarized in Table 4–1. First, however, we wish to caution you against creating such curricula around your own ideas of what is important about a group, without first investigating materials or scholarship produced by and about members of the groups. Your own ideas may distort how other groups see themselves and their own experience.

When trying to teach about people of color, for example, White teachers commonly draw on their own interpretation of the European ethnic experience to decide what is relevant to teach, usually without being aware of doing so. The result is a curriculum that may actually be irrelevant to what people of color see as important. Alba (1990) investigated the symbolic meaning that White Americans have attached to ethnicity today. He wondered why EuroAmericans continue to express interest in ethnicity in spite of the fact that European ethnicity in the United States—*unlike racial group membership*—no longer structures life chances to any significant degree. He found that EuroAmericans view ethnic identity as a matter of individual choice. They stress the commonality of ethnic immigrant histories and value expressions of ethnicity that can be shared across ethnic lines, especially food, holidays, and festivals. Many equate ethnicity with one's private family history, rather than viewing it as a group's collective experience. Whites often do not connect ethnicity with social structures, such as neighborhoods, friendship groups, occupations, or political organizations.

The resulting curricula end up focusing on customs—such as food, holidays, and folk tales—brought from the old country. Another common theme is family heritage—where (what country) students' families came from and what customs the family has retained, such as recipes. Some teachers even interpret Native

Americans within a European-immigrant framework, presenting Native Americans as the first wave of immigrants. By omission, such lessons imply that race no longer structures access to resources in the United States and that America's racial groups stand in equal status to one another, differentiated only by old world customs in which anyone can participate. Even lessons about role models can, by focusing on an individual's achievements and ignoring her or his difficulties in attaining them, suggest that the system is open equally to anyone who will try.

Women's studies units often focus on famous women, without providing much suggestion that sexism still exists nor any analysis of sexism. Disability-awareness lessons often describe characteristics of people with disabilities, without critiquing the social context that reinforces barriers. The problem with such lessons is that they often do not develop ideas that group members who have studied their own history and experience consider important about themselves.

The Single-Group Studies curriculum usually contains a history of the group. For racial groups, the history might explain reasons for immigration (e.g., of Asian Americans) or enslavement (in the case of African Americans). The history might also provide information on early relationships with White settlers (e.g., in the cases of Native Americans and Mexican Americans) or, in the case of Native Americans, the history of legal settlements and conflicts with Whites.

A group's great heroes and heroines, both past and present, are very often discussed in detail, as well as the group's creations in the fields of arts, letters, and sciences. For example, the background, struggles, and achievements of noted authors, musicians, scientists, and civic workers are provided. In addition, many of the Single-Group Studies programs include selections of art, music, and other cultural expressions. Traditional and contemporary perspectives are offered to provide insight into the group's culture. For example, Mexican Americans are known to have very strong extended-family ties and certain views related to male and female behavior. One can see these concepts reflected in the art and literature of Mexican Americans. Appalachia has a rich culture which the dominant society stereotypes as "hillbilly"; studying that culture reveals the existence of great strength and creativity in mountain people. Deaf Studies includes coursework in, for example, the deaf theater.

Also studied are experiences that the group has had with discrimination as well as how the group has dealt with discrimination, such as the internment of Japanese Americans during World War II, the Trail of Tears that Native Americans experienced during their forced immigration, the work of Rosie the Riveter in the defense plants during World War II, and the role of labor unions in collective bargaining. Many courses or programs contain information addressing diversity within the group; for example, women's studies may address the problems and strengths arising from the fact that the group is made up of both women of color and White women. Puerto Rican studies may discuss the relationship of skin color to job opportunities. Discussions of stereotyping, myths, and cultural and institutional bias are also included.

Philosophical world views of the group are usually studied. For example, women's studies programs often study feminist philosophy, or African-American

Studies may study African-American political thought. Finally, contemporary issues of concern to the group are usually studied. For example, women's studies usually address economic inequalities between the sexes, the status of gays and lesbians, and women's health care. Chicano studies may address the status of agricultural workers in the Southwest as well as the illegal-alien issue. Disabilities studies may examine implications of the Americans with Disabilities Act.

Single-Group Studies programs may be put together somewhat differently. Nevertheless, they all have important components of history, group culture, and contemporary issues. At the university level, students may take anything ranging from a single course to an undergraduate major to a Ph.D. program. The packaging of content at the university level varies widely. For example, in a review of women's studies programs, Schmitz (1985) noted.

> At minimum, the curriculum includes an Introduction to Women's Studies and a series of departmentally based courses such as Women in Literature, Psychology of Sex Roles, or Feminism and Philosophy. A mature program with a line budget and paid administrator might also offer a variety of senior seminars on aspects of feminist theory and field work practica, as well as intermediate-level interdisciplinary courses to supplement departmental offerings. (p. 1)

Chicano studies programs developed at first mainly through courses in history and the social sciences. Mature programs today include coursework in these areas as well as Chicano literature, folklore and theater, bilingual education and other education issues, and Chicano political theory (Garcia, Lomeli, & Ortiz, 1984).

Students can complete an undergraduate minor in American Indian studies from the University of Wisconsin–Eau Claire. Students are required to take at least 15 semester credits from the following core courses:

Introduction to American Indian Studies

Introduction to American Indian Expressive Cultures

Introduction to the Literature of the American Indian

American Indian History

The American Indian in Literature and Film

Native Art of the Americas

Studies in American Indian History

Students may also choose 9 credits from a list of elective courses such as Race and Ethnicity in the U.S. and Directed Studies of Minority Groups.

At the K–12 level, the entire curriculum could conceivably be designed around a single group. In fact, usually it is—White Americans, mostly males. Afrocentric schools are engaged in rewriting their curricula so that they are based mainly on African American studies rather than White studies. Short of rewriting the entire curriculum, one can construct Single-Group Studies courses. More and more, however, courses are centering upon multiple groups and are interdisciplinary in nature. For example, in Madison, Wisconsin, a sampling of four area high schools revealed that ethnic studies classes do exhibit these characteristics. In one of the high schools, the course offering remains much the same; the historical experiences of African Americans alone constitute the curricular focus. In comparison, though, the three other high schools offer courses which are multiple group and interdisciplinary in emphasis. The following course description, taken from one of those courses, illustrates this trend and reads as follows:

> This course is offered to students interested in studying American ethnic history and contemporary social issues about *Native Americans, African Americans, Asian Americans, Hispanic Chicano Mexican Americans and European Americans*. This course additionally explores cultural contributions such as *music, art, and literature* ... This course provides students a multicultural perspective on American ethnic groups. [emphasis ours]

Thus, courses still holding the traditional title, "Ethnic Studies," are metamorphasizing into multiculture, multidiscipline undertakings.

At the K–12 level, although numerous curriculum guides and supplemental materials exist, relatively few in-depth courses of study have been published. Materials for African-American studies are the most well developed. For example, the *African American Baseline Essays*, produced by Portland Public Schools in Oregon, provide background information for teachers that conceptualize from an Afrocentric perspective the following six disciplines: art, literature, social studies, mathematics, science, and music. Two texts—*African American Literature* (1992) and *The African American Experience* (Harley, Middleton, & Stokes, 1992)—are available for classroom use for literature and history courses, respectively. After reviewing *The African American Experience*, one of our students commented that the book is very much like a traditional history text except that it focuses on African American rather than White people; this conclusion helped the student to realize that texts he was used to seeing can be viewed as "White studies."

The last decade has seen the production of materials about Indian reservations and in Indian programs across the country. For example, the state of Wisconsin publishes a curriculum guide entitled *Classroom Activities in Chippewa Treaty Rights* (Satz, Gulig, & St. Germaine, 1991) for teaching about Chippewa–U.S. government treaties, and Anoka-Hennepin School District in Minnesota publishes an extensive collection of materials entitled *Inside the Culture* for teaching about Native culture, especially in relationship to science and literature. Districts outside Puerto Rico are only beginning to produce good Latino studies materials; one textbook publishing company has published a textbook entitled *Mexican American Literature* (Tatum, 1990). Women's studies materials tend to focus mainly on famous women or career exploration; teachers with a background in women's studies can find enough materials to create good courses or units, but by themselves most available materials have limited focus.

Although many school districts, teachers and parents have been, and continue to be, wary of including curriculum discussing gay, lesbian and bisexual issues, there is a growing body of literature and materials aimed at this. A number of books, articles and journal special issues have been published in the last few years which address incorporating sexual orientation into the curriculum of schools (for example, see Barnard, 1994; Chandler, 1995; *Harvard Educational Review*, 1996; Loutzenheiser, 1996; Woog, 1995). Organizations interested in improving the educational experiences of gay, lesbian, and bisexual students such as GLAAD, Project 10, and the Gay, Lesbian, and Straight Teachers Network have also made curriculum materials available. Books written by or for gay, lesbian, and bisexual students such as *Two Teenagers in Twenty* (Heron, 1994) or *Am I Blue? Coming Out from the Silence* have been useful in bringing the youth perspective into the classroom, allowing students to connect with those who are in some way "like them" and to better understand the experiences of growing up and living as gay, lesbian, or bisexual individuals. In addition, an increasingly valued resource for curriculum development is archival material; use of primary historical sources provides an avenue for social groups not traditionally represented in the curriculum to counter invisibility and establish voice and place.

Instructional Strategies

Curriculum has generally been a more central concern to Single-Group Studies than have instructional strategies. However, when a program teaches students who are mainly or only members of the group being studied, how one teaches may become a concern.

Afrocentric schools specifically try to use instructional strategies that are culturally congruent with African American culture. In Chapter 2 we discussed some differences between the learning styles of African Americans and White Americans, and we will not repeat that discussion here. However, educators often try to design an entire program, including how material is presented, so that it fits students culturally. In an ethnographic study of eight teachers, for example, Ladson-Billings (1994) documents the characteristics of what she refers to as "culturally relevant pedagogy" for African American students.

Women's studies programs have developed what is known as "feminist pedagogy" and, in a variety of institutional settings, educators are constantly in the process of developing and reshaping a teaching environment responsive to women (Maher & Tetreault, 1994). Essentially, feminist pedagogy is a teaching approach that attempts to empower women students. The main idea is that women are socialized to accept other people's ideas. In the traditional classroom, women students read text materials that were written mainly by men, providing a male interpretation of the world. Over time, women learn not to interpret the world for themselves. In the feminist classroom, women learn to trust and develop their own insights.

The feminist teacher may assign material to read and encourage students to generate discussion and reflections about the material. Discussion and personal reflection are an important part of the process, during which "control shifts from me, the teacher, the arbiter of knowing, to the interactions of students and myself with the subject matter" (Tetreault, 1989, p. 137). To have students learn to analyze materials and to think for themselves is as important as what they learn. Also, the teacher may not make assignments in the traditional sense but rather generate material for students to reflect upon. Such material may consist of writings by students about topics of importance to them or items students bring into class for consideration. Through discussion, the teacher attempts to help students build connections between their personal experiences and larger issues—allowing them, for example, to analyze strategies that are used by some men to retain control. Similarly, the teacher helps students to understand the importance of context—personal background, community, and group membership—in analyzing present learning problems. Out of this process the teacher hopes to build confidence in women students—in thinking for themselves, in listening to their inner voices, and in speaking up. Students who have experienced feminist pedagogy notice that great importance is placed on discussion—the free sharing of personal experiences and reflections—and more emphasis is given to the creation of meaning than the acquisition of the "right" answer.

Implementation

When planning a program and designing a curriculum, a teacher must make certain decisions about the relationship of that curriculum to the rest of the school program; these decisions have implications for planning and teaching. One decision is whether Single-Group Studies will be separate from the regular curriculum or integrated with it in an attempt to provide a more balanced program. Currently, when Single-Group Studies are implemented, the separate approach is usually used, often with superficial renderings of groups' experiences, such as a day to celebrate a particular heroine or hero, a unit during a special time (e.g., Black History Week), a festival, or ethnic cookouts. We have observed that the major implementation strategy for Single-Group Studies in the public schools is the four Fs: fairs, festivals, food, and folk tales. Usually, when a Single-Group Studies program is introduced in this manner, there is no well-thought-out reason for having it separate. There is also no in-depth study of the group itself. Perhaps it seems easier to add special activities and lessons to the existing instructional plan. However, such add-ons are usually devoid of any strategy to change the existing program substantially, even though the substantive change of school curricula is a primary goal of serious Single-Group Studies practitioners, whether they advocate integration or separatism.

Most advocates of Single-Group Studies—especially those teaching at the elementary and secondary levels—recommend integrating their study into the content of the mainstream curriculum. This approach encourages including information about the group's historical and cultural experience in courses such as social studies, government, history, literature, art, and music. Actually, the use of this strategy moves us closer to implementing one of the approaches to multicultural education that are examined in Chapters 5 and 6. Not to move in this direction, advocates argue, would make the Single-Group Studies curriculum supplementary to the main curriculum. Banks (1997) argues, "If ethnic content is merely added to the traditional curriculum, which in many ways is ineffective, efforts to modify the curriculum with ethnic content are likely to lead to a dead end" (p. 83). Banks's argument is consistent with data reported in an Education U.S.A. survey (cited by Giles, 1974) and voiced by a number of teachers today—that most educators believe the best way to handle material on racial groups is to make it an integral part of the regular kindergarten-through-12th grade (K–12) curriculum.

Integration has a flip side, however. The major problem is that "without such centers of intellectual work and hubs for political struggle, the culture and experiences of the marginalized will be marginalized even more systematically," especially if content about the group is absorbed into courses taught by individuals who are not trained in the study of that group (Lauter, 1991, p. 165). Single-Group Studies need to be researched and developed as areas in their own right. Perhaps after women's studies, for example, has become as well developed as the more traditional men's studies, then integration would make sense. However, to push prematurely for integration would greatly overwork women's studies scholars by giving them two jobs rather than one (i.e., redesigning traditional knowledge for a traditional set of colleagues in addition to conducting research on women). It would also weaken the efforts of women to develop new conceptual frameworks for understanding, because research and curricula currently have very well entrenched frameworks that would resist displacement by fledgling ideas (Bowles & Klein, 1983). Another argument for separatism is that educators believe that they need to offer older students separate courses to make up for all the years that this area of study was excluded from their education (National Schools Public Relations Association, 1970).

Afrocentric, or African American immersion, schools represent a serious attempt to implement the Single-Group Studies approach because of the failure of schools to successfully educate African American children. Although Afrocentric public schools received considerable publicity during the early 1990s, Ratteray (1990) notes that over 400 independent African American schools exist, a few being over 100 years old. The main rationale for the existence of such schools is that "current practice, even in desegregated settings, effectively excludes African American males [and females, to a lesser degree] from the mainstream culture" (Leake & Leake, 1992, p. 25).

Desegregated schools still operate on a Eurocentric model, and many African American students experience serious alienation. Rather than continuing to accept poor academic achievement and cultural marginality, the African American communities in several large school districts decided to try public African American centered schools. The main purpose is to help students develop a strong sense of self, high achievement, and worthy goals for the future. While Afrocentric schools continue to exist, the discourse surrounding Afrocentrism has, in many ways, shifted. Increasingly, more credence is given to the idea of building coalitions across differences. As such, the need for collective educational forms and political agendas which address the knowledge and experience of multiple communities (e.g., gay men and lesbians, Native Americans) is gaining recognition. In many high schools, for example, "ethnic studies" courses, which at one time focused only upon a single group, such as African Americans, are now adopting a curriculum which addresses a range of issues and their relationship to multiple groups. Thus, while many remain committed to single-group centered perspectives, such as Afrocentrism, discussion as well as practice reveals an evolution toward the study of multiple groups, and increasingly, the importance of teaching which is relevant to a diverse student population is being recognized. In many ways, then, the ideal of Afrocentric education is being gradually displaced by an alternative valuing of multiplicity and an emerging discourse on cultural relevance.

In Chapter 2, we noted that most bilingual education programs could be subsumed under the Teaching the Culturally Different approach. One can also find a few bilingual-bicultural education programs that have more in common with Single-Group Studies than with any other approach. Essentially, such programs include a strong curriculum that emphasizes the culture of the group with which the language is associated, their purpose being the enhancement of students' competence in that culture. Trueba (1976) distinguishes between bilingual education and bilingual-bicultural education. The main purpose of bilingual education is usually to teach English to children whose home language is not English. Bilingual-bicultural education, on the other hand, seeks to teach children as much about the Hispanic, or Chinese, or Indian culture, for example, as about the dominant Anglo culture. When bilingual-bicultural programs are open to children of diverse backgrounds and seek to promote what Ramirez and Castaneda (1976) have called "cultural democracy"—the equal status of two cultures and of the people who represent those cultures—the program is a variant of Single-Group Studies. Kjolseth (1976) argues that this type of program involves the political mobilization of the ethnic community: Members of the community are as involved in the development and implementation of the program as are members of the dominant group. The program is "two-way with members of both the ethnic and nonethnic groups learning in their and the other's language" (p. 126); the cultures of both groups are stressed equally in all curricular areas; and the program "encourages a democratic forum for the resolution of conflicts and differing interests within and between the ethnic and nonethnic communities" (p. 127).[1]

A second decision that must be made in implementing a Single-Group Studies program is how many disciplines will be involved and in what relationship to each other. The teacher has essentially three choices: using a single discipline, using a multidisciplinary approach, and using an interdisciplinary approach. The least complex, and probably the most common approach in high schools, is the single-discipline approach. This means, for example, that a history teacher develops units or an entire history course in African-American history, or a literature teacher develops units or a course in Asian-American literature.

The multidisciplinary approach involves teachers or professors in several disciplines, each contributing a unit or a course to a Single-Group Studies program. For example, an Indian studies program may have courses in anthropology, art, history, and religion. A women's studies program may offer courses in biology, literature, history, and psychology. Boneparth (1978) offers an argument in favor of this approach, saying that it would facilitate moving from a separate to an integrated program:

---

[1]We disagree with Kjolseth's equating the dominant group with a nonethnic group. To us, there is no such thing as a nonethnic group. White ethnics who have "melted" and who no longer have strong ties to European countries—which is probably the group Kjolseth refers to as nonethnic—can be considered ethnically EuroAmerican: Their ancestors came from Europe, and their culture has European roots that have developed a distinctive American character. EuroAmericans can be distinguished visually as well as culturally from, for example, African Americans.

The rationale for the multidisciplinary approach is clear: the traditional disciplines have universally ignored women and have failed to integrate the study of women into their course offerings. Therefore, outside efforts to push the discipline into a concern with women are necessary and well spent. (p. 23)

The interdisciplinary approach is the most complex. It requires integrating two or more disciplines into the study of issues of concern to a group. For example, in an African American studies program using the interdisciplinary approach, teachers of history, literature, and art could develop a study of artistic expression by African American people throughout history, examining the impact of historical events on works of art and literature. Using the interdisciplinary conceptual approach is important, Banks (1973, 1997) argues, because it helps students make reflective decisions so that they can institute social change. He believes that the social science disciplines (e.g., sociology and anthropology) must be brought together and that analytical concepts within these disciplines (e.g., values and norms) must be used to help make decisions about complex societal problems such as racism or sexism. He states:

A social studies curriculum which focuses on decision-making and the African American experience must be *interdisciplinary*; it should incorporate *key* (or organizing) concepts from all of the social sciences. Knowledge from any one discipline is insufficient to help us make decisions on complex issues such as poverty, institutionalized racism and oppression. To take effective social action on a social issue such as poverty, students must view it from the perspectives of geography, history, sociology, economics, political science, psychology, and anthropology. (p. 156, emphasis ours)

How Single-Group Studies are taught often depends on the availability of materials and the preparation of the teachers. These factors are especially important at the elementary and high school levels, where the instructors may or may not have had the opportunity to develop the area of specialization.

Teachers must also be aware that students may be sensitive to materials and embarrassed to ask questions about their culture or about racial or sexual dynamics. Therefore, the teacher, says Butler (1981), "should always be approachable and should frequently encourage students to take advantage of his/her office appointment hours to discuss topic papers [or] clarify classroom discussion" (p. 117). Finally, the most important ingredient for teaching Single-Group Studies, we have found, is the teacher's attitude—the awareness, commitment, and dedication of the teacher to the kind of job he or she thinks needs to be done.

The following vignette illustrates two teachers using the Single-Group Studies approach.

SEÑOR RICARDO GOMEZ AND MS. KATHY BENNETT

As Ricardo entered the school, he had mixed emotions. He was very pleased and proud that his college days were behind him and that he had his teaching certificate. He was sad and annoyed that in 1 week he would be 28 years old and just getting his first real job. Sometimes he counted the 2 years he had spent in Vietnam as a real job and other times he didn't. He felt he had really grown up in Nam. He had lost his two best buddies, Juan and Pedro, and had gotten banged up pretty badly himself—badly enough to remain in the hospital for 6 months.

The three young men had joined the Marines the day they had graduated from Lakeview High School. So many of his Hispanic brothers, he now thought, had lost their lives in Vietnam. Before Ricardo could allow that thought to go any further, a little kid hollered up to him, "Are you the new P. E. teacher?" Ricardo said, "No, I am the new social studies teacher."

Kennedy Junior High School was located in a suburb of a large metropolitan area. The school was in an upper-middle-class area, with a student population of 88% White, 4% African American, 2% Asian, and 6% Hispanic. All the students of color were bused in from the inner city.

In a short time, Ricardo established himself as one of the "good" teachers at Kennedy. He was assigned three classes in American history and one in world geography. The students liked and respected him, and the other teachers saw him as friendly and professional but also as a man in a hurry.

Ricardo had been a history buff for as long as he could remember. He was very interested in what the past teaches us about the present and future. In short order, his classroom took on an attractive and museumlike appearance, with pictures and historical artifacts everywhere.

George Glenn had been the principal of Kennedy Junior High School for 6 years. One of his responsibilities was evaluating all of his teachers, especially the new ones. According to district policy, he had to observe new teachers at least three times over the school year. When Mr. Glenn came to observe Ricardo, he was informed that he was to see a lesson on the fall of the Alamo. What Mr. Glenn saw was not a lesson that featured Davy Crockett and his rifle Betsy along with some Texans as fallen heroes of the Alamo; rather he saw a lesson that featured the Mexican general Santa Anna and his army putting down a revolt against the Mexican government. Around the room were bulletin boards, posters, and other classroom artifacts that featured aspects of the Mexican American culture.

Later, during their conference, Ricardo explained to Mr. Glenn how important he thought it was to provide his students with a broad perspective of history. He said that he believed it was his responsibility as a Hispanic American to include in his teaching not only the Anglo perspective of American history, but also the Hispanic perspective. He asked Mr. Glenn why more attention wasn't given to Hispanic cultures in the daily practices of the school. He said that the school curriculum and activities were exclusively Anglo in policy and practice. Mr. Glenn was taken aback by Ricardo's comments and had difficulty responding. Ricardo continued, saying that not only were the Hispanics in the school being cheated by not having their history taught, but so were the other students, especially the Anglos, many of whom displayed ethnocentric attitudes. Mr. Glenn nodded his head and concluded the conversation by saying that they should talk about this matter again soon and that he had another observation to make in 5 minutes.

Kathy Bennett had been vice-principal of Kennedy for 12 years. In fact, she had been Mr. Glenn's mentor teacher when he started teaching. Kathy was becoming increasingly disenchanted with her job and the school system in general. She had been passed over for a principalship so often that she now believed that receiving a promotion could never happen. The "word" on her was that she was too aggressive and would not fit in with the other administrators—all of whom were male. Kathy and her friends never would have described her as aggressive; rather they saw her as a person who insisted on being in charge of her own life and who knew what she wanted and where she wanted to go.

Kathy did have personal and professional concerns related to the career goals of the female students at the school. Many of them, she believed, were too passive and too much into playing the role of helpless female. Their career goals were very traditional. It was as if they were living in the 1940s and early 1950s. Kathy had started an after-school club called "You Too Can Do." In the club meeting room were pictures and posters of women in both traditional and nontraditional jobs. There were books by female authors and stories of famous and not-so-famous women who had really taken charge of their lives without relying on males. "You Too Can Do" met twice monthly. During each meeting, there was usually a discussion of some work accomplished by a woman or a guest speaker who addressed some aspect of feminism.

Mr. Glenn was aware of Kathy's club and her special attention to the female population of the school; but he tried to ignore this activity because she was fair with the boys and it did not particularly interfere with her job. However, Mr. Glenn was not personally assertive in helping her get a principalship, as he had been with Robert Wilson, his vice-principal before Kathy.

As Mr. Glenn left Ricardo's room, he saw Kathy in the hall and asked her to come and chat with him. He said he was concerned about Ricardo's curriculum and teaching. He described what he had observed in Ricardo's room, and as he did, he became more upset. Kathy told him that although she had never seen Ricardo teach, she had heard that he was "different." However, she said, the students for the most part enjoyed his approach. She then added, "You know, I have similar feelings about the girls and feminist issues in the school." Upon hearing that comment, Mr. Glenn looked at Kathy with a facial expression that turned from puzzlement to annoyance, and he said, "I have an observation to do. We can continue this discussion later."

Ricardo and Kathy continued, each in his or her own way, to influence their students' education. Ricardo's lessons always contained both the Anglo and Hispanic perspectives, and Kathy's "You Too Can Do" club continued to meet and discuss feminist issues.

Mr. Glenn, meanwhile, tried to ignore the teaching behavior of these two staff members. However, he often suggested to Ricardo in a friendly manner that he would probably prefer teaching in the urban barrio.

CRITIQUE   To critique Single-Group Studies is to realize that many positive statements can be made about this approach to multicultural education. The Single-Group Studies approach can be seen as a beginning, because people must first understand themselves before they can hope to understand others. Banks (1997) puts it this way: "Another important goal of ethnic studies is to help individuals clarify their ethnic identities and function effectively within their own ethnic community. This must occur before individuals can relate positively to others who belong to different racial and ethnic groups" (p. 21). Single-Group Studies can also be described as a beginning because the civil rights movement of the 1960s started with one group—African Americans—demanding their social, political, and economic rights, and from that beginning, other groups also demanded their rights. Although the struggles of women and labor groups were not new, their demands to be included in the curriculum as legitimate groups for study were articulated with renewed—and, in many cases, new—vigor. Gay and lesbian studies literally helps people articulate an identity and set of experiences that are usually silenced; the programs give impetus to a growing civil rights struggle based on sexual orientation. The Single-Group Studies approach has generated ethnic pride and a desire to discover one's roots. Congress was so swayed by this interest in ethnic heritage that in 1972 it passed legislation enacting the Ethnic Heritage Studies Program. Similarly, Title IX of the Elementary and Secondary Education Act (ESEA) and the Women's Educational Equity Act came about because women demanded equality.

For the teacher who doesn't have a strong knowledge of gender issues, class issues, or race diversity, the Single-Group Studies model serves as a helpful starting place. For the teacher working with a student population that is basically Asian or Hispanic, for example, the Single-Group Studies approach provides a beginning point to help students develop pride in who they are and understand how their group has been victimized. Ricardo Gomez's Hispanic students, for example, knew little about themselves as Hispanic people before enrolling in his class. They learned some Hispanic culture informally at home, but in school they had never been taught their own history, literature, and so forth. In fact, constituting only 6% of the student body, these students were ignored in the curriculum and treated as invisible by the school.

The Single-Group Studies approach does have certain limitations, however, and what one sees as its limitations depends on one's perspective. From the perspective of advocates of the Teaching the Culturally Different approach, the Single-Group Studies approach spends too little time on the things that subordinate groups need most and too much time on things that will not help them. This model has been criticized further for keeping students of color and White female students out of the mainstream and for promoting cultural separatism. Critics fear that minority students, for example, will fail to acquire a sufficient grasp of mainstream culture if they spend too much time studying their own culture. A knowledge of African-American history, for example, will not help much on the SATs or in a traditional American history class; and the system requires success in the traditional curriculum, not in the study of oppressed groups. One can argue that this requirement vividly illustrates how the system oppresses some groups, but advocates of Teaching the Culturally Different reply that teachers must nevertheless prepare students to succeed within the system, because such an approach is the most realistic course of action.

From the perspective of Human Relations advocates, Single-Group Studies can be seen as counterproductive. Human Relations advocates support studying the contributions of diverse groups, but they fear that the study of oppression will only exacerbate tension and hostility. Furthermore, they believe that studying separate groups separately will not promote unity. Rather than examining painful issues in our past, Human Relations advocates prefer to seek ways of drawing people together in the present. For example, Kathy Bennett's students will, at one time or another, experience anger toward men as they learn how women have been oppressed. Some of this anger will probably be directed toward male students, male teachers, brothers, and fathers. Similarly, Ricardo's Hispanic students will experience anger toward Whites and may display some hostility toward White students and teachers in the school. Human Relations advocates prefer that students learn to appreciate their similarities and their cultural differences and learn to interact as unique individuals, rather than exploring the pain and injustice of past oppression and victimization.

To those who accept and support the intent of Single-Group Studies, the main limitation is that the approach leaves the regular curriculum unreformed. Connell (1993) emphasizes, "Social justice is not satisfied by curriculum ghettos. Separate-and-different curricula have some attractions, but leave the currently hegemonic curriculum in place. Social justice requires … *reconstructing the mainstream*" (p. 44). Of course, this result is not the fault of advocates and practitioners of the approach, for most are keenly aware of the need to reform the curriculum. It is precisely this need that prompted the development of the Single-Group Studies countercurricula. Nevertheless, as a separate program of its own, Single-Group Studies allows the rest of the education program to proceed on a "business as usual" basis. For example, Mr. Glenn had no intention of changing anything in his school and tried hard to ignore Kathy and Ricardo. As long as their activities could be compartmentalized into a separate course or an after-school activity, they were tolerable. In this and other cases, champions of the status quo can argue that students are being provided with ethnic, gender, or class-relevant experiences and that teachers such as Ricardo and Kathy are being allowed to "do their thing." Too often, such programs exist as add-ons, supplemental to the main business of the school. As such, they tend to draw as students only members of the group being studied. For example, African American studies programs ideally should be taken by members of all racial groups, and teachers within such programs see as much need for changing White attitudes toward African Americans as for educating African Americans about African Americans. However, when African American studies programs are supplemental and elective, as they almost always are, they are attended mainly by African Americans. Although some students who are members of dominant groups find such courses enlightening and worthwhile, others feel threatened, particularly when they are in the minority as class members, and find it more comfortable to avoid such courses. Those students who may need reeducation the most can comfortably stay away, pursuing their education in the unchanged mainstream.

Another problem is that Single-Group Studies programs do not necessarily work together. The goal of most advocates of Single-Group Studies is curriculum reform that would involve the inclusion of studies about the various groups into the curriculum. Ultimately, of course, this approach would require rewriting the curriculum, because its main conceptual frameworks currently derive from studies of upper-middle-class, White males. Also, at present the goal of curriculum reform is more likely to appear in the form of rhetoric than actual demonstration. Most writings about Single-Group Studies suggest including other groups, but rarely in the examples they provide has this goal been accomplished. For example, ethnic studies often focus on the males of a given ethnic group; labor studies often focus on White, working-class males; and women's studies often focus on White, middle-class, heterosexual women. Bowles and Klein (1983) acknowledge this point when they say that women's studies, as it presently exists, "has its own problems with heterosexism, classism and racism in its predominantly White programs—all inherited from patriarchal culture" (p. 5). Ricardo's study of Hispanics, as another example, emphasized the male Hispanic experience; most likely Ricardo was not even aware of this narrowness of focus. Further, Kathy's study of feminism centered around the concerns of White, middle-class, heterosexual females. While not intending to exclude others, each of these teachers prioritized the concerns of one group and, in so doing, implicitly accepted other existing biases.

There is often confusion among teachers as to when they are really using a Single-Group Studies approach. We have observed teachers who believed they were using this approach when they taught a 2- or 3-week unit, for example, on Asian Americans—their main substantive attempt to teach about a group other than Whites for the entire school year. Advocates of Single-Group Studies would tell such teachers that they are not implementing Single-Group Studies but rather what we described in Chapter 1 as "business as usual." Single-Group Studies is an in-depth, comprehensive study of a group. Superficial lessons about groups do not really meet the goals and objectives of Single-Group Studies and may only promote stereotyping. Furthermore, they leave the rest of the teacher's teaching devoted as always to upper-middle-class White male studies, or business as usual. However, if such teachers taught the unit on Asian Americans and also taught similar units on other groups, then advocates of the approach would probably argue that the teacher had Single-Group Studies as part of his or her curriculum, if for no other reason than that the teacher was at least limiting the time spent on White male studies so as to have comparable time to spend on other groups. The phrase *time on task*, one very familiar to teachers, represents an important aspect of teaching any of these approaches to multicultural education.

Finally, some educators reject the idea of Single-Group Studies because they themselves have only seen it implemented as an add-on approach, usually in social studies. For example, teachers in math or music may view it as an additive approach that is not very practical because it takes too much time and is not very relevant outside social studies. However, we would argue that a mainstream curriculum in any subject area already does reflect the perspective and experiences of a group—the dominant group. As such, it is not neutral or universal. Your choice is not whether cultural groups will inform the education program, but rather which groups.

REFERENCES

African American literature: Voices in tradition. (1992). New York: Holt, Rinehart, & Winston; Harcourt Brace Jovanovich.

Afro-American Studies Department Curriculum. (1970). Pamphlet. Madison, WI: University of Wisconsin–Madison, Department of Afro-American Studies.

Alba, R. D. (1990). *Ethnic identity.* New Haven: Yale University Press.

Allen, P. G. (1986). *The sacred hoop.* Boston: Beacon Press.

Apple, M. W. (1993). *Official knowledge: Democratic education in a conservative age.* New York: Routledge.

Apple, M. W. (1996). *Cultural politics and education.* New York: Teachers College Press.

Aronowitz, S. (1992). *The politics of identity.* New York: Routledge.

Asante, M. K. (1990). *Kemet, Afrocentricity, and knowledge.* Trenton, NJ: Africa World Press.

Banks, J. A. (1973). Teaching black studies for social change. In J. A. Banks (Ed.), *Teaching ethnic studies* (pp. 149–179). Washington, DC: National Council for the Social Studies.

Banks, J. A. (1981). *Multiethnic education: Theory and practice.* Boston: Allyn & Bacon.

Banks, J. A. (1997). *Teaching strategies for ethnic studies* (6th ed.). Boston: Allyn & Bacon.

Barnard, I. (1994). Anti-homophobic pedagogy: Some suggestions for teachers. *Radical Teacher, 45,* 26–28.

Bauer, M. D. (Ed.) (1994). *Am I blue?: Coming out from the silence.* New York: HarperCollins.

Bernal, M. (1981). *Black Athena: The Afroasiatic roots of Western civilization* (Vol. 1). New Brunswick, NJ: Rutgers University Press.

Boneparth, E. (1978). Evaluating women's studies: Academic theory and practice. In K. O. Blumhagen & W. D. Johnson (Eds.), *Women's studies* (pp. 21–30). Westport, CT: Greenwood Press.

Bowles, G., & Klein, R. D. (1983). Introduction: Theories of women's studies and the autonomy/integration debate. In G. Bowles & R. D. Klein (Eds.), *Theories of women's studies* (pp. 1–26). London: Routledge & Kegan Paul.

Bowles, S., & Gintis, H. (1976). *Schooling in capitalist America.* New York: Basic Books.

Butler, J. E. (1981). *Black studies: Pedagogy and revolution.* Lanham, MD: University Press of America.

Chandler, K. (1995). *Passages of pride: Lesbian and gay youth come of age.* New York: Times Books.

Churchill, W. (1992). *Fantasies of the master race: Literature, cinema, and the colonization of American Indians.* Monroe, ME: Common Courage Press.

Connell, R. W. (1993). *Schools and social justice.* Philadelphia: Temple University Press.

Cortada, R. E. (1974). *Black studies.* Lexington, MA: Xerox College Publishing.

Cross, W. E., Jr. (1991). *Shades of black: Diversity in African-American identity.* Philadelphia: Temple University Press.

Cubberly, E. P. (1909). *Changing conceptions of education.* Boston: Houghton Mifflin.

Deyhle, D. (1995). Navajo youth and Anglo racism: Cultural integrity and resistance. *Harvard Educational Review, 65*(3), 403–444.

Douty, A. (1950). American workers' education in action. Paris: Economic Cooperation Administration. Mimeographed paper. Cited in R. Dwyer (1977), Workers' education, labor education, labor studies: An historical delineation. *Review of Educational Research, 47,* 179–207.

Dupris, J. C. (1981). The national impact of multicultural education: A renaissance of Native American Indian culture through tribal self-determination and Indian control of Indian education. In *Proceedings of the Eighth Annual International Bilingual Bicultural Conference* (pp. 69–78). Rosslyn, VA: InterAmerica Research Associates.

Dwyer, R. (1977). Workers' education, labor education, labor studies: An historical delineation. *Review of Educational Research, 47,* 179–207.

Freire, P. (1970). *Pedagogy of the oppressed.* New York: The Seaburg Press.

Gaard, G. (1992). Opening up the canon: The importance of teaching lesbian and gay literature. *Feminist Teacher, 6*(2), 30–33.

Garcia, E. E., Lomeli, F. A., & Ortiz, I. S. (1984). *Chicano studies: A multidisciplinary approach.* New York: Teachers College Press.

Garcia, R. L. (1982). *Teaching in a pluralistic society.* New York: Harper & Row.

Gates, H. L., & McKay, N. (Eds.). (1997). *The Norton anthology: African American literature.* New York: Norton.

Giles, R. H., Jr. (1974). *Black studies programs in public schools.* New York: Praeger.

Graber, B. (Ed.). (1997). Constitution of the National Women's Studies Association. *Women's Studies Newsletter, 5*(1–2).

Grant, C. A., & Sleeter, C. E. (1989). *Turning on learning.* New York: Merrill/Macmillan.

Guerra, M. H. (1973). Bilingual and bicultural education. In M. D. Stent, W. R. Hazard, & H. N. Rivlin (Eds.), *Cultural pluralism in education* (pp. 27–34). New York: Appleton-Century-Crofts.

Harley, S., Middleton, S., & Stokes, C. M. (1992). *The African American experience: A history.* Englewood Cliffs, NJ: Globe.

Heller, S. (1992). Worldwide 'diaspora' of peoples poses new challenges for scholars. *Chronicle of Higher Education, 38*(9), A7–9.

Helms, J. E. (Ed.). (1990). *Black and white racial identity: Theory, research and practice.* Westport, CT: Greenwood Press.

Heron, A. (1994). *Two teenagers in twenty.* Boston: Alyson.

Kjolseth, R. (1976). Bilingual education programs in the United States: For assimilation or pluralism? In F. Cordasco (Ed.), *Bilingual schooling in the United States* (pp. 122–140). New York: McGraw-Hill.

Ladson-Billings, G. (1994). *The dreamkeepers: Successful teachers of African American students.* San Francisco: Jossey-Bass.

Lauter, P. (1991). *Canons and contexts.* New York: Oxford University Press.

Leake, D. O., & Leake, B. L. (1992). Islands of hope: Milwaukee's African American immersion schools. *The Journal of Negro Education, 61*(1), 24–29.

Linn, M. C., & Hyde, J. A. (1989). Gender, mathematics and science. *Educational Researcher, 18*(8), 17–27.

Loutzenheiser, L. W. (1996). How schools play smear the queer. *Feminist Teacher, 10*(2).

Maher, F., & Tetreault, M. (1994). *The feminist classroom: An inside look at how professors and students are transforming higher education for a diverse society.* New York: Basic Books.

Mazumdar, S. (1989). A woman-centered perspective on Asian American history. In Asian Women United of California (Eds.), *Making waves: An anthology of writings by and about Asian American women* (pp. 1–24). Boston: Beacon Press.

Muñoz, C., Jr. (1984). The development of Chicano studies 1968–1981. In E. E. Garcia, F. A. Lomeli, & I. D. Ortiz (Eds.), *Chicano studies: A multidisciplinary approach* (pp. 5–18). New York: Teachers College Press.

Nakanishi, D. T., & Leong, R. (1978). Toward the second decade, a national survey of Asian American studies programs. *Amerasia Journal, 5*, 1–2.

National Schools Public Relations Association. (1970). *Black studies in schools.* Special report. Washington, DC: Author.

A national survey of lesbian and gay college programs. (1990/91). *Empathy, 2*(2), 53–56.

Newton, J. H. (1939). *Education for democracy in our time.* New York: McGraw-Hill.

Nochlin, L. (1971). Why are there no great women artists? In V. Gornick & B. K. Moran (Eds.), *Woman in sexist society* (pp. 480–510). New York: Basic Books.

Norman, R. (1975). The neutral teacher? In S. C. Brown (Ed.), *Philosophers discuss education* (pp. 172–187). Totowa, NJ: Rownan & Littlefield.

Pagano, J. A. (1990). *Exiles and communities: Teaching in the patriarchal wilderness.* Albany, NY: SUNY Press.

Paley, N. (1995). *Finding art's place: Experiments in contemporary education and culture.* New York: Routledge.

Palladino, G. (1997). Telling labor's story. *Labor's Heritage, 8*(3), 4–17.

Pentony, D. V. E. (1971). The case for black studies. In J. E. Blassingame (Ed.), *New perspectives on black studies* (pp. 60–72). Urbana: University of Illinois Press.

Portland Public Schools. (1989). *African American Baseline Essays.* Portland, OR: Author.

Ramirez, M., & Castaneda, A. (1976). *Cultural democracy, bicognitive development, and education.* New York: Academic Press.

Ratteray, J. D. (1990). African-American achievement: A research agenda emphasizing independent schools. In K. Lomotey (Ed.), *Going to school: The African-American experience* (pp. 197–208). Albany, NY: SUNY Press.

Rutenberg, T. (1983). Learning women's studies. In G. Bowles & R. D. Klein (Eds.), *Theories of women's studies* (pp. 72–78). London: Routledge & Kegan Paul.

Satz, R. N., Gulig, A. G., & St. Germaine, R. (1991). *Classroom activities in Chippewa treaty rights.* Madison, WI: Department of Public Instruction.

Schmitz, B. (1985). *Integrating women's studies into the curriculum.* Old Westbury, NY: Feminist Press.

Sears, J. T. (1992). The impact of culture and ideology on the construction of gender and sexual identities. In J. T. Sears (Ed.), *Sexuality and the curriculum* (pp. 139–156), New York: Teachers College Press.

Sleeter, C. E., & Grant, C. A. (1991). Race, class, gender, and disability in current textbooks. In M. W. Apple & L. K. Christian-Smith (Eds.), *The politics of the textbook* (pp. 78–110). New York: Routledge.

Spender, D. (1981). Education: The patriarchal paradigm and the response to feminism. In D. Spender (Ed.), *Men's studies modified: The impact of feminism on the academic disciplines* (pp. 155–173). New York: Pergamon.

Spring, J. (1973). Education as a form of social control. In C. Karier, P. Violas, & J. Spring (Eds.), *Roots of crisis: American education in the twentieth century* (pp. 30–39). Chicago: Rand McNally.

Spring, J. (1997). *The American school: 1642–1996.* New York: McGraw-Hill.

Suzuki, B. H. (1980). *An Asian-American perspective on multicultural education: Implications for practice and policy.* Paper presented at the Second Annual Conference of the National Association for Asian and Pacific American Education, Washington, DC.

Tatum, B. D. (1992). Teaching about race, learning about racism: The application of racial identity development in the classroom. *Harvard Educational Review, 62*(1), 1–24.

Tatum, C. (Ed.). (1990). *Mexican American literature.* New York: Harcourt Brace Jovanovich.

Tetreault, M. K. T. (1989). Integrating content about women and gender into the curriculum. In J. A. Banks & C. M. Banks (Eds.), *Multicultural education: Issues and perspectives* (pp. 124–144), Needham Heights, MA: Allyn & Bacon.

Trinh, T. M. (1991). *When the moon waxes red*. New York: Routledge.

Trueba, E. T. (1976). Issues and problems in bilingual bicultural education today. *Journal for the National Association of Bilingual Education, 1*, 11–19.

Tyack, D. (1966) Forming the national character. *Harvard Educational Review, 36*, 29–41.

Westkott, M. (1983). Women's studies as a strategy for change: Between criticism and vision. In G. Bowles & R. D. Klein (Eds.), *Theories of women's studies* (pp. 210–218). London: Routledge & Kegan Paul.

Woodward, J. R., & Elliott, M. (1992, May/June). What a difference a word makes! *The Disability Rag*, 14–15.

Woog, D. (1995). *School's out: The impact of gay and lesbian issues on America' schools*. Boston: Alyson.

CHAPTER FIVE

Multicultural Education

How can we have a Multicultural Education approach to multicultural education? We realize that this may be a bit confusing, so allow us to explain. *Multicultural Education* is a popular term and a growing field of study. The term itself is one educators use increasingly to describe education policies and practices that recognize, accept, and affirm human differences and similarities related to gender, race, disability, class, and (increasingly) sexual orientation. Because of the popularity of the term and what it advocates, many educators who use other approaches (e.g., Teaching the Exceptional and the Culturally Different) say they they are practicing multicultural education. Thus, it is important to clarify what most advocates of the Multicultural Education approach mean when they use the term.

GOALS

Based on a review of the literature on multicultural education, Gollnick (1980) has described it as having five goals:

1. Promoting the strength and value of cultural diversity
2. Promoting human rights and respect for those who are different from one-self
3. Promoting alternative life choices for people
4. Promoting social justice and equal opportunity for all people
5. Promoting equity in the distribution of power among groups

Although various educators emphasize and highlight one or two goals more than the others, most who advocate this approach embrace all five.

At present, many people who use this approach deal only with race and ethnicity (Banks, 1994, distinguishes in this regard between multicultural and multiethnic education) or only with gender (often termed sex equity, nonsexist education, or gender-fair education). Increasingly, those interested in mainstreaming are beginning to apply this approach to disability, although those interested primarily in social class tend not to adopt this approach for reasons we will explain later. Nevertheless, even though different terms may be used when educators discuss different groups, they advocate similar goals for their group, draw on much the same theories for achieving those goals, and recommend similar or identical practices in schools. Recognizing this, some educators explicitly give equal attention to multiple groups (Banks & Banks, 1997; Cushner, McClelland, & Safford, 1996; Gollnick & Chinn, 1998). Others who focus on one form of diversity do at least acknowledge other forms of diversity (Hernandez, 1989). This chapter will discuss race, gender, and disability, because these forms of diversity can be integrated and, increasingly, educators are doing so.

The Multicultural Education approach began in the late 1960s and grew energetically during the 1970s. Three forces converged during the mid-1960s and gave birth to this approach: The civil rights movement matured, school textbooks were critically analyzed, and assumptions underlying the deficiency orientation (described in Chapter 2) were reassessed. The civil rights movement began as a nonviolent way of changing laws that oppressed specific racial groups; by the late 1960s, it had become an energetic movement joining all Americans of color and directed toward self-determination and empowerment. An institution that was severely criticized at this time was the schools: As schools were desegregated, it became apparent that curricula were written solely or primarily about Whites. It also became apparent that many teachers knew little about students of color and treated cultural differences and not having English as a first language as deficiencies needing to be remediated. As Gay (1983) describes, "the student activists, abetted by the efforts of textbook analysts and by the new thinking about cultural differences, provided the stimulus for the first multiethnic education programs" (p. 561) (see also Grant & Ladson-Billings, 1997).

During the 1970s, these early ideas about school reform were tried and developed in many classrooms. Educators received encouragement and support from a variety of sources. Ethnic groups all around the United States developed expressions of their heritage and identity. The women's movement got well under way. Support for diversity was provided by a number of court cases and federal legislation such as the *Lau* decision supporting bilingual education, the Ethnic Heritage Act funding multiethnic curriculum development, and the adoption by many states of goal statements supporting teaching for cultural pluralism. These kinds of support diminished somewhat in the 1980s, as governmental policies became very conservative and an increasing number of critics of multicultural education became active, arguing that multicultural education was divisive and would be "disuniting" to the country. Also, lean economic conditions in the United States and a diminishing international status caused policy makers and educational administrators to argue that schools should return to the basics and put aside any curriculum that was thought to take students away from mathematics, science, reading, and writing. This argument, for the most part, continues even as we prepare to enter the 21st century. Schools are strongly encouraged to emphasize the basics, with special attention to science, math, and technology. In order to ensure the centrality of the basics, curriculum decisions have increasingly been moved from the hands of teachers and placed in the hands of test and policy makers.

Nevertheless, the Multicultural Education approach has continued to develop conceptually, and its popularity has continued to grow. Presently, multicultural education is an educational concept that most educators must profess to understand, even if they know little or nothing about it, because policy mandates require the inclusion of multicultural content in their courses (e.g., Wisconsin's human relations code points for teacher education students, California's multicultural standards for teacher education students, and Minnesota's multicultural and gender equity for public schools). Further, *multicultural education* has become a household term because of its increasing popularity in the media.

IDEOLOGY AND MULTICULTURAL EDUCATION

We distinguish in this chapter between theory and ideology because the Multicultural Education approach, more than the others, has experienced a mixing of the two concepts that can be confusing. Essentially, ideology prescribes what ought to be, whereas theory describes how social systems or human psychology actually works. Does *equal opportunity* describe a theory or an ideology? What about *cultural pluralism*? These are terms frequently employed by advocates of this approach. To understand and evaluate more clearly what advocates mean, we have divided our discussion into first ideology and then theory.

Newman (1973) describes an ideology as prescribing what "ought to be," and Mannheim (1956) says that ideologies are "those complexities of ideas which tend to generate activities toward changes in the prevailing order" (p. xxi). The large discrepancy between what ought to be and the current prevailing order in society encourages proponents of the Multicultural Education approach to argue for its implementation in school policies and practices.

Some of the earlier writings in multicultural education were based on the belief and knowledge that there is no one model American (Hunter, 1974); that the United States is a pluralistic nation, and its racial and cultural diversity needs to be recognized and prized (Stent, Hazard, & Rivlin, 1973); that women's history and point of view have been systematically ignored and omitted from the schools (Spender, 1982); and that poor people and people with disabilities have been rendered invisible. Advocates saw a need to correct the beliefs and ideas espoused by the prevailing order and to make school policies and practices affirm American diversity.

The vision of what ought to be was a major inspiration for the intellectual and emotional activities of the early advocates of this approach. The ideology of Multicultural Education is one of social change—not simply an integration into society of people who have been left out, but a change in the very fabric of that society. This ideology has two main components: cultural pluralism and equal opportunity. These components are noted as both societal goals and school goals in Table 5–1 and are described below.

Cultural Pluralism

Advocates of Multicultural Education often compare U.S. society to a tossed salad or a patchwork quilt. Both metaphors suggest the use of an array of materials and objects of various sizes, shapes, and colors. Each ingredient is dependent on the others, but each is still unique; together the ingredients form a collective total that

TABLE 5–1.
Multicultural Education

Societal goals:	Promote social structural equality and cultural pluralism (the United States as a "tossed salad")
School goals:	Promote equal opportunity in the school, cultural pluralism and alternative life styles, respect for those who differ, and support for power equity among groups.
Target students:	Everyone
Practices:	
Curriculum	Organize concepts around contributions and perspectives of several different groups; teach critical thinking, analysis of alternative viewpoints; make curriculum relevant to students' experiential backgrounds; promote use of more than one language
Instruction	Build on students' learning styles; adapt to students' skill levels; involve students actively in thinking and analyzing; use cooperative learning
Other aspects of classroom	Decorate classroom to reflect cultural pluralism, nontraditional sex roles, disabled people, and student interests
Support services	Help regular classroom adapt to as much diversity as possible
Other schoolwide concerns	Involve lower-class and minority parents actively in the school; encourage staffing patterns to include diverse racial, gender, and disability groups in nontraditional roles; make use of decorations, special events, and school menus that reflect and include diverse groups; use library materials that portray diverse groups in diverse roles; include all student groups in extracurricular activities, and do not reinforce stereotypes; make sure discipline procedures do not penalize any group; make sure building is accessible to disabled people

is distinguished by its diversity. There are a number of formal definitions of cultural pluralism in the education literature. Although these definitions vary, all suggest that cultural pluralism includes the maintenance of diversity, a respect for differences, and the right to participate actively in all aspects of society without having to give up one's unique identity.

The National Coalition for Cultural Pluralism (1973) described the concept as

A state of equal coexistence in a mutually supportive relationship within the boundaries or framework of one nation of people of diverse cultures with significantly different patterns of beliefs, behaviors, colors, and in many cases with different languages. To achieve cultural pluralism, there must be unity with diversity. Each person must be aware of and secure in his [her] own identity, and be willing to extend to others the same respect and rights that he [she] expects to enjoy himself [herself]. (p. 14)

Explicit in the definitions of cultural pluralism that have been advanced are references to race and ethnicity. Recently, advocates of the Multicultural Education approach have also begun arguing that because gender and class are also very important determinants of what happens, how it happens, and why it happens in society, these status attributes must also be considered in conceptualizing pluralism.

Those who advocate applying cultural pluralism to gender desire a society in which gender does not even hint at a particular sex role image and where females are evaluated not in comparison to males but in relationship to the best practices. For example, many women who enter into the corporate structure emulate the performance style of the successful male, trying to "make it in the man's world" instead of deciding what works for them in the world of work and basing their style on that. In the realm of educational administration, Bloom and Munro (1995) reveal the conflicted positions in which female school administrators find themselves as they seek to fulfill their roles successfully while not enmeshing themselves in masculinist discourses. Conflicts such as these are at the heart of why advocates of applying cultural pluralism to gender contend that both males and females should have equal opportunity for the occupation or profession of their choice, that domestic roles should be flexible and not defined by gender, and that society's socializing practices for the young should be nonsexist.

Androgyny provides one model of nonsexist choice making. As Ferguson (1977) explains:

> An androgynous person would combine some of each of the characteristic traits, skills, and interests that we now associate with stereotypes of masculinity and femininity ... He or she would have the desire and the ability to do socially meaningful productive activity (work), as well as the desire and ability to be autonomous and to relate lovingly to other human beings. (pp. 45–46)

This model opens up choices of roles and personality traits to both sexes. As Tavris and Wade (1984) observe:

> When people speak of liberating women and ending discrimination, they are generally thinking of how to get women out of the home and into the work force; they are generally not thinking of how to get men to do more at home. (p. 352)

Cultural pluralism related to gender means that males, as well as females, should have a gender-free repertoire of roles and styles to choose from. It also means that neither sex should be forced into a heterosexual lifestyle; people should be able to choose a heterosexual, gay, lesbian, or bisexual lifestyle without recrimination.

Many advocates of this approach agree on the need for a society in which poverty, as well as racism, does not exist. Their vision of society would expunge the need for governmental assistance, eliminate reliance on substandard housing, and ensure the provision of suitable clothing and health care for every individual. However, descriptions of how to make this vision a reality present a frontal attack on racism and only an indirect attack on class. Advocates of this approach seem to view race and class as overlapping factors that are mostly one and the same.

How much diversity and choice are possible in a society that still maintains a sense of cohesiveness? In the late 1980s, this question launched a tidal wave of attacks on Multicultural Education, which we review briefly in the critique section of this chapter. Advocates of the Multicultural Education approach maintain that U.S. society has never had real cohesiveness nor consensus about a common culture because many segments of society have been locked out of decision making. For example, White, middle-class educators sometimes look back to a supposed Golden Age of harmony and consensus during the early 1950s, wondering if an interest in pluralism has destroyed the consensus that was enjoyed then. However, during the early 1950s were African Americans actually full participants in society and could they freely voice concerns from their perspectives? The answer is no. Native Americans during that time were dealing with a U.S. policy of termination of tribal status, Mexican American children were being punished for speaking Spanish in school, and Japanese Americans were trying to deal with the fact that they had been put in concentration camps because they appeared "too different." Women were being returned to the home from the workplace and encouraged to stay there. Gay and lesbian people usually hid in the closet because their life styles were so unacceptable to most Americans. In other words, diversity was suppressed and discouraged; people who did not fit the dominant conception of how life should be lived were not supported; and people of color were denied entrance into many facets of American life. The question advocates of Multicultural Education ask is, Given the real diversity that exists in American society, how can we learn to support and respect that diversity rather than suppress and deny it?

Equal Opportunity

Equal opportunity is the other main pillar of the ideology of Multicultural Education. Equal opportunity as a legal right in education was established in 1954 in *Brown v. Board of Education*. In that decision, Chief Justice Warren wrote:

> In these days it is doubtful that any child may reasonably be expected to succeed in life if he [or she] is denied the opportunity of an education. Such an opportunity, where the state has undertaken it, is a right which must be made available to all on equal terms.

Since that decision, exactly what school practices constitute equal opportunity has been an issue of considerable debate, and as Gee and Sperry (1978) put it, "equal educational opportunity may mean all things to all people" (p. E-9).

The "business as usual" position is that because it is illegal to deny students access to education on the basis of race, sex, language, or disability, schools that comply with equal opportunity laws and court decisions such as Title IX, PL 94–142, and *Lau v. Nichols* are providing equal opportunity. According to O'Neill (1977):

> On this view, once the rules governing admissions to places of education, appointments to jobs and promotions are fair, a society is an equal-opportunity society ... If women are not barred from engineering school on account of their sex, then they have equal opportunity to become engineers—and the fact that very few do so cannot be attributed to any inequality of opportunity. (p. 179)

Advocates of the Multicultural Education approach do not see it as sufficient simply to remove legal barriers to access and participation in schooling. So long as groups do not gain equal outcomes from social institutions, those institutions are not providing equal opportunity. So long as White, middle-class children succeed and leave school with higher achievement scores than other children, so long as disproportionate numbers of boys enter mathematics and science fields and girls enter human service or domestic work after schooling, so long as children leave school seeing White male contributions as most important, schools have not provided equal opportunity. O'Neill (1977) argues that "an equal-opportunity society on the substantive view is one in which the success rates of all major social groups are the same" (pp. 181–182).

Plenty has been written from a Multicultural Education perspective about what equal educational opportunity should mean in schools as it relates to race, culture, language, gender, and disability. We will summarize the main ideas.

Advocates of equal educational opportunity related to gender wish to promote for members of both sexes an equal opportunity to choose occupational roles and life styles, to express feelings and interests, and to be rewarded for work. Gough (1976) voices these goals in raising questions about the extent to which an education program is nonsexist:

> Does it give girls the freedom to have "doctor" and "professor" in their matrix of career choices along with "truck driver," and "telephone lineperson," or whatever else suits their interests and talents? Does it make boys comfortable with expressing gentleness, grief, delight in small children, dislike of athletics? (p. 33)

In other words, the whole spectrum of roles, careers, emotions, and behavioral patterns should be equally available to male and female alike, without regard to gender.

Schools should not only encourage children to make choices free of sex role conditioning, schools should themselves reflect equal opportunity. In Chapter 1, we described ways in which they often do not. The conditions in schools that Stockard et al. pointed out in 1980 are still very much the conditions in schools as we get ready for the new millennium,

> In the elementary school, the principal is probably a man and the first grade teacher a woman ... Men often teach science, social studies, and math; women more often teach English and foreign languages. ... Where allowed to take elective classes, although there is an increasing improvement toward gender balance, girls and boys based upon their gender still differentiate between the course they take ... Principals are usually men, and superintendents and assistant superintendents are almost certainly men.
>
> ... Among the nonprofessional, virtually all members of the clerical and secretarial staff are women; men are usually employed as custodians. (pp. 3–5)

Advocates of equal educational opportunity related to disability generally wish to see all children with disabilities educated in the least restrictive environment, and they particularly wish to see the regular classroom accommodate differences better than it usually does. For example, Reynolds and Birch (1988) explain that,

> Mainstreaming means providing special educational and related services to exceptional children while they attend regular classes in schools ... It requires profession-

als to acquire new ideas and skills and it calls for changes in school organizations, educational policies, and funding systems. (p. 1)

Kohler and Rusch (1995), in the *Handbook of Special and Remedial Education*, write that, whereas the concept of mainstreaming

> exemplified the notion of "fixing" students, the more contemporary *regular education initiative* (REI) supports the emerging focus upon *individuals*. Mainstreaming typically involved educating students in regular classrooms with supoort services provided by a "resource" teacher. Support services were focused on bringing the performance of the mainstreamed student up to the level expected of all students in the classroom. Thus, mainstreaming tended to address the deficits of students in their attempts to perform in a typical academic curriculum. (p. 115)

Inclusion, or "inclusive education," in contrast,

> focuses on *individual* goals and abilities of students with disabilities within regular education classrooms. With this focus on individuals rather than on subject matter, course content and associated performance standards may vary for particular students. Although inclusive education remains embroiled in controversy, more and more communities are attempting to include their students with disabilities in regular education classrooms. Research on student performance in inclusive classrooms is in its beginning stages; however, to date, data indicate that teachers who have participated in inclusion have positive perceptions and see benefits to their students, both with and without disabilities. (Giangreco, Dennis, Cloninger, Edelman, & Schattman, 1993, p. 115; Janney, Snell, Beers, & Raynes, 1995)

Many would argue that schools and classrooms that do not provide for differences in learning style, rate, interest, and so forth actually make children disabled by defining them as deviant. Ysseldyke, Thurlow, Graden, Wesson, and Algozzine (1983) have found that the main determinant of whether a child is classified as disabled is whether a regular education teacher was bothered enough by the child to refer him or her for psychoeducational evaluation:

> From 3% to 6% of the school-age population is referred each year for psychoeducational evaluation. Of those referred, 92% are tested. Of those tested, 73% are declared eligible for special educational services. …When we investigated the specific determinants of referral, we found that teachers tend to refer students who bother them. (p. 80)

According to the Multicultural Education approach, equal educational opportunity should mean that regular classrooms accommodate a wide enough spectrum of human diversity so that only those children who would be seen as disabled in virtually any social setting (e.g., children who are blind or severely retarded) would be seen as exceptional in school. Such classrooms would prevent large numbers of children from ever being labeled as disabled and would welcome for at least a portion of their school day those who truly are disabled.

Advocates of equal educational opportunity related to race, culture, and language make arguments very similar to those we have already discussed. The central ideas are that children should have an equal chance to achieve in school, choose and strive for a personally fulfilling future, and develop self-respect, regardless of home culture or language. Sizemore, writing in 1979, describes some very large barriers that schools erect for children of color that would undercut students of color receiving equal opportunity:

> Incredibly, the curriculum of a diverse population is based on the characteristics, life experiences, and culture of one minority: the Anglo-Saxon affluent Protestant group. Characteristically, the monolingual, monocultural, and unidimensional curriculum which created cell block classrooms with single age groupings evolved. (p. 341)

Gay (1979) pointed out that this situation often leads children of color to "experience alienation and isolation in American schools" (p. 327). To provide equal opportunity for children of all American cultural backgrounds, Sizemore (1979) proposes that the classroom should be "multilingual, multicultural, multimodal, and multidimensional in its focus" (p. 348). Such a classroom would support curriculum content drawn from a variety of cultural backgrounds, the development of more than one language, varied instructional styles and systems for grouping students, and evaluative measures that respect differences in cultural background. As Gay (1979) argues:

> Children who are secure in their identity, feel good about themselves, and are excited about what is happening in the classroom, are more likely to engage eagerly in learning activities and achieve higher levels of academic performance than those who find the classroom hostile, unfriendly, insensitive, and perpetually unfamiliar. (p. 327)

THEORY AND MULTICULTURAL EDUCATION

If advocates of Multicultural Education champion equal opportunity, choice, and cultural pluralism, what theoretical propositions inform us as to how this vision can be realized and how schools can help realize it? First, let us define what we mean by *theoretical propositions*. Writing about theories of cultural pluralism, Newman (1973) says that theory explains "how a phenomenon has arrived historically, how it works or what its meaning is empirically, and, under given circumstances, what one may expect in the future" (p. 50). Writing about theories of gender relations, Tavris and Wade (1984) explain that theory "attempts to account for sex differences"—why they exist and the circumstances under which relationships between men and women change (p. 119).

Advocates of Multicultural Education as it relates to race and ethnicity have written much more about ideology than about theory—more about what ought to be than about why things are as they are and under what conditions things change in the desired direction. However, supporting theories from the fields of sociology and anthropology have usually been adopted by educators. Advocates of a Multicultural Education approach to gender, on the other hand, have written more about the theory of how sex roles are learned than about ideology. The two main kinds of theories that support the ideology of Multicultural Education are cultural pluralism theories and cultural transmission theories.

Theories of Cultural Pluralism

William Newman (1973) has provided a comprehensive discussion of theories of cultural pluralism and their use by sociologists. We will briefly summarize four main theories and show their relevance to the Multicultural Education approach.

The first theory is assimilation. Newman expresses it with "the formula A + B + C = A, where A, B, and C represent different social groups and A represents the dominant group" (p. 53). The theory holds that when minority cultural groups come into contact with a majority cultural group, over time the values and life styles of the minority groups are replaced by those of the majority group. Newman shows that while some sociological studies support this theory (such as studies of second-generation immigrants), other studies do not (such as studies of third-generation immigrants or of the ethnic resurgence of the 1960s, 1970s and 1980s). In other words, some degree of cultural assimilation usually occurs, but often it is limited and even reverses itself after a time. Cultural assimilation is not a rule of American life.

According to Multicultural Education advocates, much schooling has been based on, and has sought to facilitate, the faulty theory of assimilation. "Business as usual" has assumed that the majority culture not only should prevail but will prevail. It has sought to promote, for example, one language and one dialect, one version of history, one literary tradition, one view of the relationship between people and nature, and so forth. In so doing, "business as usual" has often contradicted reality. For example, for many years, schools, especially in the Southwest, had an English-only policy in an effort to erase the Spanish language and Mexican culture. However, rather than dropping Spanish, thousands of children quit (and often were forced out of) school. Spanish has continued to be spoken throughout the Southwest. During the 1970s, bilingual education was increasingly implemented, although there have been heated debates about whether its purpose is primarily to teach English or to teach both languages (Cummins, 1981a, 1981b; Fillmore & Valadez, 1985; Krashen, 1981; Skutnabb-Kangas, 1981; Trueba, 1976). In an ethnography of a Chinese-English bilingual program, Guthrie (1985) shows that regardless of school policy, there are both a need and a desire to maintain the Chinese language within the Chinese American community; assimilationist school practices that deny this reality are misinformed and often place children and teachers in the middle.

Children are often the victims of assimilationist school policies, particularly when "business as usual" teaches children that the home culture is inferior or un-American, when it disrupts a child's ability to function in his or her own community, or when it alienates children and causes them to reject school. Assimilationist policies can drive a wedge between the child and his or her family, which can interfere with normal socialization. This problem is particularly troublesome when teachers tell students whose first language is not English to refrain from speaking their native language in the home in order to practice English; not only does this practice impair communication development, but it weakens the family's power to teach its values and beliefs to the child. Assimilationist school policies are also harmful when they reinforce the mistaken idea in the minds of majority-group children that their home culture is the only true American culture and that everyone else wants to or should think, behave, and speak as they do.

Sometimes, children recognize that the school version of reality is incorrect. For example, one of the authors was recently told of an incident in an elementary school. The children were completing some reading exercises that contained content describing a world with definite sex roles. One of the questions read:

Which of the following gifts would a girl not receive at a birthday party?

    a. A doll
    b. A toy gun
    c. A makeup kit
    d. A tea set

The students replied that the answer that the test developers wanted was "a toy gun" but that this answer was not really true. Unfortunately, children usually do not see through school knowledge that conflicts with what they know. In such cases, they may doubt what they have learned at home, try to reconcile conflicting views of reality, or reject the school because the teachers seem stupid.

The second theory Newman (1973) describes is amalgamation, which he represents with the formula $A + B + C = D$, where "D represents an amalgam, a synthesis of these groups into a distinct new group" (p. 63). Newman points out that although many people have articulated this concept as the ideal of the melting pot, the theory of amalgamation describes very little of intergroup relations. One can point to infrequent examples of amalgamation, such as Mexican culture being an amalgam of Spanish and Indian cultures, but such examples are the exception. For cultures to blend, the groups should be of roughly equal status and the people should desire to mix. In the United States, ethnic groups are definitely not all of the same status. Because it has so little relevance for group life in America, amalgamation has little or no relevance to school policy.

The third theory Newman describes is classical cultural pluralism, "expressed in the formula $A + B + C = A + B + C$, where A, B, and C represent different social groups that, over time, maintain their own unique identities" (p. 67). Newman argues that this theory does not explain all of ethnic life in America, but it explains enough that it needs to be taken seriously. Most American cities and many suburban areas contain distinct ethnic enclaves that do not disappear over time. In fact, some have become stronger, and some ethnic and religious communities maintain themselves in spite of dispersed membership. For example, a Jewish family that moves to North Dakota immediately joins the only local synagogue and develops ties with the few other Jewish families in town. As another example, the African American community maintains some of its solidarity and cultural distinctiveness, in spite of dispersed membership, by developing Black radio stations, magazines, and newspapers.

Yet, as Newman points out, this theory is inadequate. It fails to account for the development of a shared American culture, for the cultural changes that groups experience over time, and for the varied experiences of different cultural groups. A more accurate theory is modified cultural pluralism: $A + B + C = A1 + B1 + C1$. As Newman illustrates, "An Italian in Italy is different from an Italian-American … A black African is different from an African-American" (p. 79). Modified cultural pluralism holds that different ethnic, religious, and racial groups will assimilate into the dominant group to some extent, but that this assimilation will vary with the group, and many groups will continue to retain unique cultural characteristics. As a description of group life in America, this theory is more accurate than the preceding three.

Modified cultural pluralism is one of the theories that supports the Multicultural Education approach. The approach advocates that, at the very least, schools should represent cultural pluralism as it actually exists in America. To the extent that it exists, the shared culture should be recognized and taught; but equally important, the cultural diversity that actually exists should also be recognized and taught to all Americans. For example, all students should be taught that there is no single American literary tradition, nor has there ever been one. Schools that teach either implicitly or explicitly that good literature is only what White men have written or that White men have been the only authors of good literature are not teaching reality. White male authors may feel that their work is superior to African American female writers, for instance, but African American women tend not to share their perspective (Hull, Scott, & Smith, 1982). Young Americans need to learn diverse perspectives about what constitutes good literature, as well as become familiar with the literature produced by diverse American literary traditions. This knowledge will not exacerbate divisiveness among cultural groups, as critics of Multicultural Education often argue; on the other hand, it may improve relationships by fostering dialogue among groups that will continue regardless of school policies and practices.

This last point is worth emphasizing. Modified cultural pluralism holds that some cultural diversity will continue to exist in a nation the size of the United States, despite attempts by the dominant group to assimilate people. Forced assimilation will only antagonize groups. If some degree of cultural diversity is natural, then it makes sense that schools embrace this diversity rather than pretending that it is not there or that it is harmful to the country.

You have probably noticed that this discussion has given little attention to disability or gender. Cultural pluralism theory has some applicability to disability in that America does contain subcultures of deaf, blind, and physically impaired people. Like ethnic groups, these groups share a common American culture, but they also maintain some group cohesion and distinctive cultural characteristics. Although necessity often plays a larger role than choice in the development of disability cultural groups, nevertheless the implications for Multicultural Education are similar. For example, wheelchair sports are well developed and command a fairly high level of participation. Physical education programs that fail even to alert young people to the existence of wheelchair sports are perpetuating a limited conception of American athletics.

When it comes to gender, cultural pluralism theory has less relevance. One can argue that males and females have distinct cultures; for example, compare the contents of *Ladies' Home Journal* with that of *Gentlemen's Quarterly (GQ)*. However, feminist advocates of the Multicultural Education approach seek to reduce rather than preserve gender cultural differences, not by assimilating females into the male world, but rather by upholding alternative interests and life styles that can be chosen by individuals without regard to gender. To provide a theoretical basis for this strategy, we turn to theories of how culture and roles are learned.

Cultural Transmission and Social Learning Theories

The ideology of Multicultural Education highlights cultural diversity and encourages awareness and knowledge about diverse alternatives. The approach does not advocate that the world is fine as it is and that children should learn more about it. Rather, the approach is born of a concern that society as it exists is unfair and detrimental to many people. Society does not afford equal opportunity to all. Furthermore, people are expected to conform to restricted definitions of what is considered normal if they want to succeed. For example, people of all ethnic backgrounds are often expected to display the behavioral and linguistic style of White, middle class Americans before they are taken seriously. Women who do not adhere to expected sex roles are labeled aggressive or masculine, whereas men who do not conform to the he-man image are often viewed as effeminate. Multicultural Education seeks to have all American children learn knowledge, values, and behavioral patterns that support cultural diversity, flexibility, and choice.

Theories of cultural transmission, social learning, and modeling provide guidance by alerting teachers to how children normally acquire society's values and beliefs. Teachers who want their students to learn values and beliefs for a multicultural society will need to change the content of what is usually transmitted to make it congruent with the ideology of Multicultural Education.

Cultural transmission theory was developed in the field of anthropology, social learning and modeling theory in the field of psychology. We will first explain how these theories are similar, then discuss their contribution to Multicultural Education.

To anthropologists, cultural transmission refers to the wide variety of ways members of a cultural group transmit their culture to the younger generation. Although some of this transmission takes place in the school, much also takes place in the home, religious institutions, and neighborhood.

Social learning theory and modeling theory (often used by scholars of sex role socialization) describe principles by which individuals learn particular behavioral patterns. In Chapter 3 we described Bandura and Walters' (1963) theory of prejudice formation; their work in social learning theory also has relevance here. Social learning theorists focus on the consequences that follow behavior patterns, and modeling theorists focus on the process of imitating role models. Social learning theory as articulated by Bandura and Walters argues that children learn alternative behavior patterns by observing adults, then learn when to imitate this behavior through reinforcement. For example, girls learn indirect and nonaggressive speech patterns by listening to older females speak; they learn to use such speech patterns themselves as others react favorably to them when they have imitated such patterns. Sex role theorists also usually discuss cognitive development theory, which we presented in Chapter 3; this theory describes the mental process of constructing stereotypes (Tavris & Wade, 1984). All these theories argue that children are strongly molded and shaped by their environments and that the values, beliefs, and behavioral patterns that young people develop result from the constant press of their social environment.

One implication of these theories is that children learn through a complex variety of messages. Often, when we think of teaching, we think of telling; both anthropologists and psychologists inform us that this way of thinking about teaching is a great oversimplification. For example, Tavris and Wade (1984) describe a host of sources of information about sex roles, including how parents treat each sex, how teachers treat each sex in the classroom, toys given to each sex, messages in children's books, messages in television, sexism in language (e.g., the "use of men or mankind to refer to humanity," p. 233), and sex-different styles of speech. Thus, a teacher might tell children that males and females are equal yet teach children that they are different and that males are more important in a variety of unconscious ways.

As another example, Spindler (1974) describes the process of cultural transmission in eight very different societies. His main point is that although the content and many of the particulars of the transmitting process differ from one society to the next, the general process is similar:

> If a child is told, sees demonstrated, casually observes, imitates, experiments and is corrected, acts appropriately and is rewarded, corrected, and … is given an extra boost in learning by dramatized announcements of status-role change, all within a consistent framework of belief and value, he or she cannot help but learn, and learn what adult cultural transmitters want him or her to learn. (p. 300)

What this process means to the teacher is that if one wants children to learn to value America's cultural diversity and to value nonsexist options, it is not enough simply to tell children that these elements should be valued. The whole environment of the school must be teaching this concept. Consider, for example, a music class in which most of the music the children are taught was written by White men and is embedded within the classical European tradition. The teacher may never say a word about which group writes the best music, but the fact that one music tradition receives the most emphasis teaches children which music is "best." If one wanted children to value diverse music traditions, one would model this concept by teaching and giving roughly equal emphasis to music written by members of diverse groups. In another example, which one of the authors actually observed, the English department in a high school offered two courses, one course entitled "Great Authors of the Past" and the other course entitled "Recent English and American Authors." The course "Great Authors of the Past" included only writings by White male authors and a few White female authors. The course "Recent English and American Authors" included both female authors and authors of color. This bifurcation of knowledge, presented in a seemingly unbiased manner, can suggest to students, among other things, the notion that great authors are only White and mostly male. If these courses are still being offered, the teachers should consider changing the titles of the courses as well as their organization and curriculum.

A second implication of cultural transmission theory has to do with the nature of culture in complex societies. Culture consists of shared understandings and beliefs, but not everyone in society shares identical knowledge and beliefs. Good-enough (1976) points out that "the different ways of doing things family to family and village to village, all become noteworthy" (p. 4). Each society consists of many subsocieties. A child does not simply learn a single, homogeneous American culture. Rather, as Goodenough argues:

> The process of learning a society's culture, or macro-culture, as I would call it, is one of learning a number of different or partially different microcultures and their subcultural variants, and how to discern the situations in which they are appropriate and the kinds of others to whom to attribute them. (p. 5)

This insight has relevance for the ideal of equal opportunity. For equal opportunity to exist, members of diverse groups need to learn the cultures appropriate to functioning successfully in various contexts. It is imperative for members of marginalized cultural groups to learn to function successfully in mainstream cultural groups. For example, children whose home language or dialect is not Standard English need to develop competence in Standard English, as well as the ability to know which situations require them to use Standard English. Schools that fail to teach members of marginalized groups the language, behavioral patterns, and knowledge of the dominant cultural group are not providing the means for more equal opportunities in society.

Nevertheless, it is also valuable to learn to function successfully in groups other than the dominant one. Banks (1994) points out that it is "very difficult for Anglo-Americans to learn to respond to nonWhites positively and sensitively if they are unaware of the perceptions of their culture that are held by other ethnic groups and of the ways in which the dominant culture evolved and attained the power to shape the United States in its image" (p. 99). To develop cultural sensitivity, Anglo Americans need to learn the cultures of other American subgroups and should learn them well enough to be able to function appropriately within at least one or two other cultural contexts.

Thus, to be successfully educated it is not enough to learn only the dominant culture. This shift in our thinking requires redefining success in schools and codifying cultural diversity into the measures we use to assess school success. For example, science from a multicultural perspective would include scientific theories of Native Americans in addition to those of the European tradition; thus, the successful student of science would have a working knowledge of more than one science tradition. The edge currently enjoyed by White, middle-class children—mastery of whose culture currently constitutes school success—would be shared with other groups.

One can also relate this idea to gender and disability. Child care, for example, tends to be a female cultural domain, while automobile repair tends to be a male domain. It is not uncommon for men and women to have nonsexist intentions, but they end up assuming traditional sex roles simply because, in the course of growing up, the women learned how to change diapers proficiently while the men mastered the fine art of tuning up an engine. Outside school, children often learn sex-specific domains of knowledge; to prepare both sexes for multiple roles, the schools would need to teach to both sexes knowledge that usually tends to be learned by only one sex.

With respect to disability, the concept of subsocieties implies that children not only learn to question stereotypes of disabled people but also learn how to function in disability cultural groups. This learning could mean becoming proficient in sign language or in wheelchair basketball and becoming aware of the norms and perspectives shared by people who use these skills.

A third implication of cultural transmission theory was already stated in Chapter 2 and will be briefly mentioned here—the concept of cultural compatibility. Educational anthropologists and psychologists have found it difficult for some children to learn what the teacher is trying to teach when the teaching style, communication style, cognitive schemata, or background experience of the teacher is different from that of the child. As anthropologist Solon Kimball (1974) emphasizes:

> New learnings always take place within the perceptive system of the individual being taught. Children from subcultural groupings other than those of the teacher face a difficult problem in adjusting, if they do, to the demands of the teacher and she [or he] in turn, to their ways of behaving and thinking. (p. 82)

A teacher implementing the Multicultural Education approach, like a teacher implementing the Teaching the Exceptional and the Culturally Different approach, would try to make the process as well as the content of learning as compatible as possible with that of the students' home culture. As a result, Multicultural Education in rural Oregon, for example, would not be identical to Multicultural Education in inner-city Chicago, because each implementation would reflect the styles of learning and experiential and contextual backgrounds of the children being taught in order to maximize their ability to learn.

RECOMMENDED PRACTICES

The Multicultural Education approach seeks to reform the entire process of schooling for all children. Unlike the Teaching the Exceptional and Culturally Different approach, this approach is not just for certain groups of students. It is for everybody, and it seeks not only to integrate people into our existing society but to improve society for all. Unlike the Human Relations approach, the Multicultural Education approach does not stop with the improvement of attitudes but seeks also to develop skills and a strong knowledge base that will support multiculturalism. Unlike the Single-Group Studies approach, it seeks to change more about schooling than just the curriculum. We have organized our discussion of recommended practices around the following typical elements of schooling: curriculum, instruction, evaluation, home/community-school relationships, staffing, and extracurricular activities. Recommended Multicultural Education practices are summarized in Table 5–1.

Curriculum
Multicultural Education advocates argue that the curriculum should be reformed so that it regularly presents diverse perspectives, experiences, and contributions, particularly those that tend to be omitted or misrepresented when schools conduct

"business as usual." Concepts should be selected and taught to represent diverse cultural groups and both sexes (Baker, 1983; Banks, 1989, 1994; Gay, 1975; Gollnick & Chinn, 1998; Grant, 1977; Grant & Sleeter, 1989; King, 1990; Nieto, 1996; Sadker & Sadker, 1982, 1994; Sleeter, 1992). Gay's argument in 1975 still holds true in 1998:

> Fragmented and isolated units, courses, and bits of information about ethnic groups interspersed sporadically into school curriculum and instructional programs will not do the job. Nor will additive approaches, wherein school curricula remain basically the same, and ethnic content becomes an appendage. (p. 176)

For example, if one is teaching poetry, one should select poetry written by members of a variety of groups. This approach not only teaches children that groups in addition to White men have written poetry; it also enriches the concept of poetry because it enables children to explore various poetic forms as well as study those elements that are common to diverse poems. It is further recommended that the contributions and perspectives that a teacher selects depict each group as the group would depict itself and show the group as active and dynamic. To make such selections a teacher must learn about various groups and become sensitive to aspects of each group's culture that are important to that group. For example, teachers wishing to include Native Americans in the curriculum sometimes choose Sacajawea as a heroine to discuss; but from the Native American perspective, Sequoya would be a preferable historic figure. Sacajawea served White interests by leading Lewis and Clark west, whereas Sequoya served the interests of the Cherokee by developing an alphabet for encoding the Cherokee language.

A related recommendation is that curricular materials and all visual displays (such as posters) be free of race, gender, and disability stereotypes and include members of all groups in a positive manner (Grant, 1977; Hernandez, 1989; Seaburg, Smith, & Gallaher, 1980; Sleeter, 1992; Tiedt & Tiedt, 1995). In this regard current materials have improved, but teachers still need to examine them closely. For example, recent studies have found that Hispanic Americans, contemporary Native Americans, and Asian Americans—particularly the female members of these groups—still often receive token representation and are sometimes stereotyped; the roles of males are still stereotyped, even though the roles of females (particularly White females) have been broadened; interpretations of history continue to reflect the interests of wealthy people, military officials, and politicians; and individuals with disabilities and people who are gay are rarely seen (Sleeter & Grant, 1991).

Advocates of the Multicultural Education approach continue to recommend that teachers make sure they are teaching complete concepts related to diverse groups, rather than simply fragments of information (Baker, 1983; Banks, 1989, 1994; Gay, 1975, 1979; Grant & Sleeter, 1989, 1996; Nieto, 1996; Sleeter, 1992). Sometimes, teachers try to represent people of color and women by grafting bits and pieces onto traditional concepts. For example, Cortes (1973) points out that it is not enough to add a few Mexicans to a representation of U.S. history that is organized around the ideas of manifest destiny and the westward flow of culture. From a Mexican perspective, the U.S. Southwest was gained through conquest, and culture has flowed northward as well as westward.

Diverse materials should be used to present diverse viewpoints. Students should become comfortable with the fact that often there is more than one perspective, and rather than believing only one version, they should learn to expect and seek out multiple versions.

For example, New York City Public Schools (1990) published a United States and New York history curriculum. The guide emphasizes four themes: "Culture/Diversity," "Movements of People," "Contributions," and "Struggle for Equality" (p. viii). Each unit examines a theme or time period from the perspectives of three or four different American sociocultural groups, such as EuroAmericans, Native Americans, and African Americans. Students are provided with diverse perspectives—then encouraged to analyze these perspectives and come to their own conclusions, rather than a textbook author's conclusion.

Some advocates recommend that as much emphasis be placed on contemporary culture as on historic culture and that groups be represented as active, real, and dynamic (Gay, 1979). For example, the women included in history, for the most part, are usually White women who are involved in so-called women's issues—for example, the suffrage movement. The information thus conveyed is only a small fraction of what could be taught about women in social studies. African American women, too, have always actively resisted oppression. Many have become involved (both historically and today) in African American women's clubs working to improve social conditions; many have had outstanding accomplishments; and many others have been (and still are) brutally victimized (Giddings, 1985). Oversimplified bits of information can be misleading and can lead to stereotyping.

Similarly, Stearns (1988) advocates the teaching of social history. According to Stearns, "social historians study not only ordinary people but also the ordinary aspects of life" (p. 142). He adds,

> The basic argument here was that groups outside the mainstream of conventional history—that is, groups that were not producers of formal or higher culture or did not include individually identifiable actors on the political scene—had a past in their own right. Further, such groups were not simply acted upon by leaders of society or even by anonymous forces such as economic cycles. Though lacking an equal share of society's power and wealth, the inarticulate definitely played a role in shaping their own values and habits. (p. 142)

All these recommendations should permeate the total curriculum. In other words, all subject areas should be taught multiculturally all the time. As Nieto (1996) puts it, Multicultural Education is a process of school reform that "permeates the curriculum and instructional strategies used in schools, as well as the interactions among teachers, students and parents, and the very way that schools conceptualize the nature of teaching and learning" (p. 307).

The language used in the curriculum and by the teacher should be nonsexist. Gollnick, Sadker, and Sadker (1982) point out the problems with using masculine nouns and pronouns, such as *caveman*, *forefathers*, and *he*, to refer to both sexes. When children hear these terms, they usually interpret them literally. When they hear the word *caveman*, they visualize a man. The teacher might protest that words such as *congressman* and *businessman* refer to man and woman alike, but to a child they do not. Not only do the words designate one sex, but real life often confirms this designation. Thus, girls who hear about congressmen and study mainly or only male members of Congress may never entertain the idea that they could one day serve in Congress themselves.

Advocates often recommend that multicultural curricula endorse bilingual education and a vision of a multilingual society. In an earlier chapter, we discussed approaches to bilingual education that are directed toward those who do not speak English. Bilingual education can also be provided to all students in a school. Trueba (1976) advocates that all Americans should become "capable of thinking and feeling in either of two cultural and linguistic systems independently, and of interacting effectively and appropriately with the two linguistic and cultural groups" (p. 14). One of the authors of this book was visiting a bilingual school in New York. He was sitting in the office when some African American students entered and addressed him in Spanish. They were surprised to realize that he (like most Americans) was limited to only one language. This example also illustrates how promoting bilingualism among students of color extends language learning from the once privileged elite culture of the middle and upper classes to all groups. Some people also recommend that sign language be recognized as a complete, legitimate language, because it is the fourth most commonly used language in the United States, behind English, Spanish, and German.

Advocates of Multicultural Education, like those of Teaching the Culturally Different, recommend that the curriculum relate to and draw on students' experiential background and the community and that examples used to explain concepts be based on students' daily life experiences. The curriculum should "bring the community into the schools and ... bring the school to the community" (Foerster, 1982, p. 125). Soto (1997) continues that line of reasoning when she argues about the academic and social importance of the schools taking the background of Hispanic students into account when planning and teaching the curriculum.

Finally, some educators address the need for access to the curriculum, recommending that schools adopt policies to ensure accessibility for all groups. For example, Gollnick and Chinn (1998) recommend that "minority students, as well as white students ... make up the college preparatory and general education classes" (p. 277). The American Association of University Women Educational Foundation (1992) recommends working actively to avoid sex-segregated enrollment in vocational electives such as industrial arts and home economics and in academic courses such as upper-level mathematics and science. Programs designed specifically for low-income and minority students, such as bilingual education, sometimes reduce these students' access to the rest of the curriculum by resegregating them within the school. Recognizing this problem, Nieto (1996) posits,

> There are ways in which the needs of limited English-proficient and mainstream students can be served at the same time. Within every bilingual program, there are opportunities for integrating students for nonacademic work. Students in the bilingual program can take art, physical education, and other nonacademic classes with their English-speaking peers. In addition, bilingual programs can be integrated

into the school rather than separated in a wing of the building, so that teachers from both bilingual and nonbilingual classrooms are encouraged to collaborate on projects. (p. 201)

Instruction

If the Multicultural Education approach is to work and the curriculum is to be provocative and challenging, teachers will need to be guided by certain instructional principles that are directly connected to the nature and purpose of the multicultural curriculum. Rodgers (1975) tells us that "the instructional program is theoretically and structurally tied to the curriculum and the way in which it is implemented and that the materials and resources play a pivotal role in the implementation" (p. 284). The instructional principles that advocates of Multicultural Education endorse come from their vision of what a school should provide.

One principle is that the student is an innately curious individual, capable of learning complex material and performing at a high skill level.

A second principle is that each student has his or her own unique learning style, and teachers should not only build on this learning style when teaching, but also help students "discover their own particular style of learning" for themselves so they can learn more effectively and efficiently (Kendall, 1983, p. 12).

A third principle is that teachers should draw on and make use of the conceptual schemes that students bring to school. For example, Hollins (1982) drawing on the work of Ausubel, argues that students come to school with good conceptual schemes. Rather than replacing these with new ones, the teacher should use and build on the students' own schemes. Because conceptual schemes are channeled through language, using the students' native language helps develop the conceptual schemes that the children bring with them to school. Trueba (1991) also posits, "Use of native language is best because critical thinking skills and cognitive structuring are conditioned by linguistic and cultural knowledge and experiences that children usually obtain in the home and bring with them to school" (p. 154). Simply put, we need to start where the students are and use what they already know.

Having high and realistic expectations for all students is a fourth instructional principle of this approach. Bennett (1995) argues that high expectations are a necessary prerequisite for equal education: "If teachers are to provide equal opportunities for learning, their expectations for student success must be positive and equitable" (p. 67). Further, it is not only the teacher who needs to have high expectations for the students; students also need to have high expectations for themselves. Similarly, Gibson (1991) says, "Teachers need to convey a sense of positive expectation for individuals and group achievement. This is especially important for those students whose lives have been surrounded by failure and whose families have conveyed to them little hope for their success in school" (p. 376).

Fostering cooperation is a fifth principle. In Chapter 3, in our examination of the Human Relations approach, we discussed the importance of instruction that teaches students to work cooperatively with others. Slavin (1986) reviews several studies of the effects of cooperative learning on student social relationships in desegregated and in mainstreamed classrooms. He notes, "In many of these studies, the Student Team Learning students began to choose their classmates as though ethnicity were not a barrier to friendship at all. This never happened in the control classes" (p. 13). In classes in which students with disabilities were mainstreamed, "the teamwork makes them 'one of the gang' instead of separate and odd" (p. 13). Bennett (1986), after reviewing research on cooperative learning, says that "research results show that student team learning improves both academic achievement and students' interpersonal relationships. All students (including high, average, and low achievers) appear to benefit" (p. 303). Fostering cooperation is particularly important for students with limited English proficiency. As Arias (1986) points out:

> Hispanic students are segregated in schools or classrooms in which children of limited English proficiency are the majority. Linguistic isolation reflects the residential isolation that limits the exposure of some Hispanic students to the native English discourse of peers. Schools frequently exacerbate Hispanic student linguistic isolation by homogeneously grouping students by language ability in classrooms for instructional purposes. (p. 50)

A sixth principle of multicultural instruction is to treat both boys and girls equally and in a nonsexist manner, both consciously and unconsciously. The importance of this principle is evident in a comment by Stockard et al. (1980), who argue that "observational studies of classroom interaction show that teachers tend to give boys both more negative and more positive feedback about their actions than they give girls" (p. 13). Although teachers may do this unconsciously, the feedback nevertheless provides boys with more opportunity to learn than girls. Similarly, *How Schools Shortchange Girls*, a study commissioned by the American Association of University Women Educational Foundation (1992) reports that "research spanning the past twenty years consistently reveals that males receive more teacher attention than do females" (p. 68) and that attention directed toward males was academically challenging and supportive more often than that directed toward females. The study notes that girls who are neglected by teachers from the preschool years on are shown to experience a drop in self-confidence as teenagers that affects their academic achievement. Further, girls are exposed more to biological sciences than physical sciences. The report also points out that teachers tend to select classroom activities and formats that favor boys' interests.

The development and fostering of a positive self-concept, a seventh principle, is just as important to this approach as to the other approaches. Bennett (1986) provides an insightful comment on the importance of self-concept and success in school:

> When a student with low self-esteem enters a classroom, self-concept becomes one of the most challenging individual differences in how he or she will learn. Because students with a negative self-image are not fully able to learn, school becomes an arena for failure that prevents them from achieving the success needed for high self-esteem. (p. 131)

Additionally, Nieto (1996) argues that students do not simply develop poor self-concepts accidentally, rather, they are the result of policies and practices of schools and society that respect and affirm some groups while devaluing and rejecting others.

There are probably many other principles of instruction that could be added here. Our purpose has not been to be exhaustive but to illuminate those instructional principles that are central to the approach.

Evaluation

Evaluation has been addressed less than curriculum and instruction, although educators who have addressed evaluation have made several recommendations. A long-standing recommendation is that standardized tests that sort and rank-order students, particularly IQ tests, should not be used because they are not culturally neutral, nor are they used in a culturally neutral way. For example, Mensh and Mensh (1991) reviewed the history and practices of IQ testing. They concluded that "the tests are not instruments for assessing individual differences, but a means for ignoring individuality and slotting children according to prior assumptions about the races and classes they belong to," and as long as such tests continue to be used, schools will continue "to justify superior and inferior education along class and racial lines" (p. 158). Instead, achievement tests should be based on the curricula the students have actually been taught, with criterion references rather than norm references, and used only to improve instruction. Tests to determine eligibility for special education (and especially those used to determine mental retardation) should be culturally sensitive, like the System of Multicultural Pluralistic Assessment developed by Mercer (Mercer & Lewis, 1977).

A related recommendation is that the evaluation of achievement should reflect a multicultural curriculum. For example, if children are taught a multicultural history curriculum, achievement testing over their mastery of history should not dwell on the accomplishments of wealthy White males. In fact, Mensh and Mensh (1991) argue that any evaluation will not be fair until the curriculum is pluralistic:

> When the schools encourage all children to aspire, provide them with equal opportunities to learn, and a curriculum that includes the contributions of the cultures and the gender whose true roles have historically been omitted, it will become possible, as the children mature, to assess their individual abilities and inclinations. (p. 158)

A third recommendation is that when students are grouped for instruction, grouping plans should serve a varied student population rather than penalizing those who do not fit some notion of "normal." Stainback, Stainback, Courtnage, and Jaben (1985) point out that the age/grade level system, coupled with standardized testing, assumes that all students of the same age should require the same amount of time to learn the same thing; those who deviate are placed in pull-out programs such as special education. They recommend that testing and grouping practices should employ criterion-referenced (rather than norm-referenced) tests, nongraded grouping arrangements, and flexible pacing and time requirements. By expecting and allowing for diversity (which is not to be confused with lowering expectations) and by providing variable ways of evaluating and grouping students, far fewer students will be seen as disabled.

A fourth recommendation is that evaluation procedures should not be used to penalize students by requiring skills that are extraneous to what is being evaluated. For example, if a science teacher wishes to assess how well students have learned science concepts, the test should not require students to read and write above their skill level; if a student cannot read some of the questions or write well enough to answer questions, the test should be given orally. (This recommendation is not meant to suggest that no one should be teaching reading and writing skills to the student, only that these skills should not interfere with the student's ability to display what he or she has learned about science.) Time limits should not be placed on tests (unless there is a good reason to do so) if such limits prevent those who work slowly from completing the test. Children who are fluent in a language other than English should be tested in their native language if their performance in English would not be as good (unless the purpose of the test is to evaluate their mastery of English).

A fifth recommendation is that assessments of students' English-language proficiency should take into account the different contexts in which school communication takes place and the different factors involved in such communication. Personality traits, such as sociability, may affect the rate and proficiency of a student's learning of English in peer-interaction situations; however, cognitive skills may be more involved in acquiring English proficiency in the classroom context (Fillmore, 1979). Cummins (1981a, 1981b) found that it takes substantially longer for a student to acquire the cognitively demanding English used in academic situations compared to the English proficiency required in social situations. Teachers have prematurely transferred students into an all-English curriculum when the students lacked sufficient cognitive and academic language proficiency to achieve. Accurately assessing the language factor, in addition to the other factors already discussed, is crucial to the educational achievement of language-minority students. Trueba (1991) suggests four recommendations that teachers should consider when working with students whose first language isn't English:

1. Place student in learning environments in which there are opportunities to evaluate and analyze failure and embarrassing (degrading) incidents related to academic performance.
2. Identify the learning skills and levels of students in specific subjects and domains, using their mother tongue, or the language in which they were instructed.
3. Construct learning experiences which are meaningful to children and congruent with their cultural and linguistic knowledge, and in which they play an important role negotiating the context and level of instruction.
4. Sensitize the school personnel to develop culturally based instructional models effective for minorities. (p. 155)

Finally, a sixth recommendation is that educators should make sure that the tests they give do not contain sex or race stereotypes or sexist language. For example, Tittle (1973) examined eight major achievement tests and found all but one to use more male than female nouns and pronouns, as well as stereotypical test items (e.g., girls cooked while boys hiked). Similarly, a recent study entitled *How Schools*

Shortchange Girls (American Association of University Women Educational Foundation, 1992) reported that standardized tests still provide more male references than female and give boys an advantage by using multiple-choice formats, rather than the essay formats that favor girls.

Home/Community-School Relationships

Advocates of the Multicultural Education approach encourage schools to maintain a strong relationship with the home and community. They believe that when it comes to the education of their children, parents and community members must be more than mere spectators, simply attending graduation ceremonies, open houses, or sporting events. Multicultural Education advocates supported the government when it endorsed and required "maximum feasible participation" of community members in federally sponsored programs. They argue that just as citizen participation is fundamental to American democracy, so is parent and community participation fundamental to school success for people of color and women (Grant, 1979; Sleeter & Grant, 1988).

Reed and Mitchell, 1975, argued that most home/community-school relationships are token in nature. They observed that, for the most part, few community services to the school exist. Those that do exist—for example, the Parent-Teacher Organization or a fund-raising group to buy an additional computer for the school—are directed by the school and usually do not represent the community as a whole. Furthermore, these efforts are led by fairly small groups that do virtually all of the planning; they see themselves and are seen by school personnel largely as "communication leaks" through which information about the school program is disseminated to the community (p. 190). Since the Reed and Mitchell report, especially in the late 1980s and early 1990s, parents and community members have been more active in school affairs. Nevertheless, the observations by Reed and Mitchell are still basically correct; parents are still very much information receivers and spectators at school events (Grant & Sleeter, 1996). Joyce Epstein (1991), the co-director of the Center on Families, Communities and Schools, and Children's Learning, put it as follows: "Today, most schools embrace the concept of partnership, but few have translated their beliefs into plans or their plans into practices" (p. 349).

Also, some school districts are trying to work with parents, but their actions are problematic. For example, they are holding conferences with parents of color (only) at the beginning of the school year in order to help students of color get off to a good start. Initially this practice may seem like a good idea, but it is flawed for several reasons: (a) It is based on the expectations of school officials that students of color will have academic difficulty. (b) The teachers tend to do most if not all of the talking, as observed at parent-teacher conferences by one of the authors. (c) Because the purposes of the conferences are generally not explained to them, the students are concerned about their parents coming to school. In the actual parent-teacher conferences observed, some students of color wondered why their parents had to come to school and the parents of their White friends were not required to do so.

Advocates of the Multicultural Education approach want to see the community involved in budgetary procedures, the selection of school personnel, and curriculum development. One advocate of such involvement explained to one of the authors:

> The most productive approach to improving education for students of color has been a school-community partnership. In this partnership, the community's contribution is to help define and illuminate the interests and needs of their children. The school, representing both the dominant culture and the education profession, then contributes to problem solving abilities. The coequality of school and community can strengthen school-community relationships and can reveal problem areas which have escaped previous identification and consequently impeded progress. (Montano, 1979, p. 152)

Resounding with many of the same community-oriented concerns, Peterson (1995) passionately describes the ongoing processes surrounding the effort to establish and democratically govern La Escuela Fratney, an elementary school situated in a diverse neighborhood in Milwaukee, Wisconsin; the experiences of teachers, parents, and community members at La Escuela Fratney reveal the rewarding but challenging dimensions of approaching the education of children as a truly collective project.

Writing on the editorial page of the *Phi Delta Kappan*'s issue on parental involvement (January, 1991), the editor, Pauline B. Gough, posited some reflections on home–school relations that advocates of the Multicultural Education approach would appreciate. She observes,

> Effective parent involvement programs include—but go far beyond—encouraging parents to read with their children. Such programs also deal with parents' needs for information on effective parenting, on available social services, on school procedures and curricula, and on how to help their youngster. At the same time, effective parent involvement programs acknowledge the fact that parents are a child's earliest and most influential teachers. Trying to educate the young without help and support from the home is akin to trying to rake leaves in a high wind. (p. 339)

Advocates of this approach, like advocates of the Human Relations and the Single-Group Studies approaches, acknowledge the importance of the school in recognizing and affirming the home/community cultures of all of its students. They embrace the idea that just as there is no one model American, there is no one model home or community. Homes are as varied and diverse as the people who make up a multicultural community.

Staffing

The Multicultural Education approach is concerned with schoolwide as well as classroom practices. One schoolwide area of concern is staffing. There are three main recommendations here. One is that staffing patterns should reflect cultural diversity and nonsexist roles (Baker, 1983; Gollnick & Chinn, 1998; Stockard et al., 1980). Thus, more than a token number of staff members should be of color, staff members of color should be administrators and teachers as well as aides and custodians, half of the decision makers should be female, and teachers should not be relegated to subject areas on the basis of sex stereotypes (e.g., there should be female mathematics teachers in addition to male mathematics teachers).

A second recommendation is that staff members should have high expectations of students. Gollnick and Chinn (1998) point out that research often shows that teachers base their expectations on student characteristics such as socioeconomic status, language, race, and sex; the Multicultural Education approach recommends hiring teachers who do not stereotype students and who have high expectations of them. Actually, no approach recommends hiring biased teachers, but advocates of this approach have been more outspoken against teacher biases than have been the advocates of other previously discussed approaches.

A third recommendation is that relations among staff members should be collegial and that a cooperative spirit should prevail. It is especially important that teachers from various programs and support services be integrated within the mainstream life of the school. Recent research on schools with bilingual education programs reveals that in effective schools, there are few divisions between the bilingual and regular school staff (Carter & Chatfield, 1986).

Extracurricular Activities
A second schoolwide area of concern is extracurricular activities. Baker (1983) recommends that schools make sure that athletic programs include students of color and women and that cheerleading teams include both sexes and students of color. She points out that female students sometimes are not actively encouraged to participate in certain sports and that students from lower socioeconomic backgrounds are often unable to participate in sports such as skiing, which requires access to facilities outside the school. Both Baker (1983) and Gollnick and Chinn (1998) recommend that clubs and organizations should not perpetuate racial or sex segregation and that positions of student leadership should not be dominated by one group. Stockard et al. (1980) point out that "males more often belong to chess, science, and lettermen's clubs and females more often belong to dance teams and aspire to be cheerleaders ... [and even] in the band, they generally play different instruments" (p. 40). Schools should work actively to avoid segregation and stereotyping in such areas.

Sports opened up considerably to girls after Title IX was passed in 1972, and now about one fourth of female students participate in sports. However, there is still quite a way to go in equalizing athletic opportunities. Boys still participate at about twice the rate of girls, and the proportion of women coaches has decreased rather than increased. Further, many sports are still sex stereotyped; students still perceive most sports as male; and, in a recent study, "figure skating, gymnastics, jumping rope, and cheerleading were the only athletic activities identified as female" (American Association of University Women Educational Foundation, 1992, p. 45). Historically significant, though, is the recent establishment of the Women's National Basketball Association (WNBA)—with the first professional game played on June 21, 1997. It will be of special importance to advocates of Multicultural Education to both support this victory as well as to follow its impact upon the gendered nature of athletics from the elementary school to team sports at the college level.

GETTING STARTED

John Martin, Marie Sanchez, and Ellen Foxley were returning to James Madison Junior High after spending 3 days at the district's multicultural inservice institute. They had been selected for attendance by their school principal, Dr. Herman Kempner, because of their interest in the concept and the school's goal for the year of implementing Multicultural Education into the classroom. James Madison Junior High was a newly constructed magnet school not too far from the city's downtown area. As a magnet school, it received a richly diverse student population, which was 18% Asian, 12% Black, 20% Hispanic, 3% Native American, and 47% White. The socioeconomic status of these students was also varied: About 55% came from families that could be considered solidly middle class, and the other 45% represented students who came from the working class. About 18% of the total student population were considered handicapped, or in need of special services. The girls outnumbered the boys by 2% this year; this percentage had fluctuated 1 or 2 percentage points in either direction over the last 5 years.

Kempner, or "Doc" as he was more often called by his colleagues, had made Multicultural Education the school goal partly because of his recent trip to Hawaii and Japan and partly because of the mounting attention to globalization as countries throughout the world prepare for the 21st century. He believed that technology and globalization created an important need for people to learn more about each other's history and culture, and to learn how to work together. He argued that the school's contribution to meeting this need would be to help students accept and affirm cultural diversity as a fact of life in the United States and to acknowledge that it is a valuable resource that should be preserved and cherished. The school had no particular overt problem caused by its different race and class groups, nor any overt problem between its special education and regular education students.

John, Marie, and Ellen had all become interested in multicultural education in different but equally fulfilling ways. John had attended an Ivy League college and had joined Teach For America. He had been assigned to an inner-city school in Los Angeles, and he had surprised himself by discovering that he really enjoyed teaching. At the completion of his assignment, he took a job at James Madison, where he has been teaching language arts for the last 20 years. Marie had grown up in a Hispanic barrio in Austin, Texas. She had attended a local university in Dallas and had fallen in love with the city. She has been teaching mathematics at the junior high school for 9 years. Ellen has been teaching social studies at James Madison for 6 years. She had come to the school after living most of her life in Alaska, where her mother was the principal in a school that had a large enrollment of Inuit students. She had worked for her mother for 2 years before deciding to see the "lower forty-eight." Early in her teaching career, she had become involved with the women's movement and had helped establish a local NOW chapter.

The workshop had provided two important commodities—time and material resources—to enable each of the three teachers to develop lesson plans for their classes. Also, it had encouraged and provided time for them to collaborate on developing schoolwide implementation plans. They shared these plans with Doc on their first day back. The schoolwide plans called for each subject-area department to assess how well content about the contributions and perspectives of men and women of different cultural groups was integrated into its curriculum and to establish a procedure for improvement where needed. The plans suggested that each teacher have the primary responsibility for his or her curriculum but that the process of designing a curriculum would be less difficult if subject-area colleagues worked together. The schoolwide plans also suggested that each teacher assess his or her own teaching style to determine to what extent it meshed with the different learning styles of the students and that the counseling staff help the teachers as needed. Finally, the plans recommended hiring more teachers of color for the core subject areas, because of the 35 core-area teachers, only two were Black and one was Hispanic.

The three teachers waited for Doc's reaction to their proposal. It was not long in coming. He said, "How do you think the teachers will respond to these area meetings and work? They have been very slow to start responding to multicultural education as a school goal, other than putting up a few posters here and there."

Ellen replied, "There is one thing I remember my mother saying: 'A successful instructional program requires a strong leader.' Doc, you know that unless you really get involved, most of the teachers will write this whole thing off as 'here today, gone tomorrow.'"

Doc sighed and said, "I know you're right. I'll put it on the agenda for this month's staff meeting, and then we'll really get into it." He then asked, "What are each of you going to do in your own classrooms?"

John replied first, saying that he had already developed several lesson plans. One set of plans for literature required him to change not only which pieces of literature he taught but also his teaching method. For example, he was going to include Mildred Taylor's *Roll of Thunder, Hear My Cry*, Scott O'Dell's *Carlotta*, Lawrence Yep's *Dragon Wings*, and Jean Craighead-George's *Julie of the Wolves*. He also was going to have these books put on tape so that students with reading problems could listen and follow along.

Marie responded that she had come up with a plan to use Emma's and Paul's wheelchairs to help teach circumferences, diameters, and radii. Also, she and John were planning a lesson together that involved mathematics and essay writing. The lesson would require students to measure various dimensions of a building and then refer to those measurements in an essay discussing how architectural facilities could be redesigned to accommodate disabled individuals.

Ellen said that she was changing her social studies unit on World War II to include the internment of Japanese Americans on the West Coast and the roles of African Americans, Hispanics, Asian Americans, and women in the war.

Doc complimented the three on their excellent ideas. He asked them to share their ideas with the staff at the next meeting. Also, he asked if they would be willing to be on call to help others get started. The meeting adjourned as the three responded yes.

CRITIQUE

Some of you may be thinking that the Multicultural Education approach solves all the problems not addressed by the other approaches. Others of you may feel dissatisfied with this approach, yet perhaps you may be uncertain about what is dissatisfying to you. Although this approach has been advocated prolifically, it has also been criticized on various grounds and from various perspectives. First, we will present criticisms of the goals of the approach from the perspectives of the three approaches discussed earlier. Next, we will present criticisms that support the approach's goals but question its implementation. Finally, we will present criticisms that the approach described in Chapter 6 tries to resolve.

Advocates of the Teaching the Exceptional and the Culturally Different approach see the Multicultural Education approach as misdirected. They believe that American society is essentially good and just and that the worst way to deal with differences in language, culture, or learning styles is to nurture them. For example, Broudy (1975) believes that the approach will cause social divisiveness and lock some groups out by allowing them to fail to develop knowledge and skills for participation. He notes that "some groups will be encouraged not to participate not only in the culture of this country but also in the intellectual and artistic achievements of the human race" (p. 175). Glazer (1981) argues that "most [immigrant groups] had not come here to maintain foreign language and culture, but with the intention … to become Americanized as fast as possible" (p. 33). He extends this argument to all groups, immigrant or not (e.g., Mexican Americans). Ivie (1979) believes that Multicultural Education sidesteps the problem of how to improve education for children who are failing. Likewise, Hirsch (1996) argues that it is the responsibility of the school to instill in all children the knowledge they will need (e.g. traditional) to succeed economically and participate in a commonly shared culture. This is especially essential, Hirsch stresses, for those students who arrive at school with deficits and whose home culture fails to instill background knowledge relevant to their education.

These critics argue that it is both undesirable and unrealistic to think that the mainstream will become pluralistic and that the best thing schools can do is to try to equip those who are poor, minority, and disabled with the skills and knowledge they will need to get a job and compete for upward mobility in the existing society. For example, they would probably fault John for teaching fewer traditional literary classics in order to include works by authors of color, Marie for taking up mathematics instruction time to discuss building accessibility for people with disabilities, and Ellen for cutting back on time spent on the political and military aspects of World War II in order to focus more on people of color and women.

The late 1980s and 1990s is seeing a well-financed and well-organized attack against the multicultural approach. As the population of the United States became more diverse and as that diversity was increasingly publicized and discussed, attention to multicultural education, and especially the Multicultural Education approach, grew. No longer was multicultural education a marginal activity: New York City rewrote its curriculum in order to be multicultural, the state of California battled over a multicultural history curriculum, and universities such as Stanford began to design a core curriculum for undergraduates that was multicultural.

The most outspoken critics of multicultural education implicitly accepted Teaching the Exceptional and Culturally Different, but they explicitly advocated assimilating everyone into a supposed national consensus and common culture. Hirsch (1987) issued an urgent call for heightened cultural literacy and the embrace of an "American" cultural and linguistic standard. Ravitch (1990) argued that multicultural education promotes particularism, in which diverse groups pull away from a common heritage; she wondered if a multicultural curriculum would lead the United States to fall apart like the former Soviet Union and Sri Lanka were doing. Schlesinger (1991) similarly posited that "the national ideal had once been e pluribus unum. Are we now to belittle unum and glorify pluribus? will the center hold? or will the melting pot yield to the Tower of Babel?" (p. 2). Many critics, particularly at the university level, argued that multicultural education promoted "political correctness," whereas the traditional Western curriculum is neutral and scholarly.

These critiques were leveled against Multicultural Education very publicly, appearing, for example, in such magazines as *Time*. The critiques attempted to portray advocates of the Multicultural Education approach as extremists, and in this way, many lay citizens were introduced to multicultural education. In contrast to these intense attacks by conservatives in the late 1980s and early 1990s, much milder critiques of the Multicultural Education approach from the perspectives of other approaches have also been advanced.

Those criticizing the Multicultural Education approach from a Human Relations perspective raise different objections. These critics believe that American society does not promote enough love and interpersonal caring for a fulfilling existence. They believe that as people learn not to stereotype others and learn to communicate with, share with, and care about those with whom they come into contact, eventually other social problems will be solved. They argue that the Multicultural Education approach becomes misdirected when it emphasizes cognitive knowledge about different groups over exploration of interpersonal feelings and social issues such as power over interpersonal issues. These critics believe that the Multicultural Education approach may give students a broad knowledge base, but that unless interpersonal relationships are stressed and experienced, attitudes and prejudices will not change. The objection is a question of emphasis. Human Relations advocates and Multicultural Education advocates usually do not leave each other in bitter disagreement but rather move in somewhat different directions.

Advocates of the Single-Group Studies approach usually agree with much of the vision of Multicultural Education, but they object that the approach weakens attention to the particular group they represent. Sometimes members of diverse groups initially embrace Multicultural Education's rainbow concept, but they become disenchanted when their own group continues to receive minimal attention while others receive more. For example, multicultural curriculum materials today usually give good representation to African Americans and White women, but they give barely a nod to Puerto Ricans or Hmong people. In addition, the issue of language, which is a central concern of bilingual educators, often remains peripheral to Multicultural Education. There is no theoretical reason why any particular group or issue should be left out; but the reality is that when attention is divided among a wide variety of groups, each group cannot receive in-depth and comprehensive treatment (at least, not without substantially lengthening the amount of time students spend in school).

A related objection of many Single-Group Studies advocates is that they do not see multiple forms of diversity as equally important. Many ethnic-studies educators see race as the basic form of oppression, while radical feminists insist it is gender, and class analysts argue that it is the economic structure. Studying multiple forms of diversity is seen as superfluous, a waste of time, and weakening to the study of the form of diversity that is of greatest concern. Ricardo Gomez (Chapter 4), for example, would be less than enthusiastic about Ellen's approach to teaching history because it would fail to mine the richness of Mexican American history to its fullest extent. Ellen would certainly do more than is usually done to portray Mexican Americans as active and visible contributors to American life, but Ricardo would want to focus more intensively on them.

Now let us examine some problems with implementation of the Multicultural Education approach. One problem we have observed is that educators often treat multiple forms of diversity, especially race and gender, as parallel but separate (Grant & Sleeter, 1986). For example, when teaching about African Americans and women, teachers often really teach about Black men and White women. Similarly, many teachers treat race and disability as isolated subjects, neglecting to examine how racism leads Whites to label unjustly people of color as handicapped. Further, many educators tend to view race, gender, and other social markers of difference as unitary, often failing to address the nonsynchronous or complex and contradictory nature of experience within groups as well as the way in which multiple characterstics intersect in shaping social life (McCarthy, 1990). The Multicultural Education approach itself does not call for such biased and essentialist treatment of diversity, but such treatment seems to occur for a number of reasons. Many educators and scholars simply become interested in one form of oppression (such as sexism) and often do not resolve their own biases related to other forms (such as racism). In addition, they often neglect to put in the increased amounts of time and effort required to learn about and integrate race, class, gender, and disability.

Another problem is that implementation requires a reeducation of the educators using the approach. The Multicultural Education approach is ambitious. For example, to teach instrumental music from a multicultural perspective, one needs to learn a wide variety of music traditions. Few of us received a multicultural education in our own schooling, so acquiring one now requires considerable commitment, time, and creativity. One cannot half-heartedly do a good job of Multicultural Education. In the vignette, the teachers were able to benefit from the time, materials, and knowledge provided at the inservice institute. They also knew that their colleagues would be unwilling to invest the necessary time and effort in the approach without the principal's strong encouragement. In addition to acquiring a broad and multicultural knowledge base in subject matter, it is also important that teachers interrogate their biographies in order to gain a deeper understanding of the way their own social positioning impacts perspective and teaching (Grant, 1991). Indeed, if multicultural education is to become a reality, teacher education will need to be more closely aligned with such initiatives; prospective teachers, for example, will need to be immersed in community settings in order to fully appreciate the culture and history of particular groups and should be given extensive mentorship opportunities with experienced teachers (Ladson-Billings, 1994).

You have probably noticed that this chapter included only bits and pieces about sexual orientation and disability and even less about social class. The dominant society currently marginalizes and suppresses gay and lesbian issues to such a degree that many multicultural educators are reluctant to mention this group. While there are a growing number of books, articles and curriculum materials available to introduce gay, lesbian and bisexual issues in the classroom (see Chapter 4 for examples), getting these materials into the schools is often still a struggle. For example, the gay and lesbian content in New York City's Rainbow Curriculum caused the entire project to be called into question. As recently as 1996, some New Hampshire teachers' jobs were threatened when they ignored a ban on the teaching of gay and lesbian issues in the classroom. Advocates for gay, lesbian, and bisexual rights argue that teachers and communities need increased practical strategies on how gay, lesbian, and bisexual issues can be integrated into and across a multicultural K–12 curriculum. Additionally, these advocates argue that educators, administrators, and parents must be encouraged to view sexual orientation as a cultural and civil rights issue which has a place within multicultural education. More recently, in the Middleton-Cross Plains School District, Wisconsin, conflicts abounded when teachers attempted to integrate readings from *One Teenager in Ten: Writings by Gay and Lesbian Youth* into a curriculum aimed at opposing injustice. These examples of homophobia illustrate the need for education about sexual orientation as well as the way conflicts related to diversity permeate society, from large, urban areas to smaller, suburban ones. Nevertheless, several multicultural scholars have begun to organize sessions at educational conferences to discuss the inclusion of sexual orientation and disability under the multicultural umbrella. The small, but steady, development of educational materials (e.g., books and articles) on homophobia in education as well as the discussions of the influence of traditional schooling on gay and lesbian students is having some impact. The dedication of an entire issue of the *Harvard Educational Review* (1996) to gay and lesbian educational issues is another example. The mainstreaming movement is slowly beginning to develop a Multicultural Education approach to disability; in time, we expect this approach to be even more influential in the area of disability. Special educators seem to have moved from focusing almost exclusively on how to teach those who are viewed as disabled, to integrating special education students with their regular education peers, and additionally asking how to make the mainstream itself more pluralistic. Marie's inclusion of people in wheelchairs in her mathematics curriculum is an example of "inclusion" that you will increasingly see in classrooms.

The small amount of attention given to social class is a serious problem with this approach. Unfortunately, social class receives only fragmented attention:

Many educators who are very concerned about race are concerned about class only to the extent that people of color are disproportionately poor; educators interested in gender are concerned about the increased pauperization of women; and Multicultural Education advocates often recommend that children have equal opportunity regardless of social-class background. However, in an ideal society, if race and gender status differences are eliminated, what about class differences? Multicultural Education advocates do not come right out and say that a classless society is preferable to one stratified by class. Nor do they say that the culture of people living at or below the poverty level is just as worthy as middle-class culture in the same way they argue that the cultures of Native Americans are as worthy as that of Anglo Americans. They argue that the people are as worthy, but they do not argue that class cultures are equally worthy and desirable. The Multicultural Education approach simply does not say very much about social class, particularly about the extent to which the ideal society should have different social classes. This lack of attention to social class was reflected in the teaching ideas proposed by John, Marie, and Ellen. The Single-Group Studies and the Social Reconstructionist approaches both offer a critique of social class; the Multicultural Education approach is relatively silent about this subject.

Disaffected Multicultural Education advocates who have moved on to the approach we will be presenting next have leveled another criticism: The Multicultural Education approach directs too much attention to cultural issues and not enough to social structural inequalities and the skills that students will need to challenge these. For example, young people in school may learn nonsexist values and roles and may learn to make choices without relationship to gender. Yet, when they leave school and enter the real world, which is still sexist, how will they respond? Sociologists often argue that they will rework their beliefs and behaviors to fit the circumstances in which they find themselves. Boys may have received as much reward in a nonsexist school for sewing as for giving orders, but out of school many will have access to rewards for more "masculine" behavior and to roles that require them to give orders, dominate, and compete. As such, Banks and Banks (1995) emphasize the need for equity pedagogy which includes teaching students not only to question dominant cultural assumptions but to participate in transforming the structure which supports inequality. Fraser (1997) also discusses the complex relationship between demands for cultural representation with those of structural transformation and redistribution. The two camps, she believes, have too frequently understood their agendas as separate when, in fact, they are closely linked.

In a similar vein, Suzuki (1984) has warned against an unbridled focus on ethnicity when the issues of greatest concern to people of color include powerlessness, racism, and poverty. He has expressed concern that multicultural education often becomes too much a celebration of differences without acknowledging the social problems that give rise to some of those differences and without dealing sufficiently with issues of social justice. Ogbu (1978) argues that many features of Black culture, for example, have developed directly in response to powerlessness and economic subordination; overemphasis on the value of cultural diversity without a serious examination of injustices in the social structure is misdirected.

REFERENCES

American Association of University Women Educational Foundation (1992). *How schools shortchange girls*. Washington, DC: American Association of University Women Educational Foundation.

Arias, M. B. (1986). The context of education for Hispanic students: An overview. *American Journal of Education, 95*, 26–57

Baker, G. C. (1983). *Planning and organizing for multicultural instruction*. Reading, MA: Addison-Wesley.

Bandura, A., & Walters, R. H. (1963). *Social learning and personality development*. New York: Holt, Rinehart, & Winston.

Banks, C. M., & Banks, J. A. (1995). Equity pedagogy: An essential component of multicultural education. *Theory into Practice, 34*(3), 152–158

Banks, J. A. (1989). Multicultural education: Characteristics and goals. In J. Banks & C. M. Banks (Eds.), *Multicultural education: Issues and perspectives* (pp. 2–26). Boston: Allyn & Bacon.

Banks, J. A. (1994). *Multiethnic education: Theory and practice* (3rd ed.). Boston: Allyn & Bacon.

Banks, J. A., & Banks, C. M. (Eds.). (1997). *Multicultural education: Issues and perspectives* (3rd ed.). Boston: Allyn & Bacon.

Bennett, C. I. (1986). *Comprehensive multicultural education* (2nd ed.). Boston: Allyn & Bacon.

Bennett, C. I. (1995). *Comprehensive multicultural education* (3rd ed.). Boston: Allyn & Bacon.

Bloom, L. R, & Munro, P. (1995). Conflicts of selves: Nonunitary subjectivity in women administrator's life history narratives. In J. A. Hatch & R. Wisniewski (Eds.), *Life history and narrative* (pp. 99–112). Washington, DC: Falmer Press.

Broudy, H. S. (1975). Cultural pluralism: New wine in old bottles. *Educational Leadership, 33*, 173–175.

Brown v. Board of Education, 347 U.S. 483, 493. (1954).

Carter, T. P., & Chatfield, M. L. (1986). Effective bilingual schools: Implications for policy and practice. *American Journal of Education, 95*, 26–57.

Cortes, C. E. (1973). Teaching the Chicano experience. In J. A. Banks (Ed.), *Teaching ethnic studies* (pp. 181–200). Washington, DC: National Council for the Social Studies.

Cummins, J. (1981a). The entry and exit fallacy in bilingual education. *Journal for the National Association of Bilingual Education, 4*, 23–60.

Cummins, J. (1981b). The role of primary language development in promoting educational success for language minority students. In *Schooling and language minority students: A theoretical framework* (pp. 3–49). Los Angeles: California State University Evaluation, Dissemination, and Assessment Center.

Cushner, K., McClelland, A., & Safford, P. (1996). *Human diversity in education: An integrative approach* (2nd ed.). New York: McGraw-Hill.

Epstein, J. L. (1991, January). Paths to partnership. *Phi Delta Kappan, 72*(5), 344–349.

Ferguson, A. (1977). Androgyny as an ideal for human development. In M. Vetterling-Braggin, F. A. Elliston, & J. English (Eds.), *Feminism and philosophy* (pp. 45–69). Totowa, NJ: Littlefield, Adams.

Fillmore, L. W. (1979). Individual differences in second language acquisition. In C. Fillmore (Ed.), *Individual differences in language ability and language behavior* (pp. 203–228). New York: Academic Press.

Fillmore, L. W., & Valadez, C. (1985). Teaching bilingual learners. In M. C. Wittrock (Ed.), *Handbook of research on teaching* (pp. 648–685). New York: Macmillan.

Foerster, L. (1982). Moving from ethnic studies to multicultural education. *The Urban Review, 14*, 121–126.

Fraser, N. (1997). *Justice interruptus: Critical reflections on the "postsocialist" condition*. New York: Routledge.

Gay, G. (1975). Organizing and designing culturally pluralistic curriculum. *Educational Leadership, 33*, 176–183.

Gay, G. (1979). On behalf of children: A curriculum design for multicultural education in the elementary school. *Journal of Negro Education, 48*, 324–340.

Gay, G. (1983). Multiethnic education: Historical developments and future prospects. *Phi Delta Kappan, 64*, 560–563.

Gee, E. G., & Sperry, D. J. (1978). *Education law and the public schools: A compendium*. Boston: Allyn & Bacon.

Giangreco, M. F., Dennis, R., Cloninger, C., Edelman, S., & Schattman, R. (1993). "I've counted Jon": Transformational experiences of teachers educating students with disabilities. *Exceptional Children, 59*, 359–372.

Gibson, M. A. (1991). Minorities and schooling: Some implications. In M. A. Gibson & J. U. Ogbu (Eds.), *Minority status and schooling* (pp. 357–382). New York: Garland.

Giddings, P. (1985). *When and where I enter: The impact of black women on race and sex in America*. New York: Bantam.

Glazer, N. (1981). Pluralism and the new immigrants. *Society, 19*, 31–36.

Gollnick, D. M. (1980). Multicultural education. *Viewpoints in Teaching and Learning, 56*, 1–17.

Gollnick, D. M., & Chinn, P. C. (1998). *Multicultural education in a pluralistic society* (5th ed.). Upper Saddle River, NJ: Merrill.

Gollnick, D. M., Sadker, M., & Sadker, D. (1982). Beyond the Dick and Jane syndrome. In M. P. Sadker & D. M. Sadker (Ed.), *Sex equity handbook for schools* (pp. 60–95). New York: Longman.

Goodenough, W. H. (1976). Multiculturalism as the normal human experience. *Anthropology and Education Quarterly, 7*, 4–6.

Gough, P. (1976). *Sexism: New issue in American education*. Bloomington, IN: Phi Delta Kappa Educational Foundation.

Gough, P. (1991, January). Tapping parent power. *Phi Delta Kappan, 72*(5), 339.

Grant, C. A. (1977). The mediator of culture: A teacher role revisited. *Journal of Research and Development in Education, 11*, 102–117.

Grant, C. A. (1979). *Community participation in education*. Boston: Allyn & Bacon.

Grant, C. A. (1991). Culture and teaching: What do teachers need to know? In M. Kennedy (Ed.), *Teaching academic subjects to diverse learners* (pp. 237–256). New York: Teachers College Press.

Grant, C. A., & Grant, G. W. (1981). A multicultural evaluation of some second and third grade textbook readers—A survey analysis. *Journal of Negro Education, 50*, 63–74.

Grant C. A., & Ladson-Billings, G. (Eds.). (1997). *Dictionary of multicultural education*. Phoenix, AZ: Oryx Press.

Grant, C. A., & Sleeter, C. E. (1986). Race, class, and gender in education research: An argument for integrative analysis. *Review of Educational Research, 56*, 195–211.

Grant, C. A., & Sleeter, C. E. (1989). Race, class, gender exceptionality, and educational reform. In J. A. Banks & C. A. Banks (Eds.), *Multicultural education: Issues and perspectives* (pp. 49–66). Boston: Allyn & Bacon.

Grant, C. A., & Sleeter, C. E. (1996). *After the school bell rings* (2nd ed.). Philadelphia: Falmer Press.

Guthrie, G. P. (1985). *A school divided*. Hillsdale, NJ: Erlbaum. *Harvard Educational Review* (1996). *66*(2). [Special issue].

Hernandez, H. (1989). *Multicultural education: A teacher's guide to content and process.* New York: Merrill/Macmillan.

Hirsch, E. D., Jr. (1987). *Cultural literacy: What every American needs to know.* New York: Vintage Books.

Hirsch, E. D., Jr. (1996). *The schools we need and why we don't have them.* New York: Doubleday.

Hollins, E. R. (1982). Beyond multicultural education. *Negro Educational Review, 33,* 140–145.

Hull, G. T., Scott, P. B., & Smith, B. (Eds.). (1982). *All of the women are white, all of the blacks are men, but some of us are brave.* Old Westbury, NY: Feminist Press.

Hunter, W. (1974). *Multicultural education through competency-based teacher education.* Washington, DC: American Association of Colleges for Teacher Education.

Ivie, S. D. (1979). Multicultural education: Boon or boondoggle? *Journal of Teacher Education, 30,* 23–25.

Janney, R. E., Snell, M. E., Beers, M. K., & Raynes, M. (1995). Integrating students with moderate and severe disabilities: Classroom teachers' beliefs and attitudes about implementing an educational change. *Educational Administration Quarterly, 31*(1), 86–114.

Kendall, F. E. (1983). *Diversity in the classroom.* New York: Teachers College Press.

Kimball, S. T. (1974). *Culture and the educative process.* New York: Teachers College Press.

King, E. W. (1990). *Teaching ethnic and gender awareness.* Dubuque, IA: Kendall/Hunt.

Kohler, P. D. & Rusch, F. R. (1995). Secondary educational programs and transition perspectives. In M. C. Wang, M. C. Reynolds, & H. J. Walberg (Eds.), *Handbook of special and remedial education: Research and practice,* (2nd ed.), pp. 107–129. Tarrytown, NY: Pergamon.

Krashan, S. D. (1981). Bilingual education and second language acquisition theory. In *Schooling and language minority students: A theoretical framework* (pp. 51–79). Los Angeles: California State University Evaluation, Dissemination, and Assessment Center.

Ladson-Billings, G. (1994). *The dreamkeepers: Successful teachers of African American children.* San Francisco: Jossey-Bass.

Mannheim, K. (1956). *Ideology and utopia* (L. Wirth & E. Shils, Trans.). New York: Harcourt Brace Jovanovich.

McCarthy, C. (1990). *Race and curriculum: Social inequality and the theories and politics of difference in contemporary research on schooling.* New York: Falmer Press.

Mensh, E., & Mensh, H. (1991). *The IQ mythology: Class, race, gender, and inequality.* Carbondale: Southern Illinois University Press.

Mercer, J. R., & Lewis, J. F. (1977). *System of multicultural pluralistic assessment.* New York: Psychological Corporation.

Montano, M. (1979). School and community: Boss-worker or partners? In C. A. Grant (Ed.), *Community participation in education.* Boston: Allyn & Bacon.

National Coalition for Cultural Pluralism. Cited in W. R. Hazard and M. D. Stent (1973), Cultural pluralism and schooling: Some preliminary observations. In M. D. Stent, W. R. Hazard, & H. N. Rivlin (Eds.), *Cultural pluralism in education* (pp. 13–25). New York: Appleton-Century-Crofts.

Newman, W. N. (1973). *A study of minority groups and social theory.* New York: Harper & Row.

New York City Public Schools (1990). *United States and New York State history: A multicultural perspective.* New York: Author.

Nieto, S. (1996). *Affirming diversity* (2nd ed.). New York: Longman.

Ogbu, J. U. (1978). *Minority education and caste.* New York: Academic Press.

O'Neill, O. (1977). How do we know when opportunities are equal? In M. Vetterling-Braggin, F. A. Elliston, & J. English (Eds.), *Feminism and philosophy* (pp. 177–189). Totowa, NJ: Littlefield, Adams.

Peterson, B. (1995). La Escuela Fratney: A journey toward democracy. In M. W. Apple & J. A. Beane (Eds.), *Democratic schools* (pp. 58–82). Alexandria, VA: Association for Supervision and Curriculum Development.

Ravitch, D. (1990). Multiculturalism: E pluribus plures. *The American Scholar, 59*(3), 337–354.

Reed, D. B., & Mitchell, D. E. (1975). The structure of citizen participation: Public decisions for public schools. In D. B. Reed & D. E. Mitchell (Eds.), *Public testimony on public schools*. Berkeley, CA: McCutchan.

Reynolds, M. C., & Birch, J. W. (1988). *Adaptive mainstreaming: A primer for teachers and principals* (3rd ed.). New York: Longman.

Rodgers, F. A. (1975). *Curriculum and instruction in the elementary school*. New York: Macmillan.

Sadker, M., & Sadker, D. (1982). *Sex equity handbook for schools*. New York: Longman.

Sadker, M. & Sadker, D. (1994). *Failing at fairness: How our schools cheat girls*. New York: Simon & Schuster.

Schlesinger, A. M., Jr. (1991). *The disuniting of America*. New York: Norton.

Seaburg, J. J., Smith, J. C., & Gallaher, T. H. (1980). Building a multicultural education media collection. *Viewpoints in Teaching and Learning, 56*, 100–104.

Sizemore, B. A. (1979). The four M curriculum: A way to shape the future. *Journal of Negro Education, 47*, 341–356.

Skutnabb-Kangas, T. (1981). *Bilingualism or not? The education of minorities*. Clevedon, Avon, England: Multilingual Matters.

Slavin, R. E. (1986). *Using student team learning* (3rd ed.). Baltimore, MD: The Johns Hopkins Team Learning Project.

Sleeter, C. E. (1992). *Keepers of the American dream: A study of staff development and multicultural education*. London: Falmer Press.

Sleeter, C. E., & Grant, C. A. (1988, Winter). Educators and parents ... partners in student academic achievement. *Multicultural Leader, 1*.

Sleeter, C. E., & Grant, C. A. (1991). Race, class, gender, and disability in current textbooks. In M. W. Apple & L. K. Christian-Smith (Eds.), *The politics of the textbook* (pp. 78–110). New York: Routledge.

Soto, L. E. (1997). *Language, culture, and power*. New York: State University of New York Press.

Spender, D. (1982). *Invisible women: The schooling scandal*. London: Writers and Readers Publishing Cooperative Society.

Spindler, G. D. (1974). The transmission of culture. In G. D. Spindler (Ed.), *Education and cultural process* (pp. 279–310). New York: Holt, Rinehart, & Winston.

Stainback, W., Stainback, S., Courtnage, L., & Jaben, T. (1985). Facilitating mainstreaming by modifying the mainstream. *Exceptional Children, 52*, 144–152.

Stearns, P. N. (1988) Social history in the American history course: Whats, whys, and hows. In B. R. Gifford (Ed.), *History in the schools: What shall we teach?* (pp. 138–161). New York: Macmillan.

Stent, M., Hazard, W., & Rivlin, H. (1973). *Cultural pluralism in education: A mandate for change*. New York: Appleton-Century-Crofts.

Stockard, J., Schmuck, P. A., Kempner, K., Williams, P., Edson, S. K., & Smith, M. A. (1980). *Sex equity in education*. New York: Academic Press.

Suzuki, B. H. (1984). Curriculum transformation for multicultural education. *Education and Urban Society, 16*, 294–322.

Tavris, C., & Wade, C. (1984). *The longest war: Sex differences in perspective* (2nd ed.). New York: Harcourt Brace Jovanovich.

Tiedt, P. L., & Tiedt, I. M. (1995). *Multicultural teaching: A handbook of activities, information, and resources* (4th ed.). Boston: Allyn & Bacon.

Tittle, C. K. (1973). Women and educational testing. *Phi Delta Kappan, 54,* 118–119.

Trueba, E. T. (1976). Issues and problems in bilingual bicultural education today. *Journal for the National Association of Bilingual Education, 1,* 11–19.

Trueba, H. T. (1991). Learning needs of minority children: Contributions of ethnography to educational research. In L. M. Malave & G. Duquette (Eds.), *Language, culture & cognition* (pp. 137–155). Clevedon, England: Multilingual Matters.

Ysseldyke, J. E., Thurlow, M., Graden, J., Wesson, C., & Algozzine, B. (1983). Generalizations from five years of research on assessment and decision making: The University of Minnesota Institute. *Exceptional Education Quarterly, 4,* 75–93.

CHAPTER SIX

Education That Is Multicultural and Social Reconstructionist

Y
ou are probably stumbling over the name of the fifth approach we will now examine—Education That Is Multicultural and Social Reconstructionist—wondering why it contains so many words. Each word contributes to our understanding of the concept. *Social reconstructionism* is a recognized philosophical orientation toward education. As Brameld (1956) puts it, reconstructionism offers a "critique of modern culture" (p. 37). It holds that "magnificent as their services to society [may] have been in the past, the major institutions and the corresponding social, economic, and other practices that developed during the preceding centuries of the modern era are now incapable of ..." (pp. 37–38), and one can end this statement by adding whatever social issue with which one is concerned. To Brameld, the social issues of concern were ending war and economic depression. To advocates of this approach to multicultural education, the social issue of concern is the elimination of oppression of one group of people by another.

As Grant (1978) has explained, the expression *Education That Is Multicultural* means that the entire educational program is redesigned to reflect the concerns of diverse cultural groups. Rather than being one of several kinds of education, it is a different orientation and expectation of the whole educational process.

Since the time that Grant used the phrase an "Education That Is Multicultural," and Grant and Sleeter added Social Resconstructionist to complete their way of articulating this approach, it has developed a small but steadily growing number of advocates. The term, Education That Is Multicultural and Social Reconstructionist, is also adopted by educators who want to identify with a more assertive and transforming educational postion.

GOALS

Reflect on the various forms of social inequality that we discussed in Chapter 1. Education That Is Multicultural and Social Reconstructionist deals more directly than the other approaches with oppression and social structural inequality based

Table 6–1.
Education That Is Multicultural and Social Reconstructionist

Societal goal:	Promote social structural equality and cultural pluralism
School goals:	Prepare citizens to work actively toward social structural equality; promote cultural pluralism and alternative life styles; promote equal opportunity in the school
Target students:	Everyone
Practices:	
Curriculum	Organize content around current social issues involving racism, classism, sexism, handicapism; organize concepts around experiences and perspectives of several different American groups; use students' life experiences as starting point for analyzing oppression; teach critical thinking skills, analysis of alternative viewpoints; teach social action skills, empowerment skills
Instruction	Involve students actively in democratic decision making; build on students' learning styles; adapt to students' skill levels; use cooperative learning
Other aspects of classroom	Decorate room to reflect social action themes, cultural diversity, student interests; avoid testing and grouping procedures that designate some students as failures
Support services	Help regular classroom adapt to as much diversity as possible
Other schoolwide concerns	Involve students in democratic decision making about substantive schoolwide concerns; involve lower-class and minority parents actively in the school; involve school in local community action projects; make sure that staffing patterns include diverse racial, gender, and disability groups in nontraditional roles; use decorations, special events, school menus to reflect and include diverse groups; use library materials that portray diverse groups in diverse roles; make sure that extracurricular activities include all student groups and do not reinforce stereotypes; use discipline procedures that do not penalize any one group; make sure building is accessible to disabled people

on race, social class, gender, and disability. As noted in Table 6–1, the approach prepares future citizens to reconstruct society so that it better serves the interests of all groups of people and especially those who are of color, poor, female, gay, lesbian, transexual, disabled, or any combination of these. This approach is visionary. Although grounded very much in the everyday world of experience, it is not trapped by this world. In fact, it is similar to the view revealed in these words by George Bernard Shaw (1921): "You see things; and you say, 'Why?' But I dream things that never were; and I say, 'Why not?'"

Brameld (1956) describes social reconstructionism as a utopian philosophy. By this statement he means "any construction of the imagination that extends beyond the here-and-now to become a far-reaching idealization of human, especially cultural, potentialities" (p. 24). He goes on to explain:

> "Utopian" does not here connote a flight from reality into a realm of totally unrealizable, fantastic perfection. The utopian attitude is not that of the impractical daydreamer who cannot bear to face the hard problems of his [or her] own day or his [or her] immediate environment. The vision of utopianism is, rather, a realizable one—a vision of what can be and should be attained in order that man [and woman] may be happier, more rational, more humane than he [or she] has ever been. (pp. 24–25)

Social reconstructionism speaks, in the words of Aronowitz and Giroux (1985), the "language of possibility. In this case, we move to the terrain of hope and agency, to the sphere of struggle and action, one steeped in a vision which chooses life and offers constructive alternatives" (p. 19).

Advocates of this approach do not loudly and clearly articulate one particular vision of the ideal society. They argue that resources should be distributed much more equally than they are now and that people should not have to adhere to one model of what is considered "normal" or "right" to enjoy their fair share of wealth, power, happiness, or respect. Nonetheless, advocates believe that it would be another form of elitism for a small group of educators to tell other people what the "right" vision of a better society is. Rather, young people, and particularly those who are members of oppressed groups, should understand the nature of oppression in modern society. Correspondingly, they should understand how their ascribed characteristics (e.g., race, class, gender) and their culture impact on that oppression, which should lead them to develop the power and skills to articulate both their own goals and a vision of social justice for all groups and to work constructively toward these ends.

This approach works toward a vision of social justice by teaching political literacy. As Freire (1985) explains:

> A political illiterate—regardless of whether she or he knows how to read and write— is one who has an ingenuous perception of humanity in its relationships with the world. This person has a naive outlook on social reality, which for this one is a given, that is, social reality is a fait accompli rather than something that's still in the making. (p. 103)

Through a process called *conscientization*, Freire believes that people should learn to question society, see through versions of "truth" that teach people to accept unfairness and inhumanity, and become empowered to envision, define, and work toward a more humane society.

This approach, more than the others, is called different things by different advocates. For example, one may encounter terms such as *emancipatory pedagogy* (Gordon, 1985), *critical teaching* (Shor, 1980), *transformational education* (Giroux, 1981), *multicultural education* (Suzuki, 1984), *antiracist teaching* (Carby, 1982; Mullard, 1980), *socialist feminism* (Jaggar & Struhl, 1993), *culturally responsive teaching* (Irvine, 1991), and *decision making and social action* (Banks, 1988). Although educators using these different terms do not advocate exactly the same things (one main difference being that some focus primarily on race, others on gender, still others on social class), their basic goals and theoretical assumptions are very similar. The term we use may be longer, but we believe it is also more descriptive of what is meant.

This approach lends itself well to integrating concerns related to race, social class, gender, disability, and forms of oppression such as homophobia. Most advocates do not achieve such integration very well, but most recognize the desirability of achieving integration. In this chapter, gender, race, and social class will be tied together, although you should be aware that such linking may not have been done in the sources cited.

Advocates of Education That Is Multicultural and Social Reconstructionist, regardless of the term they use for the approach, agree on several theoretical assumptions about the nature of society and the nature of learning.

ASSUMPTIONS AND THEORY

This approach reverses much common-sense thinking about the relationship between individual beliefs and behavior and the larger social order. People often believe that if individuals become more humane, better skilled, more literate, or more civil, society as a whole will become more just. The first two approaches that were discussed rest heavily on this thinking, and the fourth approach considered contains some of this thinking. A fundamental assumption from the field of sociology, however, is that the reverse of this concept is true: Individuals shape their beliefs and behavior to fit their niche in the social structure. Similarly, one's niche in society or the social and cultural cues received from that niche influence one's performance or how the performance is viewed and accepted by others. Try to change individuals and they will quickly return to their old ways if the world they experience remains unchanged.

For example, middle-class people often wonder why housing in many low-income neighborhoods becomes so run down. Sometimes well-intentioned people try to teach the low-income residents techniques for home maintenance, assuming the condition of their housing is the product of a lack of knowledge and a lack of concern. (Even more naive attempts to help include preaching to the residents on the value of keeping their homes up.) Often, however, the residents are contending with other factors, such as absentee landlords who own the property, charge high rents, and do not themselves maintain the property that they own. The residents may not perceive that it is worthwhile to invest their own meager earnings in maintaining property that does not belong to them or make repairs and additions that will become the property of a landlord who has demonstrated a lack of regard for the tenants, especially if they are unsure of how long they will actually remain living there. If one is really concerned about the condition of such housing, often more pertinent issues to address are landlord policies and access to purchasing affordable, low-cost housing.

The assumption is that if we change peoples' world significantly, then their attitudes, beliefs, and behavior will change accordingly. The question that arises is:

Who is supposed to change society, if not individuals? Advocates of this approach argue that individuals need to learn to organize and work collectively in order to bring about social changes that are larger than individuals.

The approach actually elaborates on this idea. We will address this concept by discussing three interrelated theories on which this approach is based: conflict theory, cognitive development theory, and a sociological theory of culture.

Conflict Theory

Conflict theory, also called critical theory, is a sociological perspective for understanding social behavior. Various versions of conflict theory have been developed by theorists such as Weber (1947, 1968), Marx (1972), and Dahrendorf (1959). There are serious disagreements between schools of conflict theory; however, we will synthesize the main points of agreement.

First, social behavior is organized much more on a group basis than on an individual basis. Weber calls major social groupings "status groups." Collins (1977) explains that "the core of such groups is families and friends, but they may be extended to religious, educational, or ethnic communities" (p. 125). Groupings do not necessarily have definite boundaries; what constitutes a group changes somewhat, depending on the situation. However, groupings do follow definite patterns, centering around family, level of wealth, geographic proximity, and religious and cultural ties. As Collins explains, groups are central to human existence because "participation in such cultural groups gives individuals their fundamental sense of identity" (p. 125).

Second, groups struggle with each other for control over resources and ideas. Collins notes that power, wealth, and prestige are the main kinds of scarce resources. You can probably think of examples of these scarce resources in your own community: jobs, land, housing, political influence, perhaps even food or water. You can also think of ideas and beliefs, like environmental issues and abortion, over which groups struggle. Groups compete because people are by nature concerned mainly with their own welfare and that of their family, and secondarily about the welfare of others who they see as being like themselves or believing as they believe. When important resources are in scarce supply, most of us are concerned primarily about attaining these resources for people close to us. People we neither know nor identify with usually receive much less concern or sympathy— often none at all.

The more scarce is the resource, the more intense is the struggle, and the more important group membership becomes. America has an ideology of individual achievement, but for the conflict theorist, this ideology masks reality. The resources with which a person starts, the opportunities open to the person, the circumstances in which the person lives, and the way others react to the person all depend to a significant extent on the groups of which that person is a member.

For example, writing about gender membership and power, Oakley (1981) writes that "power is unequally distributed in most societies, and depends not only on personal qualities of the individual but on social position. Different people occupy different social positions and men occupy a different position in society from women" (p. 281). A woman may attempt to achieve power within a community, but her individual efforts are shaped partly by her gender: As a mother, her time may be limited by domestic responsibilities; some men in the community may refuse to take orders from her; and her stand on gender-related issues may polarize would-be constituents on the basis of sex. The more influential and coveted is the position she seeks, and the more she acts as an advocate for women, the more one is likely to see sex stereotyping and denigration of women occurring to "keep her in her place." Former Labor Secretary Lynn Martin refers collectively to the attitudes, prejudices, and patterns of action that keep women and people of color from being rewarded top management positions as a "glass ceiling." In a study of the rise of anorexia, Wolf (1991) argues that the gains women made during the 1970s challenged male privileges such as access to the highest-paying jobs. The result was a backlash to keep women "in their place" by diverting women's attention to personal "self-improvement" rather than collective advancement. The ideal woman in media became much thinner, stressing to women how important looks are, how inadequate most women's bodies are, and what beauty products and diet regimens are necessary in order to become attractive.

A third idea is that to solidify, extend, and legitimate its control, a dominant group structures social institutions to operate in ways that will maintain or increase the group's own advantage. However, the group tries to establish and promulgate rules of society in such a way that most people will think the system is fair. For example, in a capitalist economy, people can gain wealth by investing extra money. The investor collects interest, dividends, or profits; the labor necessary for accumulating that money is performed by someone else. The more extra money one has, the wealthier one can become. The secretary who barely earns enough to make ends meet will have little or no capital to invest; the corporate executive will very likely have quite a bit. Yet, most people accept this system as fair because they believe that everyone has an equal opportunity to invest; it just so happens that those who need money the most rarely have any capital to invest.

As another example, Abberley (1987), a sociologist who is disabled, argues that dominant groups oppress disabled people in an effort to control access to jobs and to convince workers of the rightness of the Protestant work ethic. People are led to believe that normal adults work full time, which is an advantage to the capitalist; people who do not work full time are viewed as abnormal, even defective. He points out that most concepts of disability are purely biological in nature and that they suggest that defective people cannot be expected to want or have the same advantages as "normal" people. For example, hearing impairment is usually understood as resulting from defects in a person's auditory system, with little consideration given to the extent to which the social environment accommodates the hearing impaired. If we view disabled people as biologically defective, we tend to assume that they should be satisfied with less from life. Abberley writes:

> By presenting disadvantage as the consequence of a naturalized "impairment" it legitimizes the failure of welfare facilities and the distribution system in general to provide for social need, that is, it interprets the effects of social maldistribution as the consequence of individual deficiency. (p. 17)

This structuring of social institutions for the benefit of dominant groups results in institutional racism, sexism, and classism. As neo-Marxist sociologists point out, the capitalist economy structures in great wealth differences and enables the class that controls production to maintain and extend its wealth. A few individuals may gain economic mobility, but the lower and working classes as a whole do not. However, because some people do become upwardly mobile, and because most people seem to act like autonomous individuals, the class system is made to seem fair. Many people do not recognize or understand how the wealthy use their wealth to control the economic and political lives of others. As Apple (1985) puts it, "We castigate a few industrialists and corporations, a small number of figures in government, a vague abstraction called technology, instead of seeing the productive and political apparatus of society as interconnected" (p. 5).

For example, Mitchell (1978) has described four structures in which women are institutionalized into a separate existence from men, an existence that enables men to extend power over women. These structures are production, reproduction, sexuality, and the socialization of children. Within each of these structures, all of which are interconnected, women's lives are made different from men's. For instance, production refers to a division of labor based on sex. Mitchell points out that in most societies, women's work is different from men's and is connected to women's role as childbearer; furthermore, women's work is usually valued less than men's work. In industrial societies, as labor moved from the home to the factory, women were increasingly segmented out of the labor force because they were given responsibility for the socialization of children, which meant they had to stay home. The fact that child raising, housework, and related jobs (such as teaching) are either unpaid or poorly paid has structured women as a group into an economically and politically oppressed position.

So far, it probably appears that social change is almost impossible. However, some conflict theorists offer a related theory that provides the promise of help: resistance theory. The main idea behind resistance theory is that people who are oppressed should not just sit back and take it. Although it is not always obvious to people exactly how they are being oppressed, they can often act in ways that oppose their oppression.

Opposition can take many different forms. Here we will make a few distinctions. One distinction is between overt behavioral opposition, which is visible to observers, and private, or mental, opposition, which is more difficult for an observer to detect. People often adapt overtly to circumstances they face while privately opposing those circumstances. Theorists such as Anyon (1983), Apple (1985), Genovese (1974), and Giddens (1979) have called this form of opposition *accommodation* or *pragmatic acceptance*. For example, many people who are bilingual accommodate English-only policies by speaking English in public, but privately they advocate bilingualism.

Resistance is a term given to overt behavioral opposition. Resistive behavior can be, on the one hand, consciously directed toward extensive and long-term social change or, on the other hand, directed toward making one's own immediate life a little better; or it can be anywhere in between. For example, the 1960s witnessed many instances of African-American resistance to racism. Rosa Parks's refusal to give up her seat on the bus triggered collective resistance on the part of the African-American community in the form of a bus boycott, which became consciously directed toward changing race relations. Collectively, African Americans reduced White control over many areas of their lives through such actions. However, not all resistance to authority is directed consciously toward extensive social change. For example, many teenagers of color, especially young men, are joining gangs partly because they see their own futures as limited because they are poor, because the adult males that they know have been marginalized and oppressed, and because their race and culture often are not accepted as equal to Whites in society's marketplaces. Although society tells them to go to school to make their life circumstances equal to that of Whites, many do not accept this injunction and therefore join gangs as a form of self-help and resistance. These teenagers' resistance to dominant social norms can be interpreted as an attempt to create more meaningful lives for themselves, although most members of their community view such behavior as harmful to their group's status. These two examples illustrate quite different forms of resistance to oppression, but what they have in common is the refusal of people to accept restrictions that the social system attempts to impose on their lives and their happiness.

The important point for teachers to realize is that many people are already engaged in some sort of struggle against oppression without necessarily having been taught social theory. Many people, often as part of a group, oppose on a daily basis what they see as unfair authority or restrictions imposed by someone else. In school, this may take countless forms, such as girls resisting being viewed as sex objects, students in wheelchairs ganging up against those who tease them, or students living below the poverty line who refuse to obey middle-class teachers with low expectations of them. Further, oppressed communities are often engaged in organized forms of resistance, although children may not yet be cognizant of the issues in the same way that adults in the community view those issues. For example, local chapters of the National Association for the Advancement of Colored People (NAACP), Indian rights organization such as HONOR, local gay rights or disability rights organizations, or local National Organization of Women (NOW) chapters often have organized strategies for addressing specific issues of discrimination.

These naturally occurring examples of resistance are a good place to start teaching about social issues because they are a part of real-life issues with which students can identify. In addition, organizations often produce newsletters that provide useful information about issues. After studying an issue, students may decide that their present form of resistance is not as effective as alternative forms. For example, resisting racism by refusing to learn and validating the low expectations some White teachers may have is not usually as effective as resisting racism by achieving academic success and learning as much as possible in order to gain a position of social power, thus making certain that others do not have to endure a similar experience. Rather than dismiss or ignore students' opposition to authority, however, educators can use this opposition as a beginning point to analyze issues.

Cognitive Development Theory

Education That Is Multicultural and Social Reconstructionist also draws on cognitive development theory, which has been developed by scholars such as Piaget (1952), Vygotsky (1986) and Dewey (1938). Cognitive development theory was discussed in Chapter 3, so we will not elaborate extensively on it here, although its implications for this approach are somewhat different. According to cognitive development theory, learning is a process of constructing knowledge through the interaction of mind and experience. Knowledge always has a concrete basis, and children need concrete experience in order to develop knowledge. Children develop knowledge by interacting mentally and to some extent physically with people and objects around them. This interaction requires active involvement. Knowledge that is poured into a passive mind is quickly forgotten. As Dewey (1938) remarked, "The educator cannot start with knowledge already organized and proceed to ladle it out in doses" (p. 82). Additionally, Vygotsky's (1986) social cognitive theory points up the importance of culture and language to facilitate learning. He believes that language is a social and cultural phenomenon that is central to the development of thinking and that cognitive development is greatly influenced by one's cultural and social environment. Knowledge that is remembered and used by children is that which relates to their interests and social and cultural milieu, is in a language that they understand, is constructed by the children (often with guidance from a teacher, parent, or another child), and includes their active involvement.

In other words, children's understanding of society and of other people is based on the world they experience and how society connects to their world. If the society they encounter is predominantly of one ethnic or racial group, children's comprehension of racism or knowledge of other groups is limited. Similarly, if children see females mainly in certain roles, their understanding of the life roles and goals of women will be limited. Simply telling children about people or problems beyond their experience may not penetrate their understanding very deeply. Children need to have direct and active involvement with the group or issue of concern. Also, if their daily experience contradicts what the teacher tells them, they will probably believe their experience, although they may parrot back what the teacher says. For example, if jobs are hard to find in the students' neighborhood and many people are unemployed, the teacher who tells them that the economy is strong and that anyone who looks can find work will not only not be believed, but will be seen as someone out of touch with their needs and interests. These ideas are similar to those discussed in earlier chapters, and they underscore the importance of paying attention to and working with children's experiential backgrounds.

With respect to social action, cognitive development theory has additional implications. Dewey (1938) agreed with Thomas Jefferson's (1779) observation that:

> Even under the best of forms, those entrusted with power have, in time, and by slow operations, perverted it into tyranny; ... the most effectual means of preventing this would be, to illuminate, as far as predictable, the minds of the people at large. (chap. 79, sec. 1)

For Dewey, a democracy requires citizens who are capable of critical thought and collective social action. However, these traits are not developed by telling people to think or by explaining the principles of democracy. They are developed by practicing critical thought and social decision making in school. Dewey saw schools as ideal laboratories for developing an informed and active citizenry because schools are social institutions inhabited by groups of future citizens. The raw material is there. He wrote:

> Most children are naturally "sociable." Isolation is even more irksome to them than to adults. A genuine community life has its ground in this natural sociability. But community life does not organize itself in an enduring way purely spontaneously. It requires thought and planning ahead. (1938, p. 56)

Most schools and classrooms do not practice democracy, nor do they develop students' powers of decision making and collective action. Nevertheless, their potential to do so is an idea that is attractive to advocates of this approach. Advocates of Education That Is Multicultural and Social Reconstructionist are often drawn to the ideas of Dewey and Piaget because they focus attention on the child's world and because they focus on social action. Advocates are also drawn to these ideas because they suggest the equalizing of power relations in the classroom.

Democratizing power relationships in the classroom does not necessarily mean turning all power over to the students. As Elshtain (1976) points out, giving students too much power over deciding what to learn and allowing them to dwell excessively on their own experience is not necessarily enlightening because the students by themselves will not necessarily come up with insights about social inequality. The teacher implementing this approach wants students to use experience to gain certain insights about the nature of society. Therefore, the teacher needs to maintain a balance between drawing on the students' world and inviting student decision making on the one hand and, on the other, helping students gain knowledge and ideas that will illuminate not only their own experience, but society in general. Additionally, and very importantly, democratizing power relationships allows students to gain some understanding of the responsibilities that come with power in a democracy, as well as the appropriate use of power in a democracy.

Theory of Culture
The previous chapter described cultural transmission theory as anthropologists have developed it. Many anthropologists, and indeed many advocates of the Multicultural Education approach, believe that behavior is guided mainly by culturally learned ideas and that society is the way it is, in large part, because of our cultural beliefs and values. Change the culture, and social institutions will change. Furthermore, many cultural practices are valuable in and of themselves and can be maintained even if the life circumstances of a group change.

Advocates of Education That Is Multicultural and Social Reconstructionist see culture somewhat differently. To them, much of everyday culture is an adaptation to life's circumstances, which have been in part determined by group competition for resources. Certainly, some aspects of culture are passed down from one generation to the next. Language is a good example: Most of us simply learn and use the language developed by our ancestors, although we may make small contributions to this language during our lifetime. Other aspects of culture are created on an ongoing, everyday basis, in much the same way knowledge is constructed. For example, Kanter (1975) has described some differences between male and female cultures in the workplace. Those who hold secretarial jobs, usually women, are rewarded by their employers with little or no career-ladder opportunities as well as relatively low salaries. Consequently, women holding such jobs gradually learn to seek some of their rewards for working from coworkers. (Making friends with other secretaries brings satisfaction that routine word processing for a small paycheck does not.) In addition, they learn to confine work to working hours, since working overtime will not advance them in a career and may not even bring overtime pay. Such women develop a culture that nurtures relationships and cooperation and that is oriented toward completing assigned work during assigned hours only. On the other hand, the bosses for whom they work, usually men, often have access to a career ladder with increased pay and power. Getting the work done and spending time outside normal work hours on work-related matters pays off more than developing relationships with coworkers. The men, therefore, develop a culture that is somewhat impersonal, intense, and competitive. Both cultures are adaptations to conditions and access to resources, which are based in part on membership in unequal groups.

As this example illustrates, culture represents a group's attempt to interpret, give meaning to, and function within shared circumstances. When this idea is viewed politically, it means that part of the substance of culture results directly from a group's material and political position. Essentially, then, one should study culture not just to appreciate and admire it, but also to understand the sociopolitical circumstances that helped give rise to it. One should recognize that members of a given group struggle to change their sociopolitical circumstances, which in turn will result in some cultural change. We will borrow from the writings of two Asian American authors to illustrate this point. In *Strangers from a Different Shore*, Takaki (1989) discusses how Asian Americans have continually struggled to gain acceptance in mainstream society. He writes:

> Asian newcomers encounter a prevailing vision of America as essentially a place where European immigrants would establish a homogenous white society and where nonwhites would have to remain "stranger" ... But the Asian immigrants chose not to let the course of their lives be determined completely by the "necessity" of race and class in America ... Throughout their history in this country, Asians have been struggling in different ways to help America accept its diversity. (pp. 472–473)

Suzuki (1977), discussing Japanese Americans, relates the idea of culture to education. He points out that many social scientists have attributed the economic and educational success of Japanese Americans to inherited cultural patterns from Japan: "strong family structure, emphasis on education, Protestant-type work ethic and high achievement motivation—values deeply rooted in the cultural milieu of Meiji-era Japan" (p. 153). Such social scientists assume that culture is an inheritance from previous generations and that Japanese-American culture is a blend of Japanese culture and Anglo culture. Suzuki argues that this view is at best only partially correct.

Japanese Americans have retained some cultural forms inherited from the Japanese, but what was retained and how it has been changed and redeveloped in the United States has depended strongly on the sociopolitical circumstances that Japanese Americans have encountered. Suzuki (1977) points out several factors that Japanese Americans have had to deal with: racism during World War II and the internment camps; the loss of possessions as a result of internment; quotas placed on Japanese immigration, which kept the Japanese American population very small; and the demand for technical workers immediately after the war. He describes how Japanese Americans tried to reestablish themselves after the war:

> It seemed prudent for them to adopt a low-profile strategy that would not attract too much attention nor elicit adverse reaction. Thus, it is understandable why the Nisei (second-generation) has been stereotyped as quiet, hardworking, non-assertive, dependable and accommodating. (p. 151)

Values and cultural patterns have provided some of the substance for interpreting and adapting to the American experience, but sociopolitical factors such as racism and economic circumstances have also been important. Japanese-American culture is continually being recreated as Japanese Americans confront, interpret, and respond to social conditions. One can apply this example to other groups as well. Culture is continually recreated as people confront their daily environments; inherited patterns of believing and behaving provide themes and forms to help interpret daily life, but culture does not simply flow through passive individuals like water through a pipe.

For this reason, Suzuki (1984) has warned that overemphasis on culture "has led some to pursue ethnicity almost for its own sake." Similarly, he argues that it has led others to believe that multicultural education consists merely of including ethnic content in the curriculum. With this belief, culture takes on limited meaning and comes to suggest only foods, festivals, fairs, and folk tales, as well as exotic or primitive life styles. Because of this overemphasis and narrow meaning, Suzuki continues, "the social realities of racism, sexism, and class inequality are often overlooked or conveniently forgotten" (p. 300). He then points out that ignoring or downplaying the importance of social structure and "the position of an ethnic group in that structure ... can lead to the mistaken and conservative view that ethnic subcultures are rooted in the past and are static and unchanging" (p. 300).

This conclusion does not suggest that culture is unimportant. The cultures of diverse groups should be studied. However, they, as well as the culture of the dominant group, should be studied not only to help develop appreciation, but also to help understand how a group relates to other groups, how a group has made sense of its own status, and how a group has attempted to compete with other groups. For example, the literature produced by men and women of different ethnic and racial groups tells us something about what it means to be poor, or to live in the barrio or ghetto, or to work in the factory or the home. The literature tells us how people have adjusted their dreams to their conditions, how people have given each other support, how they have resisted oppression. These ideas may not always be stated explicitly, but implicitly they are there and can be examined.

RECOMMENDED PRACTICES

Education That Is Multicultural and Social Reconstructionist has much in common with the Multicultural Education approach, and it also borrows from the other three approaches. However, it is a distinctly different approach. We will first describe and discuss four practices that are unique to it, then briefly discuss practices drawn from previously discussed approaches. Table 6–1 summarizes recommended practices that are specific to this approach, as well as practices it shares with other approaches.

Practicing Democracy

Americans believe in the ideals of democracy, which are written into documents such as the Constitution, the Bill of Rights, and the Declaration of Independence. However, advocates of Education That Is Multicultural and Social Reconstructionist point out that most schools do not actively encourage democracy. For example, Banks (1981) points out that there are major "contradictions between the values expressed in our national documents and the ways in which minority groups are treated in the United States" (p. 154). Barbagli and Dei (1977) condemn schools for teaching students to acquiesce to authority rather than to exercise it:

> The more hierarchical and rigid these [teacher-pupil] relationships are, and the more they are characterized by the concentration of decisions in the hands of the teacher and by a rigid control on the behavior of the pupils, the more easily will the latter acquire attitudes of docility and submission to authority. (p. 426)

In schools, the practice of democracy often does not go beyond reading the Constitution and learning about the three branches of government in a social studies class. However, advocates of Education That Is Multicultural and Social Reconstructionist point out that practicing democracy also means learning to articulate one's interests, to openly debate issues with one's peers, to organize and work collectively with others, to acquire power, to exercise power, and so forth. Mann (1974) argues as follows:

> Since political power is a ubiquitous fact of social existence, and since a democracy depends for its vigor and justness upon equitable distribution of power, it is proper that the citizens' schools offer extensive opportunities for learning about how political power operates. (p. 147)

It is not enough just to know that the Constitution exists or that the law says that Americans are equal: Citizens need to learn to make these ideas work for them. This concept is particularly important for members of oppressed groups. Writing about oppressed ethnic and racial groups, Banks (1981) argues that:

> They must also develop a sense of political efficacy, and be given practice in social action strategies which teaches them how to get power without violence and further ex-

clusion … Opportunities for social action, in which students have experience in obtaining and exercising power, should be emphasized within a curriculum that is designed to help liberate excluded ethnic groups. (p. 149)

To Freire (1985), this practice would produce women and "men who organize themselves reflectively for action rather than [women and] men who are organized for passivity" (p. 82).

Shor (1980) talks about helping students become subjects rather than objects in the classroom. According to this view, students should learn to direct much of their learning and to do so responsibly, rather than always being directed by someone else. This is not to say that teachers should abdicate and simply let students do whatever they want. Such a response can result in chaos or "trivial pursuit." Rather, teachers should guide and direct so that students can grow and develop a sense of responsibility in the way they make decisions. McPhie (1988) argues that students should have the opportunity to debate issues and make decisions that affect their immediate lives, both directly and through representation, as long as those decisions abide by the principle of hierarchical authority. He points out that educators have allowed student-government elections to become too much of a popularity contest, with a carnival atmosphere, and that little is done to teach students how to effectively lobby to promote change (p. 152).

Many argue that empowering students is the most effective, not to mention the most ethical, way of dealing with discipline. For example, Van Avery (1975) writes:

Our society thinks that "more discipline" will make a better world and certainly better schools. But doesn't the cry for discipline really translate to, "Let's try to help people act in a responsible manner"? This society desperately needs people who accept responsibility, not simply accept discipline. (p. 177)

By learning to obey others, young people may learn discipline but not responsibility, because obedience does not require examining situations, thinking through alternative courses of action, or forecasting the consequences of various courses of action.

Consider the example of a junior high social studies teacher who has built into his curriculum opportunities for student decision making and student exercise of power, specifically so that his students, who are working class and racially diverse, can practice affecting an institution. After teaching students about various forms of government, he has the class select a form to use to govern the class (the usual selection being representative democracy). Under his guidance, the class then practices that form for a period of time. He also has the class run schoolwide elections: They organize balloting, make campaign posters, plan campaign strategies, and so forth. He provides opportunities for them to select topics to research in small groups and to plan their research strategies. Again, he guides their thinking so that their decisions are usually workable, and when their decisions are not workable, the students understand why not and what might work better next time.

Practicing democracy also has implications for how teachers interact with the communities they serve. A teacher or a school committed to democracy makes a point of involving parents in deciding on the goals and educational practices of the school. The parents and the community are viewed both as partners and as valuable resources. The community actively works to connect with the school and to extend the programs and experiences begun during the school day. For example, the community library staff and the school teaching staff work together in preparation for students to visit their state capital. Parents are accepted as valuable members of their son's or daughter's educational team. They are seen as able to contribute much more than telling their children to go to school, to listen to the teacher, and to behave. The utter centrality of providing students with the opportunity to develop and participate in the democratic life of schools and involving teachers, parents, and community members in collaborative, educational efforts is illustrated quite compellingly in a recent publication highlighting schools engaged in attempts to democratize education (Apple & Beane, 1995).

Analyzing the Circumstances of One's Own Life

Earlier, we discussed the concept of resistance; here we develop its implications. Anyon (1981) explains that people have a practical consciousness that coexists with a theoretical consciousness. Practical consciousness refers to one's common-sense understanding of one's own life, of how the system works, and of "everyday attempts to resolve the class, race, gender and other contradictions one faces" (p. 126). Theoretical consciousness refers to dominant social ideologies, explanations that one learns for how the world works that purport that the world is fair and just as it is. These two sets of consciousness do not always mesh; most of us learn to believe a mixture of them. For example, children are taught that America is the golden land of opportunity and that anyone can get ahead by working hard. Yet poor children whose parents work hard for low wages know that this teaching does not necessarily apply to their own families; children of color learn firsthand that racism often thwarts their opportunities. Nevertheless, schools proclaim the dominant ideology, rarely giving much attention to insights that run counter to it that may develop in everyday life.

Advocates of Education That Is Multicultural and Social Reconstructionist recommend that schooling help students analyze their own lives in order to develop their practical consciousness about real injustices in society and to develop constructive responses. Metcalf and Hunt (1974) believe that this approach would appeal to most young people, who "are particularly critical of established educational practice" (p. 138). Let us consider some examples.

Freire (1985) has long used this approach to help South American peasants learn to read, having them learn words that will help them examine limitations placed on their own lives, such as vastly unequal land distribution. Most reading texts bear no relationship to their lives, teaching only the dominant group's version of reality; Freire either does not use these texts or teaches students to question them. Shor (1980) has used this same approach in several ways, such as having his students examine hamburgers for nutritional value and then examine who benefits economically when we eat junk food rather than food that is good for us. Kobrin (1992) has implemented a collaborative project with four public-school teachers in which students are taught to become historians and are also taught the importance of being able to use history to understand and shape the problems of their own lives.

Similarly, Gere, Fairbanks, Howes, Roop, and Schaafsma (1992) describe how teachers in language-as-social-construct classrooms use this method to teach their students about political aspects of schooling, including how to address political topics in the classroom. These teachers seek to empower their students because they believe that all people have a vested interest in the decisions that govern their lives. Additionally, as the result of a study of young women taking business-education courses, Valli (1986) suggests that the courses, which in the past have been virtually silent about the class and gender oppression experienced by secretaries, should be changed in order to help young women examine the marginal status of these jobs, as well as the ways in which such jobs perpetuate the subordination of working-class women. Another opportunity for change could be to help Hispanic students analyze the impact of current immigration legislation on themselves and their communities, examining its effect on undocumented workers as well as on those who have been citizens for years. Students could survey their neighborhoods for patterns of employment among adults and also for ties, if any, with relatives in Puerto Rico, Mexico, Cuba, and so forth. In the area of mathematics, Tate (1995) encourages teachers to adopt culturally relevant teaching methods and focuses upon the way a particular teacher and her students used math to analyze community problems (e.g., tax incentives which supported the location of liquor stores near the school) and to influence change through the production and public sharing of quantitative data (e.g., maps and graphs presented to the city council).

So far, the idea of analyzing students' own life circumstances probably seems most relevant to students who are members of oppressed groups. Advocates of this approach recognize that the dominant, standard curriculum is more congruent with the lives of middle- and upper-middle-class White students than it is with the lives of other students. However, members of advantaged groups can also learn from their own lives how their privileged position allows them advantages that others cannot afford or gain access to. For example, middle-class White students can analyze housing patterns in their community to determine where the various racial, ethnic, and social class groups live. To look into the basis of housing patterns, they can interview someone from Fair Housing or some realtors; they can also investigate how zoning laws are made and by whom. To examine the effects of housing patterns, they can compare two different neighborhoods in terms of access to schools, access to public transportation, or access to bank loans. It is imperative, in fact, that students reflect on the ways "whiteness" bestows upon them particular privileges. In this way, students may come to recognize their own complicity in forms of oppression, the destructive impact it has upon their own humanity, and the need for them to contest injustice in all its forms (Frankenburg, 1993; Sleeter, 1994; Tatum, 1994).

Metcalf and Hunt (1974) believe that most young people are critical to some extent of the world their elders have created and are open-minded about investigating social problems. This phenomenon has become increasingly evident in recent times as many civic and political leaders posit that the present generation is exploiting the natural and monetary resources of future generations. Advocates of this approach recommend that the curriculum incorporate "a study of an important social movement, rejection by youth, and that this study emphasize examining, testing, and appraising the major beliefs caught up in the movement" (Metcalf & Hunt, 1974, p. 138).

Students should analyze not only their own lives but also their responses to life circumstances. For example, many children who live at or below the poverty level, many gay and lesbian students, and many students of color give up and drop out, recognizing that society and the school are strongly biased against them. Although their interpretation of society may be quite correct, their response is not constructive. They are not, according to Hale (1982), seeing school as a place to gain an education for struggle and survival. Dropping out, having babies, taking drugs, joining a gang, and other behaviors may be active forms of opposition, but these forms do not empower the young to change the circumstances that they are facing. Criticizing aspects of the student revolt of the 1960s, Aronowitz and Giroux (1985) argue that "if students are to be empowered by school experiences, one of the key elements of their education must be that they acquire mastery of language as well as the capacity to think conceptually and critically" (p. 158). What these authors are stressing is the need for young people to recognize those responses that will empower them, probably requiring them to use school to develop the skills needed to work for social change and to better their own lives. Writer bell hooks (1994) envisions schooling as a means for liberation, advocating a pedagogy which empowers both teachers and students to actively oppose dominance both inside the classroom as well as outside.

Teachers who are unsure of how to begin helping students analyze inequality in their own lives might start by subscribing to social action publications produced by oppressed groups, such as *The Crisis*, *Third Force*, *MS*, *The Disability Rag*, or *off our backs*. These publications often frame current issues in ways that ensure that leaders of oppressed groups see them, and they provide a blueprint of exactly what to look at locally, in one's own community.

Developing Social Action Skills

This third recommended practice links the first two: It brings democratic political skills to bear on issues involving race, class, and gender inequalities in the students' everyday world. Bennett (1986) defines social action skills as "the knowledge, attitudes, and skills needed to help bring about political, social, and economic changes" (p. 212). She argues that ignoring the fact that some groups "are unable to gain, maintain, and effectively use political power, to ignore this goal, is to make a sham out of the rest of multicultural education" (p. 212).

We should first repeat that advocates of Education That Is Multicultural and Social Reconstructionist do not expect children to reconstruct the world. Rather, these advocates view schools as connected with other institutions in society, either working with most institutions to reinforce inequality or working with opposition movements to institute change. Suzuki (1984) argues that "the schools cannot avoid transmitting values ... The only honest position educators can take is to impart values they believe reflect their vision of the highest achievable human ideals"; educators should recognize that "while the schools cannot operate independent of the prevalent culture, they can still play a significant role in the process of social change" (pp. 303–304).

Advocates of this approach view the school as a laboratory or training ground for preparing a socially active citizenry. Bennett (1986) argues that this preparation should begin at the kindergarten level in classrooms operating democratically, as described earlier. Thus, students learn to begin seeing themselves as powerful agents within a social institution. Elementary school children can begin to examine issues and consider courses of action to take. For example, a reading text by Myers, Banfield, and Colon (1983) features stories that deal with issues of discrimination and oppression, written in terms children can understand. The stories also show people actively working to confront these issues, offering role models of active involvement. Discussion questions invite students to consider similar issues in their own life experiences. Follow-up action projects ask children to investigate, for example, the sexist advertising of toys in their own community and to make their findings and feelings known to local advertisers.

Primary-grade teachers often ask if their age group of students can participate in social action. The answer is that they can and actually do participate in social action frequently, for example, when they lobby to get home and school rules changed to meet their interests and needs. A recent example of such participation may help substantiate this statement. Several students in a first-grade class, who were tired of drinking white milk each day, wondered why they could not have chocolate milk sometimes—at least one or two days a week. These students joined with the rest of their classmates and approached their teacher with this idea. They were told by their teacher that the school did not order chocolate milk. The students asked, "Why couldn't the school order it sometimes?" They argued that the same brand of milk they received at school was available in the store as both white milk and chocolate milk. Some students said their parents bought them chocolate milk. Their teacher then informed them that the lunchroom manager had to decide this matter. The students asked if they could write the manager a letter and explain how they felt. They did, and to make what could be a long story short, the students are now receiving chocolate milk twice a week.

Older students can engage in more sophisticated social action projects. Banks (1981) recommends a variety of projects:

> Conducting a survey to determine the kinds of jobs which most minorities have in local hotels, restaurants, and firms, and if necessary, urging local businesses to hire more minorities in top level positions.
>
> Conducting boycotts of businesses that refuse to hire minorities in top level positions ... Conducting a survey to determine what local laws exist (and how they are enforced) regarding open housing, discrimination in public accommodations, etc., and if necessary, developing recommendations regarding changes which should be made in the laws or in the ways in which they should be implemented. Presenting these recommendations to appropriate public officials and pressuring them to act on the recommendations. (pp. 123–124)

Some advocates recommend that the schools should work with local community groups involved in reconstructive action rather than work in isolation, because this would help young people become involved with real struggles taking place around them (Aronowitz & Giroux, 1985).

Anyon (1981) explains that the purpose of these kinds of activities is to politicize students' resistance—to help students turn oppositional activity into constructive political activity. She explains that these sorts of activities should also help students develop "a collective self-love of themselves as a class made up of Blacks, Whites, members of both sexes, and various ethnicities" (p. 129); social action centers around group change strategies.

There are a number of curriculum guides available to teachers to help them teach students social action skills. For example, the Martin Luther King, Jr., Center on Nonviolent Social Change has developed a curriculum guide to infuse Dr. King's principles of nonviolent social action into the curriculum. The teaching guide *Open Minds to Equality* (Schniedewind & Davidson, 1983) provides first a step-by-step series of activities to build group cooperation, then collective skills in analysis of local issues and taking action. *The Kid's Guide to Social Action* (Lewis, 1991) shows young people how to take various kinds of actions such as writing letters, organizing petitions, and making persuasive speeches.

Coalescing

One of the main differences between the Education That Is Multicultural and Social Reconstructionist approach and the Single-Group Studies approach is that the former approach promotes coalescing across race, class, and gender lines, as Anyon's statement illustrates. There are some very good reasons for learning to form coalitions. One reason is that race, social class, and gender often should not be treated as separate issues. As we have pointed out elsewhere, not only do these issues all involve common concerns of oppression, but people are all members of a gender, a social class, and a racial group, and separating the issues is often somewhat artificial (Grant & Sleeter, 1986).

Another reason advocates call for coalescing is that this process makes for a more powerful group. For example, although the poor may be economically weak as a power base, they gain strength when joined by middle-class people of color and additional strength if joined by White women. Advocates have noted that disenfranchised groups sometimes find themselves fighting over crumbs, whereas if they worked together, they might all be able to achieve more.

Furthermore, coalescing guards against a kind of chauvinism that can result when issues of race, class, and gender are dealt with separately. Giroux (1983) has observed that much neo-Marxist work that challenges social class contains "reactionary racial and gender views" which often, "although allegedly committed to emancipatory concerns, ends up contributing to the reproduction of sexist and racist attitudes and practices" (p. 287).

Forming coalitions is not easy. Throughout our nation's history, groups have attempted to coalesce, often fragmenting as a result of internal competition. For example, Davis (1981) has examined the struggle for suffrage for people of color and women, arguing that White, middle-class women distanced themselves from

African American people when they feared that African American men rather than White women would achieve voting rights. Roediger (1991) explored the dynamics underlying the formation of the White working class during the post-Revolutionary period, ultimately revealing how the tendencies of White laborers to define themselves against and forge an identity in relationship to an enslaved Black class inhibited them from recognizing the economic system accountable for the exploitation of both. Advocates warn that people need to recognize and struggle against all forms of oppression, keeping in mind that the common goal is eliminating oppression rather than simply furthering one's own interests. This awareness involves learning how to handle compromise and how to cooperate with members of diverse groups. It also involves continually examining one's own biases and recognizing sources of one's own advantages.

For example, women continue to be divided along race and class lines so long as White, middle-class women refuse to deal with their own racism and classism. Similarly, African Americans, Hispanics, and Asians find themselves divided along gender and class lines to the extent that middle-class males of all colors fail to take seriously the concerns of women and lower-class members of their racial groups. Many people take homophobia so much for granted that they scoff at the idea of fighting for gay rights along with civil rights for other groups.

One promising approach to coalition building is using the school as a base for local social action projects that draw together diverse groups to accomplish something for the community. The school can serve as a coalescing point if community input is regarded seriously and not just as a rubber-stamp PTA. For example, Carter and Chatfield (1986) describe a school that included students who were White middle class, Mexican migrant, Filipino, and Southeast Asian. The school became involved with helping a senior citizens' community nearby, and this action helped the school develop cohesion and identification with a common community.

Commonalities with Previous Approaches

Education That Is Multicultural and Social Reconstructionist embraces the recommended practices of the Multicultural Education approach because, like the Multicultural Education approach, it advocates that the school and the classroom reflect and celebrate diversity. For both approaches, the curriculum—including materials, visual displays, films, guest speakers, and content taught orally—should represent experiences, perspectives, and contributions of diverse groups and should do so in a conceptual rather than in a fragmented way. The curriculum should be thus formulated all the time, in all subject areas. Nonsexist language should be used, and bilingualism or multilingualism should be endorsed. The curriculum should be equally accessible to all student groups; grouping practices or teaching procedures that enable only certain groups of students access to high-status knowledge or better teaching should be avoided. Teachers should build on students' learning styles rather than assuming that all learn best in the same way, and they should maintain high expectations for all students. Cooperative learning should be used to develop skills and attitudes of cooperation. Sexist teacher behavior should be avoided, and teachers should work to develop positive self-concepts in all students. (Incidentally, educators warn that White male students often find the approach discussed in this chapter threatening to their own self-concepts, and they strongly suggest that teachers work to affirm these students as individuals and include them in social reconstructionist efforts.) Biased evaluation procedures should be avoided; evaluation should be used for improving instruction, not for sorting and ranking students. Home/community-school relationships should be developed, and parents should be actively involved, particularly if they are at or below the poverty level and/or minority. Staffing patterns should reflect cultural diversity and offer a variety of role models for males and females of different race and class backgrounds. Finally, extracurricular activities should not perpetuate race and sex stereotypes.

Education That Is Multicultural and Social Reconstructionist shares with Single-Group Studies its social-issues emphasis, its concern with representing the interests of oppressed groups, and its desire to mobilize young people to work actively for social justice. It shares with the Human Relations approach an interest in developing cooperation among students and a concern for developing student self-concept. It also shares a desire to eliminate stereotyping, but it does not view as particularly effective the use of lessons about stereotyping or attempts to deal with stereotyping without changing the social sources of stereotypes. As with Teaching the Exceptional and Culturally Different, this approach agrees that teaching should start where students are, relate to their experiential background, build on the language and learning style they bring from home, and develop more effectively students' mastery of basic skills, but it diverges from that approach in its long-term purpose.

PUTTING IT INTO ACTION

Elizabeth Harvey was having mixed emotions about her upcoming 40th birthday. She was happy and also unhappy to be celebrating the big "four-O," but she also felt special because her best friend from college, Beth, was flying in to celebrate the day with her. College, she thought to herself, seems so long ago; but with Beth, they would relive the good memories. Liz had been a campus activist. She was one of the student leaders, who fought to give the students a choice of a non-Western Civilization course. The faces of the students who had worked with her to make the non-Western course happen were mentally passing before her, when a distant bell interrupted the reminiscing. The ringing of the bell signaled her that her ninth-grade U.S. history class would convene in 3 minutes. She quickly washed and stored her coffee cup, gathered up her papers, and headed out of the teachers' lounge and up the stairs to greet her class.

The class was composed of 28 students: 13 were White, 8 were African Americans, 6 were Hispanic (3 Mexican Americans, 2 Puerto Ricans, and 1 Guatemalan refugee), and 1 was a Native American (Winnebago tribe). The socioeconomic status of the students was working class students or students living below the poverty line. The students were typical of those found in many classrooms. Their achievement levels and reading scores spanned a wide range: 10 of the students were reading on or above grade level, 12 were reading between one and two grades below grade level, and 6 were reading at the sixth-grade level. This class was typical of the classes Liz had taught at O'Henry during her 7 years of teaching there.

Directly across the hall from Liz, Erick Cosby taught general science. He and Liz were the same age and often joked about their big four-O birthdays. Erick had grown up in Nashville, Tennessee, and had come to Central City after spending 4 years in the army before he was honorably discharged because of a service-related accident. The student composition of Erick's class was very similar to that of Liz's class, except that he had 2 White students in wheelchairs, 8 Hispanics, 6 African Americans, and 2 Hmong.

Next door to Liz's room was Ross Wisser's room. Ross had been teaching English at O'Henry for the last 20 years. He was divorced, lived alone, and was a sports enthusiast. He spent most of his free time following Central City's four major sports teams. He often team taught with Liz and Erick because he liked their style and liked teaming up on some units or assignments.

Because Liz, Ross, and Erick taught the same classes of students, they often worked together to plan activities and assignments that would combine English, social studies, and science. Presently, Erick's classes were studying health, Liz's classes were studying city government and local agencies, and Ross's classes were studying general composition. The philosophy and style of teaching of all three teachers were geared to challenge and involve the students as much as possible in curriculum planning and instructional processes and to include activities and experiences that would take into account the students' home background and place in the economic structure, as well as any so-called learning or physical disabilities. All three also believed that if their students were going to succeed in life, the students needed to know how the system worked and develop the skills and knowledge necessary to take charge of their own lives.

Earlier that day, during their planning period, Erick had persuaded Liz and Ross to use County Hospital as their theme of study. He argued that the recent controversy about closing the facility was receiving a good deal of media coverage. The mayor's office and city council were locked in dispute over whether to close the hospital and have its services picked up by the other hospitals in the area, renovate it so that the community could keep its own hospital, or build a new hospital at a site closer to the center of town. He maintained that this lively debate would be excellent for Liz's unit. The students could learn not only about the different branches of city government and the way laws are passed but also how the members of the council, the mayor, and the different factions within the council bargain and compromise to get their way. The students could also study how people often vote along racial lines and how the benefits and rewards that a councilperson's district will receive often give direction to the way he or she votes.

Erick added, "You know, there is considerable debate as to which companies will get the contract for either the renovation or new construction, and one aspect of the debate centers upon the minority representation of the companies bidding for the contract." He suggested that Ross have the students write letters to the newspaper expressing their views on the subject as well as interview people in the neighborhood. He also suggested that the students publish their own newspaper about the topic. Ross added that he could borrow a TV mini-camera so that the students could learn to do real, live TV interviews.

Erick said that he would ask the students to contact doctors and other health personnel to get their views on the role of science in this decision-making process, investigating any medical factors that emerge as for or against the proposed plans. He added, "Results of the students' work could be printed in the newspaper they will publish. What the students learn from this process may not influence the way things at City Hall go on this issue, but it may influence what goes on in City Hall and in the students' lives regarding future issues."

Liz and Ross quickly agreed, telling Erick it was a super idea and now they should begin to get down to details. Liz suggested that they reserve the little theater for the next day, bring all three classes together to see what the students think of the idea, and if students like the idea, begin to organize around the three subjects. She said, "We can explain what each student's requirements are, as well as give students the opportunity to work in areas of their own interest."

"One requirement," said Ross, "is to get the students to work together in groups, and to make certain that they are integrated across the lines of race, gender, and class. Also, we don't usually have a problem with the kids with disabilities fitting in, but let's make certain they are really a part of the groups."

Liz said, "I believe it is important that we guide the class in a way that students learn how the system works and how they can make it work for them."

Erick said, "Anywhere you go in this world, there are people making decisions that will affect your life. You need to know and understand this fact and learn to become a part of the process. Otherwise, those decision makers will make many of your life decisions for you."

The final bell sounded, and it was time for Liz to start her U.S. history class. She completed greeting her class, and as she moved to close the door to her room, she guardedly called out to Erick, who was doing the same thing across the hall, "Happy four-oh, ol'friend!" Erick pushed the button on his wheelchair, turning himself into direct view of Liz, and said, "The same to you, ol'friend. Let's go and see what they think about the new unit and get ready for our joint meeting tomorrow."

CRITIQUE   We opened this chapter by noting that this approach is called different things by different people and that most advocates are still working on integrating race, social class, and gender. This point represents a difficulty that the approach currently faces and will reflect how we critique it.

In a review of the literature on multicultural education, we found fewer works discussing this approach than any other (Grant, 1992; Sleeter & Grant, 1987). Actually, advocates come to this approach from a variety of camps. Some have come from the Multicultural Education approach; some have come from Black studies, women's studies, Asian American studies, or some other Single-Group Studies approach; some have come from bilingual education after rejecting the remedial/compensatory model that many programs follow; some are disaffected neo-Marxists who see social class critiques as too limited; some are social reconstructionists who have only begun to apply this philosophy to race, class, and gender (and who perhaps had applied it mainly to peace education, world hunger, or ecology). As a result, the literature developing the approach is rather scattered, and advocates often do not recognize or dialogue with each other. Earlier we noted that coalition building is not easy; it is also not automatic among advocates of this approach.

The result is that the educator who wants to learn about the approach may become frustrated attempting to do so, partly because material is housed under different titles and partly because it is not abundant. In addition, there is relatively little material giving teachers specific guidance in what to do. We located some well-developed theoretical material (though little that integrated race, class, and gender) and a few very specific teaching guides (Myers et al., 1983; Schniedewind & Davidson, 1983) but very little connecting theory with practice in an open-ended fashion that would guide a teacher in developing his or her own plan of action.

As a result, one finds very few explicit critiques of this approach. The philosophy of social reconstructionism has been critiqued, as have been specific writings developing ideas in this approach, but the approach itself has rarely been the subject of thoughtful critique. We suspect it is more often simply ignored by those who view it as too radical or too advanced to bother with. Therefore, we have had to fashion this critique ourselves. We will first raise four general problems with the approach, then objections from each of the other four approaches.

One problem is with the role of the school in building a "new social order" (Counts, 1982). Counts asks if the school dare take such action; skeptics ask if it can. There is good reason to question whether it can. Schools are instruments of society, charged with the mission of preparing the young to take their place in society. As Chapter 1 explained, schools do a good job of reproducing the existing society. Expecting them to do otherwise may be unrealistic. Advocates of this approach usually counter, as Suzuki did earlier in this chapter, that schools alone cannot change society; however, they can collaborate with other institutions in doing so, and because teachers cannot avoid taking a stance toward society, the issue is what stance a teacher will take. We think it is an open question as to how much impact schools can have on social change: This approach or variations of it have not been implemented frequently enough for anyone to know what results can be expected.

A second problem discussed by Duck (1980) involves the contradiction between having students think for themselves and persuading them to think like the teacher. The approach does advocate taking seriously what students think, but students often do not recognize as problems what the teacher sees as problems, nor do students always agree with interpretations or solutions the teacher may promote. This situation is due in large part to students' lack of experience, background, or exposure, as well as to teachers who do not fully understand how to proceed or who protect vested interests they may have in the status quo. Duck warns that teachers can become extremists who do not tolerate students' views. This issue is one that reconstructionist educators face, and most recognize a tension here.

In the vignette, Erick, Liz, and Ross will have to face this issue if some of their students decide that the County Hospital should be closed and that the people it now serves should make do with other medical facilities. Without necessarily stating it to their students, the three teachers believe that closing the hospital will hurt low-income people, that this action is unfair, and that taxpayers should be willing to make certain that all communities that make up the city have equal access to comparable medical facilities. In setting up the unit, the three will need to decide how much coverage to give to arguments in favor of closing the hospital and how to respond to students who agree with those arguments.

A third problem is in the implementation more than in the approach itself. It is quite possible for an educator to sensitize students to social issues, then leave the students hanging—feeling frustrated and hopeless about what they can do about these issues. Shor (1980) has noted that critical teaching can blow up in a teacher's face if the teacher has not thought carefully how students may be feeling and has not planned for the constructive release of energy. For example, if students recognize the problems inherent in capitalism, they will not necessarily see what can be done short of tearing down our whole economic structure (which a class of students is powerless to do and for which they probably do not have a full-blown alternative system and a strategy for getting that system instituted). There are constructive actions one can take toward much more circumscribed problems, such as dealing with the provision of medical care for the poor in one's own community, but the teacher needs to be ready to deal with this issue. This problem is the reason why the unit described earlier in the vignette focused on a specific local issue and on the local politics deciding that issue. By the same token, however, Erick, Liz, and Ross would want students to see how this issue is connected to larger race and class struggles, rather than viewing it simply as an isolated local problem.

A related implementation problem is that the teacher must be focusing on social structural problems ("the system") more than on individual attitudes in order to be actually implementing this approach. In our experience, teachers and preservice students often say they prefer this approach over the other four, but their implementation has more in common with the Human Relations approach than with this approach. Teachers who themselves have not been involved in social movements or social protests, or who are not members of social action organizations, usually do not have sufficient background or experience to understand and work well with this approach. Such teachers tend to reduce problems of social structural inequality (such as the lack of decent-paying jobs or housing discrimination) to individual attitudes or the lack of student effort (Sleeter, 1992). Earlier we noted that publications produced by social action organizations provide a useful starting point for many teachers.

A fourth problem is how to build the coalitions that this approach advocates. Little has been written or studied about how coalitions among diverse groups can be built. How one brings together labor unions, middle-class Mexican Americans, and Southeast-Asian refugees, for example, is a challenge; helping them recognize and identify common ground is not an easy task.

Now for criticisms from the vantage point of the other approaches. The main objections raised by advocates of Teaching the Exceptional and the Culturally Different are that this approach seeks too much (and too unrealistic) change and diverts students who live at or below the poverty line and students of color from what they really need. Many educators do not see society as fundamentally flawed and believe that this approach exaggerates problems such as racism. (Those who say this, from our experience, are usually White and middle- or upper-class.) They, as well as others who agree with the magnitude of society's problems, argue that this approach gets students away from mastery of the skills and knowledge they will need to "make it." A principal of an urban high school recently told us how important he thought it was that his students acquire the skills to get a job or go to college in order to have a productive role in a society stacked against them; he cautioned that educational approaches such as the one described in this chapter would take time away from that preparatory work, as well as encouraging students to expect social changes that will not be forthcoming.

Human Relations educators fear that this approach will aggravate conflict and tension among people, escalating rather than reducing problems. Even though the approach values cooperation, Human Relations educators are concerned that too much open discussion of past and present injustices will fuel the fires of hate and distrust and that social action projects will promote confrontation. They fear that acts performed in the name of reconstruction will promote anarchy rather than fashioning a better society.

Advocates of the Teaching the Exceptional and the Culturally Different approach as well as of the Human Relations approach take issue with a fundamental premise of social reconstructionism: that the mainstream of society needs serious restructuring in order to be minimally fair to all Americans. Single-Group Studies and Multicultural Education advocates agree with that premise; their objections center around strategy rather than the goal. Advocates of Single-Group Studies feel that the approach discussed in this chapter bogs down in building coalitions across groups, to the extent that efforts toward change become ineffective. For example, although bilingual educators share some similar concerns with sex-equity advocates, there are also major differences of priority between the two groups. Joining forces might make for a stronger front, but hashing out a mutually agreeable common agenda can consume much of the energy of both groups. Historically, coalitions, if they are formed at all, have been fragile. Thus, groups with partially overlapping concerns may wish each other well but choose not to try to work together.

Finally, Multicultural Education advocates generally embrace the intent of this approach but view its feasibility with skepticism. To advocates of Education That Is Multicultural and Social Reconstructionist, the Multicultural Education approach is too limited and usually not assertive enough. However, to many business-as-usual educators, the Multicultural Education approach is radical. Multicultural Education advocates know that it is hard to get teachers and administrators seriously interested in implementing their approach. Education That Is Multi-cultural and Social Reconstructionist would be even harder to sell, more controversial, and more different from business as usual. We have also observed a certain amount of elitism among some social reconstructionists who see themselves as "correct" and Multicultural Education advocates as too accommodating. This attitude of elitism fosters distrust between the two approaches, which compounds disputes over goals, assumptions, and strategies.

Our last chapter explains which approach we favor and why. Most of the objections raised about the different approaches center on differences in priorities, assumptions, and perspectives. It cannot be proved that one approach is right and the rest are wrong. Our choice results from our own study of society, our own interactions with people, and our own convictions about which actions will go the farthest toward improving society. If you disagree with us or with your colleagues, we encourage open dialogue, since this is an excellent stimulus to further learning and growth.

REFERENCES

Abberley, P. (1987). The concept of oppression and the development of a social theory of disability. *Disability, Handicap, and Society, 2,* 5–20.

Anyon, J. (1981). Elementary schooling and distinctions of social class. *Interchange, 12,* 118–132.

Anyon, J. (1983). Intersections of gender and class: Accommodation and resistance by working class and affluent females to contradictory sex-role ideologies. In S. Walker & L. Barton (Eds.), *Gender, class and education* (pp. 19–38). Barcombe, England: Falmer Press.

Apple, M. W. (1985). *Education and power* (Ark ed.). Boston: Routledge & Kegan Paul.

Apple, M. W., & Beane, J. A. (1995). *Democractic schools.* Alexandria, VA: Association for Supervision and Curriculum Development.

Aronowitz, S., & Giroux, H. A. (1985). *Education under siege.* South Hadley, MA: Bergin & Garvey.

Banks, J. A. (1981). *Multiethnic education: Theory and practice.* Boston: Allyn & Bacon.

Banks, J. A. (1988). Approaches to multicultural curriculum reform. *Multicultural Leader, 1*(2), 1–2.

Barbagli, M., & Dei, M. (1977). Specialization into apathy and political subordination. In J. Karabel & A. H. Halsey (Eds.), *Power and ideology in education* (pp. 423–431). New York: Oxford University Press.

Bennett, C. I. (1986). *Comprehensive multicultural education.* Boston: Allyn & Bacon.

Brameld, T. (1956). *Toward a reconstructed philosophy of education.* New York: Holt, Rinehart, & Winston.

Carby, H. (1982). Schooling in Babylon. In Centre for Contemporary Cultural Studies, *The empire strikes back: Race and racism in 70's Britain* (pp. 183–211). Wolfeboro, NH: Longwood.

Carter, T. P., & Chatfield, M. L. (1986). Effective bilingual schools: Implications for policy and practice. *American Journal of Education, 95,* 26–57.

Collins, R. (1977). Functional and conflict theories of educational stratification. In J. Karabel & A. H. Halsey (Eds.), *Power and ideology in education* (pp. 118–136). New York: Oxford University Press.

Counts, G. (1982). *Dare the school build a new social order?* New York: John Day.

Dahrendorf, R. (1959). *Class and class conflict in industrial society.* Stanford: Stanford University Press.

Davis, A. Y. (1981). *Women, race, and class.* New York: Random House.

Dewey, J. (1938). *Experience and education.* New York: Macmillan.

Duck, L. (1980). *Teaching with charisma.* Boston: Allyn & Bacon.

Elshtain, J. B. (1976). The social relations of the classroom: A moral and political perspective. *Telos, 27,* 97–110.

Frankenberg, R. (1993). *The social construction of whiteness: White women, race matters.* Minneapolis: University of Minnesota Press.

Freire, P. (1985). *The politics of education: Culture, power, and liberation* (D. Macedo, Trans.). South Hadley, MA: Bergin & Garvey.

Genovese, E. (1974). *Roll, Jordan, roll: The world the slaves made.* New York: Pantheon.

Gere, A. R., Fairbanks, C., Howes, A., Roop, L., & Schaafsma, D. (1992). *Language and Reflection.* New York: Macmillan.

Giddens, A. (1979). *Central problems in social theory.* Berkeley: University of California Press.

Giroux, H. A. (1981). *Ideology, culture and the process of schooling.* Barcombe, England: Falmer Press.

Giroux, H. A. (1983). Theories of reproduction and resistance in the new sociology of education: A critical analysis. *Harvard Educational Review, 53,* 257–293.

Gordon, B. M. (1985). Toward emancipation in citizenship education: The case of African-American cultural knowledge. *Theory and Research in Social Education, 12,* 1–23.

Grant, C. A. (1978). Education that is multicultural—Isn't that what we mean? *Journal of Teacher Education, 29,* 45–49.

Grant, C. A. (1992, April). *Best practices in teacher preparation for urban schools.* Paper presented at the meeting of the American Educational Research Association, San Francisco, CA.

Grant, C. A., & Sleeter, C. E. (1986). Race, class and gender in educational research: An argument for integrative analysis. *Review of Educational Research, 56,* 195–211.

Hale, J. E. (1982). *Black children, their roots, culture, and learning styles.* Provo, UT: Brigham Young University.

hooks, b. (1994). *Teaching to transgress: Education as the practice of freedom.* New York: Routledge.

Irvine, J. J. (1991, February). *Culturally responsive pedagogy: Myth and misperception.* Paper presented at the American Association of Colleges of Teacher Education Annual Conference, San Antonio, TX.

Jaggar, A. M., & Struhl, P. R. (Eds.). (1993). *Feminist frameworks* (3rd ed.). New York: McGraw-Hill.

Jefferson, T. (1779). *A bill for the more general diffusion of knowledge.* Report of the Revisors, State of Virginia.

Kanter, R. M. (1975). Women and the structure of organization: Exploration in theory and behavior. In M. Millman & R. M. Kanter (Eds.), *Another voice* (pp. 34–75). Garden City, NY: Anchor-Doubleday.

Kobrin, D. (1992, Winter). My country, too: A proposal for a student historian's history of the United States. *Teachers College Record, 94*(2), 329–342.

Lewis, B. A. (1991). *The kid's guide to social action.* Minneapolis, MN: Free Spirit.

Mann, J. (1974). Political power and the high school curriculum. In E. W. Eisner & E. Vallance (Eds.), *Conflicting conceptions of curriculum* (pp. 147–153). Berkeley, CA: McCutchan.

Marx, K. (1972). *Capital* (Book 1). London: J. M. Bent.

McPhie, W. E. (1988). Teaching American democracy in American public schools. *Social Education, 52*(2), 152.

Metcalf, L. E., & Hunt, M. P. (1974). Relevance and the curriculum. In E. W. Eisner & E. Vallance (Eds.), *Conflicting conceptions of curriculum* (pp. 136–146). Berkeley, CA: McCutchan.

Mitchell, C. (1978). Woman's estate. In A. M. Jaggar & P. R. Struhl (Eds.), *Feminist frameworks* (pp. 130–141). New York: McGraw-Hill.

Mullard, C. (1980). *Racism in society and schools: History, policy, and practice.* Occasional Paper No. 1, Centre for Multicultural Education of London, Institute of Education.

Myers, R. A., Banfield, B., & Colon, J. J. (1983). *Embers: Stories for a changing world.* Westbury, NY: Feminist Press; and New York: Council on Interracial Books for Children.

Oakley, A. (1981). *Subject women.* New York: Pantheon.

Piaget, J. (1952). *The language and thought of the child.* London: Routledge & Kegan Paul.

Roediger, D. R. (1991). *The wages of whiteness: Race and the making of the American working class.* New York: Verso.

Schniedewind, N., & Davidson, E. (1983). *Open minds to equality.* Upper Saddle River, NJ: Prentice-Hall.

Shaw, G. B. (1921). *Back to Methuselah,* Pt. 1, Act I.

Shor, I. (1980). *Critical teaching and everyday life.* Boston: South End Press.

Sleeter, C. E. (1992). *Keepers of the American dream.* London: Falmer Press.

Sleeter, C. E. (1994, Spring). White racism. *Multicultural Education,* 5–9.

Sleeter, C. E., & Grant, C. A. (1987). An analysis of multicultural education in the U.S.A. *Harvard Educational Review, 57,* 421–444.

Suzuki, B. H. (1977). The Japanese-American experience. In M. J. Gold, C. A. Grant, & H. N. Rivlin (Eds.), *In praise of diversity: A resource book for multicultural education* (pp. 139–162). Washington, DC: Teacher Corps.

Suzuki, B. H. (1984). Curriculum transformation for multicultural education. *Education and Urban Society, 16,* 294–322.

Takaki, R. (1989). *Strangers from a different shore.* Boston: Little, Brown.

Tate, W. F. (1995). Returning to the root: A culturally relevant approach to mathematics pedagogy. *Theory into Practice, 34*(3), 166–173.

Tatum, B. D. (1994). Teaching white students about racism: The search for white allies and the restoration of hope. *Teachers College Record, 95*(4), 462–476.

Valli, L. (1986). *Becoming clerical workers.* London: Routledge & Kegan Paul.

Van Avery, D. (1975). The humanitarian approach. *Phi Delta Kappan, 57,* 177–178.

Vygotsky, L. S. (1986). *Thought and language.* (E. Hamsman & G. Vankan, Eds. and Trans.). Cambridge, MA.: MIT Press.

Weber, M. (1947). *The theory of social and economic organization.* (A. M. Henderson & T. Parsons, Trans.; T. Parsons, Ed.). Glencoe, IL: Free Press.

Weber, M. (1968). *Economy and society.* New York: Bedminster Press.

Wolf, N. (1991). *The beauty myth.* New York: Morrow.

CHAPTER SEVEN

Our Choice: Education That Is Multicultural and Social Reconstructionist

By now, you probably have a sense of which approach to multicultural education you prefer. We have tried to present and critique the approaches thoroughly and objectively enough to help you make your own choices. At the same time, we cannot remain neutral and detached. We do have a strong sense of which approach we believe goes the furthest toward providing better schooling as well as creating a better society. Furthermore, based on our own experience in schools, our research on schools, and our long-standing study of multicultural education, we feel we have an obligation to share our thinking.

Our thinking is based largely on social conditions that persist and that limit and often damage or destroy the lives of many people. A significant segment of American society has always been poor, and the size of this group in recent years has been growing rather than diminishing. Globally, poverty and hunger are more the norm than is the wealth so many of us take for granted. Racism in the United States is still in many ways as intact now as it was decades ago, and as the population of color in the United States grows, one can predict increased competition among racial groups. The family structure in the United States continues to change as more women enter the work force, but family role changes and cooperative networks are not emerging on a large scale. For example, rather than involving husbands and the extended family more actively in child care, many families simply reduce the time spent on child care when the mother takes on additional roles. These are some of the trends and persistent problems that concern us.

People tend to live in small, rather insulated worlds with others who share their advantages or disadvantages. Consequently, the educator who is experiencing a relatively comfortable and privileged life may have difficulty fully appreciating and understanding the very real problems faced, for example, by the Mexican-American father searching desperately for work, the single mother wondering how to make ends meet, or the laid-off worker who feels powerless as the local factories close down. Nevertheless, these problems exist, and they are part of the very fabric of American society. There may be periodic improvements of a superficial

217

nature, and these may be widely publicized, but the character and magnitude of the problems have not changed much in the past two or three decades.

The revolt in Los Angeles following the April 1992 acquittal of police brutality against Rodney King and the verbal debates between Blacks and Whites after the O. J. Simpson verdict in 1996 reveal the depth of social divisions that exist in the United States. Although many believe that such divisions no longer exist and that the nation has realized its democratic aspirations, the evidence reveals otherwise. Many Americans, including many of our students, viewed these events as isolated and unfortunate but also as unpredictable as a hurricane. Now that the revolt is past and the trial has concluded, such "incidents" have been moved to the recesses of the public mind.

To us, this revolt after the acquittal of the police epitomized the reasons why Education That Is Multicultural and Social Reconstructionist must be taken seriously. About a year before the revolt, some educators in Southern California told one of us that the rest of the nation has time to address its social injustices and to take its diversity more seriously than California has done. The poverty, joblessness, retrenchment, and despair that spawned the outbreak were long in the making, and they were visible to people who lived or worked in inner-city areas every day. In fact, we use the term *revolt* deliberately. The term *riot* suggests a disorganized overreaction to an immediate event. The term *revolt* suggests an uprising against a long-standing system of deprivation.

People who were surprised by the revolt and who viewed its main solution as tighter law enforcement have not been looking closely at the systematic impoverization of large segments of the U.S. population. Across the nation, growing segments of the population and of American youth are feeling locked out, powerless to change their lives, robbed of dignity, and silenced. We believe that it is essential to the survival of the nation that social justice issues be taken seriously. The approach to multicultural education presented last in this book is most explicit in its serious treatment of social justice issues. The importance of a position that is both Multicultural and Social Reconstructionist is illustrated, we think, by reactions to President Clinton's 1997 initiation of an agenda aimed at bettering race relations. Forming an advisory panel on race, Clinton hopes to steer the nation in a direction more accepting of diversity. Yet many have criticized his efforts, complaining that his agenda aspires to change public attitudes while lacking any substantive goals, such as enacting policies, allocating funds, or developing social programs for, say, housing, education, or jobs. Roger Wilkins, a professor of history at George Mason University, states, "I don't believe that exhortation—when you are dealing with the poorest people in this society and the historical forces that created their desperation—is going to do it" (Mitchell, 1997). Although the implications of President Clinton's efforts remain to be seen, opinions surrounding his political agenda aimed at promoting a harmonious multiracial society underscore the significance of combining recognitions of diversity with concrete proposals and social action centered upon socially reconstructing a system which unjustly disadvantages many of its citizens.

Let us return to the hypothetical class of students with whom we opened the first chapter. How should they be taught? Before proceeding with business-as-usual techniques or with any of the approaches to multicultural education, the teacher should consider these students in relationship to the society in which they live today and will live as adults. As they grow up, what is in store for these students? Which approach to education might make a genuine difference?

Half of the students are girls, half are boys. If present trends continue, virtually all of them will attempt to join the labor force as adults. The girls may be only dimly aware of this statistic, but most of them will wind up with two careers: child raising and housekeeping, as well as holding down a low-paying job. Many of the girls will be heads of households fighting to stay above the poverty line; the African American girls who find themselves as heads of households will have a better than 50-50 chance of living in poverty. Many of the boys, though economically better off, will find themselves psychologically alienated or living apart from their children, in some cases even feared by their children. Many will find themselves forced to make a decision about becoming involved in a gang and living up to the responsibility which gang membership entails. Many will find themselves trapped in jobs they dislike but must keep for the sake of their role as breadwinner. Some will become angry and resentful of their wives and beat them. Some of the girls will have babies at a young age and find themselves without a partner to share in the raising of the child. Some girls can look forward to being battered wives. Some of the students already know these things because their parents experience them. To try to adhere to the image of *feminine* that is being sold to them, some of the girls are already beginning to starve themselves or surgically remake their bodies. Nevertheless, at this point, most of the students believe that adulthood holds a happy marriage with clearly divided responsibilities and a comfortable income (Sidel, 1988).

The first approach discussed in this book—Teaching the Exceptional and the Culturally Different—which is an improvement over business as usual, would address one of the current problems by equipping girls better to compete with boys in male-dominated areas, especially in fields requiring mathematics, science, and computers. This strategy will help a few girls, maybe 1 or 2 out of 15. However, it does not address the dual career that most women must take on, which causes many not to consider entering full time, demanding professions that conflict with domestic responsibilities. It also does not help homemakers to receive a full reward for their work. Nor does it address the low wages paid for jobs that women dominate. Moving women out of secretarial work into the sciences, for example, does nothing to raise the pay of secretaries; it only increases the competition for more lucrative jobs. Further, it ignores backlash attempts to control women.

The second approach examined in this book—Human Relations—would help build better cross-sex understanding, which one hopes would lead to better communication and more respect between the sexes. Again, however, economic problems and role responsibilities would tend to remain intact, probably disrupting relationships among men and women. Similarly, this approach would support Rodney King's question, "Can't we all get along?" However, the approach does not develop discussion and action on economic and political inequalities that often lead to not getting along.

Women's studies (part of the third approach discussed, that of Single-Group Studies) would help students examine sexism and mobilize them (mainly the girls) to challenge it. Although this type of approach has greater potential than the approaches previously discussed (and certainly greater potential than business as usual) for preparing students to recognize and struggle against institutional sexism, it is limited. Women's studies focuses on a single form of human diversity and does not necessarily attend to issues such as poverty (which is also a very important problem) or racism (which the girls of color will face). It also often excludes men, unintentionally presenting sexism as a problem only for women.

The fourth approach examined in this book—Multicultural Education—would address sexism by promoting nonsexist role and job choice and by giving as much attention to the female experience as to the male experience in the curriculum. It would also include the experiences of women of color as well as those of White women, the experiences of poor women as well as those of middle-class women. It would attempt to eliminate a sexist division of labor in the home and encourage the young to choose careers without reference to masculine versus feminine roles. Still, this approach has limitations—the biggest being that it does not prepare students to take steps to change the rules of the game that incorporate sexism into society. We will illustrate this point with three structures that help perpetuate sexism.

First, many careers, particularly those with the greatest pay, do not lend themselves well to maintaining an active role in parenting. The very existence of careers that greatly reduce available hours for parenting is one structure that helps maintain sexism, because such careers automatically exclude their holders from active parenting and because women are assumed to have primary responsibility for child care. Men greatly outnumber women in such careers, and their wives end up with most of the parenting responsibility.

A second structural rule of the game that reinforces sexism is the nuclear family, in which the woman's primary role is child caretaker and the man's is breadwinner. Even if young people start married life believing they will share roles, they later often divide roles by sex as the result of a lack of alternatives. For example, when children are young, either one parent stays home part of the day or the family pays for day care, which can cost as much as or more than many women make at work. Thus, the woman usually stays home. The extended family, familiar to many people of color, can provide more alternatives because more adults are in the home who can share roles, lessening the need to shift domestic work to one adult. Although the extended family is growing in popularity, the nuclear family is offered as the norm and is legitimated in the structure of houses and in the tax structure. To encourage and support greater role flexibility as well as foster attitudes that support nonsexist role sharing, one would want to legitimate the extended family as well as the nuclear family.

A third structural problem is the institution of domestic help. Many career-oriented people who can afford it hire domestic help to do the jobs for which the husband and wife do not have time, or they make use of services such as day care. In and of themselves, these are good options, but these jobs pay very poorly and are usually filled by women, often women of color. Furthermore, jobs such as "cleaning lady" rarely provide benefits such as health insurance or retirement pay. These are more rules of the game that society accepts and plays by that continue to trap many women.

The approach discussed last—Education That Is Multicultural and Social Reconstructionist—would help students examine these sorts of issues and begin to think of ways of challenging them. In so doing, the approach offers several advantages. First, it speaks to issues that currently impact on many of the students and eventually will impact on all of them. For example, students who may see little relevance in studying economics see considerable relevance when economics is used to help them understand changes in the availability of jobs locally or the reduced availability of government loans for college. Second, it encourages students to take an active stance—to take charge of their lives. It helps them connect what they are doing now with their future lives as adults but in a way that does not fit them into the status quo with all its problems; rather, it teaches them to challenge the status quo. Finally, this approach helps them learn to work collectively to speak out, be heard, and effect change. Furthermore, unlike Single-Group Studies, this approach attempts to join the White girls with the girls and boys of color and the middle-class students with those of the lower class as they examine common or related concerns.

Three of the students in our hypothetical class are Hispanic. If present trends continue, and especially if schools continue with business as usual, one and possibly two of the three will not graduate from high school. They will leave mainly to help take care of their families but also because many will experience alienation in school. Culturally, the school will connect only partially with their own life experience, and most, if not all, of the teachers and authority figures will be White. As teenagers, all three may have to look for jobs, but at least one will not find a job. Unable to find a job and alienated from school, one of these students may choose to join a gang, because gangs can sometimes offer a source of identity, an underground economy, a source of income, and a means of controlling something, even if it is only a city block. As adults, the family income of these three Hispanic students will average only about 75% of the family income of their White peers. One of the students will probably live in poverty, and the other two will live in the lower middle class. All three will continually feel caught in a cultural tug of war that will probably intensify. As the Hispanic population becomes the largest American racial-minority group, Mexican culture will gain a firmer foothold. Whites will probably continue to respond by asserting the primacy of English and the legitimacy of Anglo-American culture. About 4.5 million American students speak Spanish at home, and language policy will increasingly be a source of tension. The Hispanic students will feel, for example, somewhat alienated from mainstream media, which renders Hispanics almost invisible except in advertisements for Mexican food, in which viewers may be invited to "feel a little Mexican" tonight. Lack of representation will be a problem in many other areas as well, such as in political decision making. Moreover, the Hispanic students as adults may find themselves competing with their former Black classmates or with recent immigrants for control over elective inner-city offices.

Teaching the Culturally Different deals with these issues mainly by trying to get Hispanics through school (which is important), helping them to learn English, and preparing them to compete for jobs. These steps are all important but are limited. This approach does not deal with the cultural tug of war, except by acknowledging that it is okay to be Hispanic as long as one can also function effectively in an Anglo world. It ignores White racism entirely; in fact, it denies it. The Human Relations approach helps all the students learn not to stereotype Hispanics, and it develops more positive attitudes about Hispanic culture. However, it does not deal with poverty and political powerlessness; it only teaches that these problems will be resolved if people communicate better and appreciate each other more.

Chicano studies would offer Hispanic students a chance to develop group solidarity with other Mexican Americans. It would offer a source of identification with school and a counter to cultural alienation, because Chicano studies embraces Hispanic culture and concerns. It would also offer a forum for examining the life circumstances and needs of Hispanics. However, the Single-Group Studies approach, in the form of Chicano studies, could subordinate and ignore Hispanic women, would not encourage Hispanics to work with other oppressed groups, and might even aggravate cross-group conflict. Further, the concerns of the many Hispanics who are not Chicano might be completely ignored.

The Multicultural Education approach would make Hispanic cultures and concerns an integral part of the curriculum, along with the cultures and concerns of other groups. It would help Hispanic students succeed in school by building on their learning styles and experiential backgrounds. It would offer all the students role models of successful Hispanic men and women and would encourage bilingualism as a norm. A good Multicultural Education curriculum would accurately represent the diversity among Hispanic groups. However, it would not offer a plan for attacking poverty and unemployment, nor would it necessarily help build the political skills and group solidarity that Hispanics need.

Education That Is Multicultural and Social Reconstructionist offers a more direct response to these concerns in addition to other benefits of the Multicultural Education approach. For example, Hispanics have a pressing need to improve their representation in decision-making roles at many institutions. Although Hispanics are developing more political clout at the local level in areas where the Hispanic population is large, they are still virtually powerless in most states and at the national level. Two issues directly affecting Hispanics are periodically debated and voted on at the national level: language policy and immigration policy. As the Hispanic population in the United States grows, as the Mexican economy continues to suffer, and as Central America continues to be a hotbed of political unrest, these two issues will probably take on greater urgency. The Free Trade Agreement with Mexico, for example, can be viewed as an Anglo attempt to divide Third World people from Americans of Mexican decent in a competition over jobs. As Anner (1991) put it, "The worst irony is that, economically speaking, low-income workers in the U.S. will be pitted against their counterparts in Mexico in competition for the same jobs" (p. 4). The approach we discussed last does not teach a certain stance on these issues so much as it encourages young people, including (and in this case especially) Hispanics, to learn how to research the issues, to mobilize, to articulate a stand, to gain access to the media, to use the legal system, and to perform other activities.

A final example relates to the issue of unemployment. It is not enough to equip people better to compete for jobs when there are not enough jobs to go around and when existing jobs are not amply available in minority neighborhoods. Youth of color should learn to seek jobs more effectively, to interview skillfully, to complete school, and to perform other job-search activities. However, future citizens should also begin to examine the job structure itself and consider improvements. For example, students could research the availability of jobs in African American, Hispanic, and White neighborhoods, and on Indian reservations. They could find out why businesses tend not to locate in lower-class neighborhoods, and they could study ways of attracting business. Students could find out how to assess hiring discrimination and how to fight it effectively. The students could analyze wage structure in relationship to the cost of living in order to understand the extent to which local employers tacitly support near-poverty existence by keeping wages low, and then they could find out how to change this situation.

It may appear that we are writing a social studies curriculum, but we are not. The topics we have suggested lend themselves to reading (one can learn reading skills by reading about virtually any topic), writing, mathematics skills, learning to use science methods, some science topics, art, and music (here we are referring to the content of song lyrics), as well as social studies.

We could continue with examples from the hypothetical class, but we suspect that our point has been made. However, there is one group whose presence and probable discomfort we would like to acknowledge: that of the White, middle-class or upper-class males. This group would be comprised of about eight members of our hypothetical class and a sizable portion of the readers of this book. We could start cataloging the problems this group will face after schooling—indeed, there are problems. (A simple example is to ask yourself what your own family income would be if the women in your family were paid as well as the men are; if such were the case, many of you would experience an improvement in your entire family's living condition.) Yet, the group composed of White, heterosexual, middle-class males will tend to have greater access to resources and more power than any other group.

How does the Education That Is Multicultural and Social Reconstructionist approach regard White, middle- or upper-class males? It regards the group mainly as a necessary potential ally. There are and always have been White males who have joined the struggle against oppression and who have worked with (rather than dominated) members of subordinate groups. Their presence and help is necessary partly because of, rather than in spite of, their membership in dominant race, class, and gender groups. At the classroom level, White male students are often willing to join with others as long as they feel valued and a genuine ethos of cooperation is fostered. As they become adults, they will be offered advantages not available to their classmates; they will need to decide whether to use their privileged status for their own benefit or for the benefit of others.

Before concluding, we issue a caution to enthusiastic readers. In our experience, readers often declare that they agree with us that Education That Is Multicultural and Social Reconstructionist is the best—without having thought through the issues for themselves. If this is your first attempt to grapple with social-justice and multicultural issues, recognize that you have taken the first step in a long process of learning. These are very complex issues. Often those who agree with us on our choice of approaches do so at a rhetorical level only: They adopt out words, but they have yet to think through the implications of these words for living and teaching. Learning any of the approaches well means learning to teach differently—and in most cases very differently—from business as usual.

Which approach is the best one is a value decision that the individual educator must make. This book has outlined the goals, assumptions, underlying values, and practices of five ways of approaching diversity in the classroom. One cannot choose not to choose, because to accept the status quo is also to make a choice. We hope that this book helps the educator in the process of making a decision that is best for him or her.

REFERENCES

Anner, J. (1991, Summer). Trading away labor rights. *The Minority Trendsletter, 4,* 3–5, 14–15.

Mitchell, A. (1997, June 16). Clinton feels sure-footed on the tightrope of race. *The New York Times*, p. A12.

Sidel, R. (1988). *On her own: Growing up in the shadow of the American dream.* New York: Penguin.

Author Index

Subject Index

Ability grouping, 24–25, 171
  and differences in curricula, 23
  in Multicultural Education
    approach, 171
  in school, 119–120
  and social status, 119–120
Abuse
  domestic, 11
  against people with disabilities, 17
Academic gaps, filling in, 58–59
Access Living, 17
Accessibility, and Multicultural
    Education approach, 168–169
Accommodation, 194
Achievement gaps, 39
Achievement tests, 171
  and determination of curricula, 23
The Adventures of Huckleberry Finn
  (Twain), 118
Affirmative action, 4
African American Baseline Essays,
  135
The African American Experience,
  135
African American immersion
  schools, 61, 138
African American studies
  instructional strategies for, 136
  materials for, 135
African Americans
  and communication, 49–50
  in desegregated schools, 138
  educational attainment of, 3
  and employment, 4
  and health insurance, 7
  in history books
    portrayal of, 128
    starting point for, 125
  and housing discrimination, 7

income/education correlation, 3, 4*t*
income of, 3
learning styles of, 19, 49
life expectancy of, 7, 8*f*
literary tradition of, 124
and morality, 42–43
in 1950s, 155
in politics, 7–9
in poverty, 5*f*
public opinion regarding, 3
and self-concept, 88
in Single-Group Studies
  curriculum, 118
and teaching styles, 59
Afrocentric schools, 138
Afrocentrism, 138
  history topics in, 127*f*
Amalgamation, 160
American Federation of Teachers, 24
American Indian studies, 134
American Sign Language (ASL), 51
Americans With Disabilities Act,
  16–17
Am I Blue? Coming out from the
  Silence, 136
Analytical learners, 48
Androgyny, 154
Anoka-Hennepin School District,
  135
Anorexia nervosa, 12
Anthropology, and cultural
  transmission, 162
Anti-Bias Curriculum, 106
Anti-Defamation League of B'nai
  B'rith, 78
Antiracist teaching, 190
Appalachian studies, 133
Arts
  and group identity, 128–129

and Single-Group studies
  approach, 133
Asian Americans, struggle for
  acceptance, 198–199
Asian American women, 129
Asian studies, development of, 123
ASL. *See* American Sign Language
Assessment
  and learning styles, 59
  and limited-English proficiency, 172
  in Multicultural Education
    approach, 171–173
Assimilation, 159–160
  and Human Relations approach,
    105
  and Teaching the Exceptional and
    Culturally Different, 69
At-risk students, 67
  descriptions of, 40–41
  determination of, 43
  language of, 42
  perceptual skills of, 41–42
Attitudes, impact of cognitive
  information on, 95
The Autobiography of Malcolm X, 118
Autonomy, definition of, 121*f*

Behavioral model, of psychological
  and mental deficiencies, 45–46
Benevolent multiculturalism, 30
Benning, Sadie, 129
Bias, changes in, 2
Bicultural education, 30
Bilingual education, 19–20, 23,
  26–27, 50–51, 68
  and assimilation, 159
  and Multicultural Education
    approach, 168
  need for, 112

Note. The letter *f* following a page number indicates *figure; t* indicates *table.*